The Author

SUSANNA MOODIE was born Susanna Strickland in Bungay, Suffolk, England, in 1803. The sixth and final daughter of a retired dock manager, she grew up in a middle-class family that encouraged the children in reading and in writing. Her sisters Agnes and Elizabeth would write *Lives of the Queens of England* and other biographies of the aristocracy, her sister Catharine Parr (later Traill) would emigrate to Canada and write several natural history books, and her brother Samuel, another emigrant to Canada, would write of the settler's life. Susanna's juvenilia include poetry and many fiction tales for young adults.

In 1831 Susanna Strickland married John Wedderburn Dunbar Moodie, a military officer who had returned to England from South Africa to explore publication projects and to find a wife. A year later, they emigrated to Upper Canada (Ontario). In *Flora Lyndsay* (1854), Susanna Moodie gives a fictionalized account of the family's move to Canada, concluding with the journey up the Saint Lawrence River.

For their first seventeen months in Canada, the Moodies lived on cleared farmland near Port Hope. In 1834 they moved to a bush farm in Douro Township north of Peterborough and near the homes of Samuel Strickland and Catharine Parr Traill. The farm was the Moodie home for five years, and *Roughing It in the Bush* (1852), describes their life in these two backwoods areas.

From 1837 to 1839 Dunbar Moodie served in the Upper Canada militia, and in 1839 he was appointed Sheriff of Victoria District (later Hastings County). His family moved to Belleville in 1840, their home until his death in 1869. After her husband's death Susanna Moodie spent her time with her various grown children and with her sister Catharine.

Susanna Moodie died in Toronto, Ontario, in 1885.

THE NEW CANADIAN LIBRARY

General Editor: David Staines

SUSANNA MOODIE

Life in the Clearings versus the Bush

With an Afterword by Carol Shields

*"I sketch from Nature, and the draught is true.
Whate'er the picture, whether grave or gay
Painful experience is a distant land
Made it mine own."*

This edition is an unabridged reprint of the first edition of
Life in the Clearings versus the Bush, published in London,
England, by Richard Bentley in 1853.

New Canadian Library edition copyright © 1989 by
McClelland & Stewart Inc.
Afterword copyright © 1989 by Carol Shields

Canadian Cataloguing in Publication Data

Moodie, Susanna, 1803–1885
Life in the clearings versus the bush

(New Canadian library)
Bibliography: p.
ISBN 0-7710-9976-2

1. Ontario – Description and travel – 1764–1850.*
2. Ontario – Social life and customs. I. Title.
II. Series.

FC3067.2.M66 1989   917.13′042   C89-093658-7
F1057.M66 1989

Typesetting by Pickwick
Printed and bound in Canada

McClelland & Stewart Inc.
The Canadian Publishers
481 University Avenue
Toronto, Ontario
M5G 2E9

to

John Wedderburn Dunbar Moodie, Esq.

Sheriff of the County of Hastings,
Upper Canada,
this work is affectionately dedicated,
by his attached friend
and wife,

Susanna Moodie.

Contents

Introduction

> "Dear foster-mother, on whose ample breast
>   The hungry still find food, the weary rest;
>   The child of want that treads thy happy shore,
>   Shall feel the grasp of poverty no more;
>   His honest toil meet recompense can claim,
>   And Freedom bless him with a freeman's name!"
>
> S.M.

IN OUR WORK of "Roughing it in the Bush," I endeavoured to draw a picture of Canadian life, as I found it twenty years ago, in the Backwoods. My motive in giving such a melancholy narrative to the British public, was prompted by the hope of deterring well-educated people, about to settle in this colony, from entering upon a life for which they were totally unfitted by their previous pursuits and habits.

To persons unaccustomed to hard labour, and used to the comforts and luxuries deemed indispensable to those moving in the middle classes at home, a settlement in the bush can offer few advantages. It has proved the ruin of hundreds and thousands who have ventured their all in this hazardous experiment; nor can I recollect a single family of the higher class, that have come under my own personal knowledge, that ever realised an independence, or bettered their condition, by taking up wild lands in

9

remote localities; while volumes might be filled with failures, even more disastrous than our own, to prove the truth of my former statements.

But while I have endeavoured to point out the error of gentlemen bringing delicate women and helpless children to toil in the woods, and by so doing excluding them from all social intercourse with persons in their own rank, and depriving the younger branches of the family of the advantages of education, which, in the vicinity of towns and villages, can be enjoyed by the children of the poorest emigrant, I have never said anything against the REAL benefits to be derived from a judicious choice of settlement in this great and rising country.

God forbid that any representations of mine should deter one of my countrymen from making this noble and prosperous colony his future home. But let him leave to the hardy labourer the place assigned to him by Providence, nor undertake, upon limited means, the task of pioneer in the great wilderness. Men of independent fortune can live anywhere. If such prefer a life in the woods, to the woods let them go; but they will soon find out that they could have employed the means in their power in a far more profitable manner than in chopping down trees in the bush.

There are a thousand more advantageous ways in which a man of property may invest his capital, than by burying himself and his family in the woods. There never was a period in the history of the colony that offered greater inducements to men of moderate means to emigrate to Canada than the present. The many plank-roads and railways in the course of construction in the province, while they afford high and remunerative wages to the working classes, will amply repay the speculator who embarks a portion of his means in purchasing shares in them. And if he is bent upon becoming a Canadian farmer, numbers of fine farms, in healthy and eligible situations, and in the vicinity of good markets, are to be had on moderate terms, that would amply repay the cultivator for the money and labour expended upon them.

There are thousands of independent proprietors of this class in Canada – men who move in the best society, and whose names have a political weight in the country. Why gentlemen from Britain should obstinately crowd to the Backwoods, and prefer the coarse, hard life of an axeman, to that of a respectable landed proprietor in a civilised part of the country, has always been to me a matter of surprise; for a farm under cultivation can always be purchased for less money than must necessarily be expended upon clearing and raising buildings upon a wild lot.

Many young men are attracted to the Backwoods by the facilities they present for hunting and fishing. The wild, free life of the hunter, has for an ardent and romantic temperament an inexpressible charm. But hunting and fishing, however fascinating as a wholesome relaxation from labour, will not win bread, or clothe a wife and shivering little ones; and those who give themselves entirely up to such pursuits, soon add to these profitless accomplishments the bush vices of smoking and drinking, and quickly throw off those moral restraints upon which their respectability and future welfare mainly depend.

The bush is the most demoralizing place to which an anxious and prudent parent could send a young lad. Freed suddenly from all parental control, and exposed to the contaminating influence of broken-down gentlemen loafers, who hide their pride and poverty in the woods, he joins in their low debauchery, and falsely imagines that, by becoming a blackguard, he will be considered an excellent backwoodsman.

How many fine young men have I seen beggared and ruined in the bush! It is too much the custom in the woods for the idle settler, who will not work, to live upon the new comer as long as he can give him good fare and his horn of whisky. When these fail, farewell to your *good-hearted*, roystering friends; they will leave you like a swarm of musquitoes, while you fret over your festering wounds, and fly to suck the blood of some new settler, who is fool enough to believe their offers of friendship.

The dreadful vice of drunkenness, of which I shall have occasion to speak hereafter, is nowhere displayed in more revolting colours, or occurs more frequently, than in the bush; nor is it exhibited by the lower classes in so shameless a manner as by the gentlemen settlers, from whom a better example might be expected. It would not be difficult to point out the causes which too often lead to these melancholy results. Loss of property, incapacity for hard labour, yielding the mind to low and degrading vices, which destroy self-respect and paralyse honest exertion, and the annihilation of those extravagant hopes that false statements, made by interested parties, had led them to entertain of fortunes that might be realised in the woods: these are a few among the many reasons that could be given for the number of victims that yearly fill a drunkard's dishonourable grave.

At the period when the greatest portion of "Roughing it in the Bush" was written, I was totally ignorant of life in Canada, as it existed in the towns and villages. Thirteen years' residence in one of the most thriving districts in the Upper Province has given me many opportunities of becoming better acquainted with the manners and habits of her busy, bustling population, than it was possible for me ever to obtain in the green prison of the woods.

Since my residence in a settled part of the country, I have enjoyed as much domestic peace and happiness as ever falls to the lot of poor humanity. Canada has become almost as dear to me as my native land; and the homesickness that constantly preyed upon me in the Backwoods, has long ago yielded to the deepest and most heartfelt interest in the rapidly increasing prosperity and greatness of the country of my adoption, – the great foster-mother of that portion of the human family, whose fatherland, however dear to them, is unable to supply them with bread.

To the honest sons of labour Canada is, indeed, an El Dorado – a land flowing with milk and honey; for they soon obtain that independence which the poor gentleman struggles in vain to realise by his own labour in the woods.

The conventional prejudices that shackle the movements of members of the higher classes in Britain are scarcely recognised in Canada; and a man is at liberty to choose the most profitable manner of acquiring wealth, without the fear of ridicule and the loss of caste.

The friendly relations which now exist between us and our enterprising, intelligent American neighbours, have doubtless done much to produce this amalgamation of classes. The gentleman no longer looks down with supercilious self-importance on the wealthy merchant, nor does the latter refuse to the ingenious mechanic the respect due to him as a man. A more healthy state pervades Canadian society than existed here a few years ago, when party feeling ran high, and the professional men and office holders visited exclusively among themselves, affecting airs of aristocratic superiority, which were perfectly absurd in a new country, and which gave great offence to those of equal wealth who were not admitted into their clique. Though too much of this spirit exists in the large cities, such as Quebec, Montreal, and Toronto, it would not be tolerated in the small district towns and villages, where a gentleman could not take a surer method of making himself unpopular than by exhibiting this feeling to his fellow-townsmen.

I have been repeatedly asked, since the publication of "Roughing it in the Bush," to give an account of the present state of society in the colony, and to point out its increasing prosperity and commercial advantages; but statistics are not my forte, nor do I feel myself qualified for such an arduous and important task. My knowledge of the colony is too limited to enable me to write a comprehensive work on a subject of vital consequence, which might involve the happiness of others. But what I do know I will endeavour to sketch with a light pencil; and if I cannot convey much useful information, I will try to amuse the reader; and by a mixture of prose and poetry compile a small volume, which may help to while away an idle hour, or fill up the blanks of a wet day.

Belleville, Canada West,
Nov. 24th, 1852.

INDIAN SUMMER.

By the purple haze that lies
   On the distant rocky height,
By the deep blue of the skies,
   By the smoky amber light,
Through the forest arches streaming,
Where nature on her throne sits dreaming,
And the sun is scarcely gleaming
   Through the cloudlet's snowy white,
Winter's lovely herald greets us,
Ere the ice-crown'd tyrant meets us.

A mellow softness fills the air –
   No breeze on wanton wing steals by,
To break the holy quiet there,
   Or make the waters fret and sigh,
Or the golden alders shiver,
That bend to kiss the placid river,
Flowing on and on for ever;
   But the little waves seem sleeping,
   O'er the pebbles slowly creeping,
   That last night were flashing, leaping,
Driven by the restless breeze,
In lines of foam beneath yon trees.

Dress'd in robes of gorgeous hue –
   Brown and gold with crimson blent,
The forest to the waters blue
   Its own enchanting tints has lent.
In their dark depths, life-like glowing,
We see a second forest growing,

Each pictur'd leaf and branch bestowing
     A fairy grace on that twin wood,
     Mirror'd within the crystal flood.

'Tis pleasant now in forest shades; –
     The Indian hunter strings his bow
To track, through dark entangled glades,
     The antler'd deer and bounding doe;
Or launch at night his birch canoe,
     To spear the finny tribes that dwell
On sandy bank, in weedy cell,
     Or pool the fisher knows right well, –
Seen by the red and livid glow
Of pine-torch at his vessel's bow.

This dreamy Indian summer-day
     Attunes the soul to tender sadness:
We love, but joy not in the ray, –
     It is not summer's fervid gladness,
But a melancholy glory
     Hov'ring brightly round decay,
Like swan that sings her own sad story,
     Ere she floats in death away.

The day declines. – What splendid dyes,
     In flicker'd waves of crimson driven,
Float o'er the saffron sea, that lies
     Glowing within the western heaven!
     Ah, it is a peerless even!
See, the broad red sun has set,
But his rays are quivering yet
Through nature's veil of violet,
Streaming bright o'er lake and hill;
But earth and forest lie so still –
We start, and check the rising tear,
'Tis beauty sleeping on her bier.

ONE

Belleville

"The land of our adoption claims
  Our highest powers, – our firmest trust –;
May future ages blend our names
  With hers, when we shall sleep in dust.
Land of our sons! – last-born of earth,
  A mighty nation nurtures thee;
The first in moral power and worth, –
  Long mayst thou boast her sovereignty!

Union is strength, while round the boughs
  Of thine own lofty maple-tree;
The threefold wreath of Britain flows,
  Twined with the graceful *fleur-de-lis*;
A chaplet wreathed mid smiles and tears,
  In which all hues of glory blend;
Long may it bloom for future years,
  And vigour to thy weakness lend."

YEAR AFTER year, during twenty years' residence in the colony, I had indulged the hope of one day visiting the Falls of Niagara, and year after year, for twenty long years, I was doomed to disappointment.

For the first ten years, my residence in the woods of Douro, my infant family, and last, not least, among the list of objections, that great want, – the want of money, –

placed insuperable difficulties in the way of my ever accomplishing this cherished wish of my heart.

The hope, resigned for the present, was always indulged as a bright future – a pleasant day-dream – an event which at some unknown period, when happier days should dawn upon us, might take place; but which just now was entirely out of the question.

When the children were very importunate for a new book or toy, and I had not the means of gratifying them, I used to silence them by saying that I would buy that and many other nice things for them when "our money cart came home."

During the next ten years, this all-important and anxiously anticipated vehicle did not arrive. The children did not get their toys, and my journey to Niagara was still postponed to an indefinite period.

Like a true daughter of romance, I could not banish from my mind the glorious ideal I had formed of this wonder of the world; but still continued to speculate about the mighty cataract, that sublime *"thunder of waters,"* whose very name from childhood had been music to my ears.

Ah, Hope! what would life be, stripped of thy encouraging smiles, that teach us to look behind the dark clouds of to-day for the golden beams that are to gild the morrow. To those who have faith in thy promises, the most extravagant fictions are possible; and the unreal becomes material and tangible. The artist who placed thee upon the rock with an anchor for a leaning post, could never have experienced any of thy vagrant propensities. He should have invested thee with the rainbow of Iris, the winged feet of Mercury, and the upward pointing finger of Faith; and as for thy footstool, it should be a fleecy white cloud, changing its form with the changing breeze.

Yet this hope of mine, of one day seeing the Falls of Niagara, was, after all, a very enduring hope; for though I began to fear that it never would be realized, yet, for twenty years, I never gave it up entirely; and Patience, who always sits at the feet of Hope, was at length rewarded by her sister's consenting smile.

During the past summer I was confined, by severe indisposition, almost entirely to the house. The obstinate nature of my disease baffled the skill of a very clever medical attendant, and created alarm and uneasiness in my family: and I entertained small hopes of my own recovery.

Dr. L——, as a last resource, recommended change of air and scene; a remedy far more to my taste than the odious drugs from which I had not derived the least benefit. Ill and languid as I was, Niagara once more rose before my mental vision, and I exclaimed, with a thrill of joy, "The time is come at last – I shall yet see it before I die."

My dear husband was to be the companion of my long journey in search of health. Our simple arrangements were soon made, and on the 7th of September we left Belleville in the handsome new steam-boat, "The Bay of Quinte," for Kingston.

The afternoon was cloudless, the woods just tinged with their first autumnal glow, and the lovely bay, and its fairy isles, never appeared more enchanting in my eyes. Often as I had gazed upon it in storm and shine, its blue transparent waters seemed to smile upon me more lovingly than usual. With affectionate interest I looked long and tenderly upon the shores we were leaving. There stood my peaceful, happy home; the haven of rest to which Providence had conducted me after the storms and trials of many years. Within the walls of that small stone cottage, peeping forth from its screen of young hickory trees, I had left three dear children, – God only could tell whether we should ever meet on earth again: I knew that their prayers would follow me on my long journey, and the cherub Hope was still at my side, to whisper of happy hours and restored health and spirits. I blessed God, for the love of those young kindred hearts, and for having placed their home in such a charming locality.

Next to the love of God, the love of nature may be

regarded as the purest and holiest feeling of the human breast. In the outward beauty of his creation, we catch a reflection of the divine image of the Creator, which refines the intellect, and lifts the soul upward to Him. This innate perception of the beautiful, however, is confined to no rank or situation, but is found in the most barren spots, and surrounded by the most unfavourable circumstances; wherever the sun shines and warms, or the glory of the moon and stars can be seen at night, the children of genius will find a revelation of God in their beams. But there is not a doubt that those born and brought up among scenes of great natural sublimity and beauty, imbibe this feeling in a larger degree, and their minds are more easily imbued with the glorious colouring of romance, – the inspired visions of the poet.

Dear patient reader! whether of British or Canadian origin, as I wish to afford you all the amusement in my power, deign to accompany me on my long journey. Allow me a woman's privilege of talking of all sorts of things by the way. Should I tire you with my desultory mode of conversation, bear with me charitably, and take into account the infirmities incidental to my gossiping sex and age. If I dwell too long upon some subjects, do not call me a bore, or vain and trifling, if I pass too lightly over others. The little knowledge I possess, I impart freely, and wish that it was more profound and extensive, for your sake.

Come, and take your seat with me on the deck of the steamer; and as we glide over the waters of this beautiful Bay of Quinte, I will make you acquainted with every spot worthy of note along its picturesque shores.

An English lady, writing to me not long ago, expressed her weariness of my long stories about the country of my adoption, in the following terms: – "Don't fill your letters to me with descriptions of Canada. Who, *in England*, thinks anything of *Canada!*"

Here the pride so common to the inhabitants of the

favoured isles spoke out. This is perhaps excusable in those who boast that they belong to a country that possesses, in an eminent degree, the attributes bestowed by old Jacob on his first-born, – "the excellency of dignity, and the excellency of power." But, to my own thinking, it savoured not a little of arrogance, and still more of ignorance, in the fair writer; who, being a woman of talent, should have known better. A child is not a man, but his progress is regarded with more attention on that account; and his future greatness is very much determined by the progress he makes in his youth.

To judge Canada by the same standard, she appears to us a giant for her years, and well worthy the most serious contemplation. Many are the weary, overtasked minds in that great, wealthy, and powerful England, that turn towards this flourishing colony their anxious thoughts, and would willingly exchange the golden prime of the mother country for the healthy, vigorous young strength of this, her stalwart child, and consider themselves only too happy in securing a home upon these free and fertile shores.

Be not discouraged, brave emigrant. Let Canada still remain the bright future in your mind, and hasten to convert your present day-dream into reality. The time is not far distant when she shall be the theme of many tongues, and the old nations of the world will speak of her progress with respect and admiration. Her infancy is past, she begins to feel her feet, to know her own strength, and see her way clearly through the wilderness. Child as you may deem her, she has already battled bravely for her own rights, and obtained the management of her own affairs. Her onward progress is certain. There is no *if* in her case. She possesses within her own territory all the elements of future prosperity, and *she must be great!*

The men who throng her marts, and clear her forests, are *workers*, not *dreamers*, – who have already realized Solomon's pithy proverb, "In all labour is profit;" and their industry has imbued them with a spirit of independence which cannot fail to make them a free and enlightened people.

An illustration of the truth of what I advance, can be given in the pretty town we are leaving on the north side of the bay. I think you will own with me that your eyes have seldom rested upon a spot more favoured by Nature, or one that bids fairer to rise to great wealth and political importance.

Sixty years ago, the spot that Belleville now occupies was in the wilderness; and its rapid, sparkling river and sunny upland slopes (which during the lapse of ages have formed a succession of banks to the said river), were only known to the Indian hunter and the white trader.

Where you see those substantial stone wharfs, and the masts of those vessels, unloading their valuable cargoes to replenish the stores of the wealthy merchants in the town, a tangled cedar swamp spread its dark, unwholesome vegetation into the bay, completely covering with an impenetrable jungle those smooth verdant plains, now surrounded with neat cottages and gardens.

Of a bright summer evening (and when is a Canadian summer evening otherwise?) those plains swarm with happy, healthy children, who assemble there to pursue their gambols beyond the heat and dust of the town; or to watch with eager eyes the young men of the place engaged in the manly old English game of cricket, with whom it is, in their harmless boasting, "Belleville against Toronto-Cobourg; Kingston, the whole world."

The editor of a Kingston paper once had the barbarity to compare these valiant champions of the bat and ball to "singed cats – ugly to look at, but very devils to go."

Our lads have never forgiven the insult; and should the said editor ever show his face upon their ground, they would kick him off with as little ceremony as they would a spent ball.

On that high sandy ridge that overlooks the town eastward – where the tin roof of the Court House, a massy, but rather tasteless building, and the spires of four churches catch the rays of the sun – a tangled maze of hazel bushes, and wild plum and cherry, once screened the Indian burying-ground, and the children of the red hunter sought for strawberries among the long grass and wild flowers that flourish profusely in that sandy soil.

Would that you could stand with me on that lofty eminence and look around you! The charming prospect that spreads itself at your feet would richly repay you for toiling up the hill.

We will suppose ourselves standing among the graves in the burying-ground of the English church; the sunny heavens above us, the glorious waters of the bay, clasping in their azure belt three-fourths of the landscape, and the quiet dead sleeping at our feet.

The white man has so completely supplanted his red brother, that he has appropriated the very spot that held his bones; and in a few years their dust will mingle together, although no stone marks the grave where the red man sleeps.

From this churchyard you enjoy the finest view of the town and surrounding country; and, turn your eyes which way you will, they cannot fail to rest on some natural object of great interest and beauty.

The church itself is but a homely structure; and has always been to me a great eyesore. It is to be regretted that the first inhabitants of the place selected their best and most healthy building sites for the erection of places of worship. Churches and churchyards occupy the hills from whence they obtain their springs of fresh water, – and such delicious water! They do not at present feel any ill-consequences arising from this error of judgment; but the time will come, as population increases, and the dead accumulate, when these burying-grounds, by poisoning the springs that flow through them, will materially injure the health of the living.

The English church was built many years ago, partly of red brick burnt in the neighbourhood, and partly of wood coloured red to make up the deficiency of the costlier material. This seems a shabby saving, as abundance of brick-earth of the best quality abounds in the same hill, and the making of bricks forms a very lucrative and important craft to several persons in the town.

Belleville was but a small settlement on the edge of the forest, scarcely deserving the name of a village, when this church first pointed its ugly tower towards heaven. Doubtless its founders thought they had done wonders when they erected this humble looking place of worship; but now, when their descendants have become rich, and the village of log-huts and frame buildings has grown into a populous, busy, thriving town, and this red, tasteless building is too small to accommodate its congregation, it should no longer hold the height of the hill, but give place to a larger and handsomer edifice.

Behold its Catholic brother on the other side of the road; how much its elegant structure and graceful spire adds to the beauty of the scene. Yet the funds for rearing that handsome building, which is such an ornament to the town, were chiefly derived from small subscriptions, drawn from the earnings of mechanics, day-labourers, and female servants. If the Church of England were supported throughout the colony, on the voluntary principle, we should soon see fine stone churches, like St. Michael, replacing these decaying edifices of wood, and the outcry about the ever-vexed question of the Clergy Reserves, would be merged in her increased influence and prosperity.

The deep-toned, sonorous bell, that fills the steeple of the Catholic church, which cost, I have been told, seven hundred pounds, and was brought all the way from Spain, was purchased by the voluntary donations of the congregation. This bell is remarkable for its fine tone, which can be heard eight miles into the country, and as far as the village of Northport, eleven miles distant, on the other side of the bay. There is a solemn grandeur in the solitary voice of the magnificent bell, as it booms across the valley in which the town lies, and reverberates among the distant woods and hills, which has a very imposing effect.

A few years ago the mechanics in the town entered into an agreement that they would only work from six to six during the summer months, and from seven till five in the winter, and they offered to pay a certain sum to the Catholic church for tolling the bell at the said hours. The Catholic workmen who reside in or near the town, adhere strictly to this rule, and, if the season is ever so pressing, they obstinately refuse to work before or after the stated time. I have seen, on our own little farm, the mower fling down his scythe in the swathe, and the harvest-man his sickle in the ridge, the moment the bell tolled for six.

In fact, the bell in this respect is looked upon as a great nuisance; and the farmers in the country refuse to be guided by it in the hours allotted for field labour; as they justly remark that the best time for hard work in a hot country is before six in the morning, and after the heat of the day in the evening.

When the bell commences to toll there is a long pause between each of the first four strokes. This is to allow the pious Catholic time for crossing himself and saying a short prayer.

How much of the ideal mingles with this worship! No wonder that the Irish, who are such an imaginative people, should cling to it with such veneration. Would any other creed suit them as well? It is a solemn thing to step into their churches, and witness the intensity of their devotions. Reason never raises a doubt to shake the oneness of their faith. They receive it on the credit of their priests, and their credulity is as boundless as their ignorance. Often have I asked the poor Catholics in my employ why such and such days were holy days? They could seldom tell me, but said that "the priest told them to keep them holy, and to break them would be a deadly sin."

I cannot but respect their child-like trust, and the reverence they feel for their spiritual teachers; nor could I ever bring myself to believe that a conscientious Catholic was in any danger of rejection from the final bar. He has imposed upon himself a heavier yoke than the Saviour kindly laid upon him, and has enslaved himself with a thousand superstitious observances which to us appear absurd; but his sincerity should awaken in us an affectionate interest in his behalf, not engender the bitter hatred which at present forms an adamantine barrier between us. If the Protestant would give up a little of his bigotry, and the Catholic a part of his superstition, and they would consent to meet each other half way, as brothers of one common manhood, inspired by the same Christian hope, and bound to the same heavenly country, we should no longer see the orange banner flaunting our streets on the twelfth of July, and natives of the same island provoking each other to acts of violence and bloodshed.

These hostile encounters are of yearly occurrence in the colony, and are justly held in abhorrence by the pious and thinking portion of the population of either denomination. The government has for many years vainly endeavoured to put them down, but they still pollute with their moral leprosy the free institutions of the country, and effectually prevent any friendly feeling which might grow up between the members of these rival and hostile creeds.

In Canada, where all religions are tolerated, it appears a useless aggravation of an old national grievance to perpetuate the memory of the battle of the Boyne. What have we to do with the hatreds and animosities of a more barbarous age. These things belong to the past: "Let the dead bury their dead," and let us form for ourselves a holier and truer present. The old quarrel between Irish Catholics and Protestants should have been sunk in the ocean when they left their native country to find a home, unpolluted by the tyrannies of bygone ages, in the wilds of Canada.

The larger portion of our domestics are from Ireland, and, as far as my experience goes, I have found the Catholic Irish as faithful and trustworthy as the Protestants. The tendency to hate belongs to the race, not to the religion, or the Protestant would not exhibit the same vindictive spirit which marks his Catholic brother. They break and destroy more than the Protestants, but that springs from the reckless carelessness of their character more than from any malice against their employers, if you may judge by the bad usage they give their own household goods and tools. The principle on which they live is literally to care as little as possible for the things of to-day, and to take no thought at all for the morrow.

"Shure, Ma'am, it can be used," said an Irish girl to me, after breaking the spout out of an expensive china jug, "It is not a hair the worse!" She could not imagine that a mutilated object could occasion the least discomfort to those accustomed to order and neatness in their household arrangements.

The Irish female servants are remarkably chaste in their language and deportment. You are often obliged to find fault with them for gross acts of neglect and wastefulness, but never for using bad language. They may spoil your children by over-indulgence, but they never corrupt their morals by loose conversation.

An Irish girl once told me, with beautiful simplicity, "that every bad word a woman uttered, made the blessed Virgin *blush*."

A girl becoming a mother before marriage is regarded as a dreadful calamity by her family, and she seldom, if ever, gets one of her own countrymen to marry her with this stain on her character.

How different is the conduct of the female peasantry in the eastern counties of England, who unblushingly avow their derelictions from the paths of virtue. The crime of infanticide, so common there, is almost unknown among the Irish. If the priest and the confessional are able to restrain the lower orders from the commission of gross crime, who shall say that they are without their use? It is true that the priest often exercises his power over his flock in a manner which would appear to a Protestant to border on the ludicrous.

A girl who lived with a lady of my acquaintance, gave

the following graphic account of an exhortation delivered by the priest at the altar. I give it in her own words: –

"Shure, Ma'am, we got a great scould from the praste the day." "Indeed, Biddy, what did he scold you for?" "Faix, and it's not meself that he scoulded at all, at all, but Misther Peter N—— and John L——, an' he held them up as an example to the whole church. 'Peter N——' says he, 'you have not been inside this church before to-day for the last three months, and you have not paid your pew-rent for the last two years. But, maybe, you have got the fourteen dollars in your pocket at this moment of spaking; or maybe you have spint it in buying pig-iron to make gridirons, in order to fry your mate of a Friday; and when your praste comes to visit you, if he does not see it itself, he smells it. And you, John L——, Alderman L——, are not six days enough in the week for work and pastime, that you must go hunting of hares on a holiday? And pray how many hares did you catch, Alderman John?'"

The point of the last satire lay in the fact that the said Alderman John was known to be an ambitious, but very poor, sportsman; which made the allusion to the *hares* he had shot the unkindest cut of all.

Such an oration from a Protestant minister would have led his congregation to imagine that their good pastor had lost his wits; but I have no doubt that it was eminently successful in abstracting the fourteen dollars from the pocket of the dilatory Peter N——, and in preventing Alderman John from hunting hares on a holiday for the time to come.

Most of the Irish priests possess a great deal of humour, which always finds a response in their mirth-loving countrymen, to whom wit is a quality of native growth.

"I wish you a happy death, Pat S——" said Mr. R——, the jolly, black-browed priest of P——, after he had married an old servant of ours, who had reached the patriarchal age of sixty-eight, to an old woman of seventy.

"D—— clear of it!" quoth Pat, smiting his thigh, with a

look of inimitable drollery, – such a look of broad humour as can alone twinkle from the eyes of an emeralder of that class. Pat was a prophet; in less than six months he brought the body of the youthful bride in a waggon to the house of the said priest to be buried, and, for aught I know to the contrary, the old man is living still, and very likely to treat himself to a third wife.

I was told two amusing anecdotes of the late Bishop Macdonald; a man whose memory is held in great veneration in the province, which I will give you here.

The old bishop was crossing the Rice Lake in a birch bark canoe, in company with Mr. R——, the Presbyterian minister of Peterboro'; the day was rather stormy, and the water rough for such a fragile conveyance. The bishop, who had been many years in the country, knew there was little danger to be apprehended if they sat still, and he had perfect reliance in the skill of their Indian boatman. Not so Mr. R——, he had only been a few months in the colony, and this was the first time he had ever ventured upon the water in such a tottleish machine. Instead of remaining quietly seated in the bottom of the canoe, he endeavoured to start to his feet, which would inevitably have upset it. This rash movement was prevented by the bishop, who forcibly pulled him down into a sitting posture, exclaiming, as he did so, "Keep still, my good sir; if you, by your groundless fears, upset the canoe, your protestant friends will swear that the old papist drowned the presbyterian."

One hot, sultry July evening, the celebrated Dr. Dunlop called to have a chat with the bishop, who, knowing the doctor's weak point, his fondness for strong drinks, and his almost rabid antipathy to water, asked him if he would take a draught of Edinburgh ale, as he had just received a cask in a present from the old country. The doctor's thirst grew to a perfect drought, and he exclaimed "that nothing at that moment could afford him greater pleasure."

The bell was rung; the spruce, neat servant girl appeared, and was forthwith commissioned to take the bishop's own silver tankard and draw the thirsty doctor a pint of ale.

The girl quickly returned: the impatient doctor grasped the nectarian draught, and, without glancing into the tankard – for the time

"Was that soft hour 'twixt summer's eve and close," –

emptied the greater part of its contents down his throat. A spasmodic contortion and a sudden rush to the open window surprised the hospitable bishop, who had anticipated a great treat for his guest: "My dear sir," he cried, "what can be the matter!"

"Oh, that diabolical stuff!" groaned the doctor. "I am poisoned."

"Oh, never fear," said the bishop, examining the liquid that still remained in the tankard, and bursting into a hearty laugh, "It may not agree with a Protestant's stomach, but believe me, dear doctor, you never took such a wholesome drink in your life before. I was lately sent from Rome a cask of holy water, – it stands in the same cellar with the ale, – I put a little salt into it, in order to preserve it during this hot weather, and the girl, by mistake, has given you the consecrated water instead of the ale."

"Oh, curse her!" cried the tortured doctor. "I wish it was in her stomach instead of mine!"

The bishop used to tell this story with great glee whenever Dr. Dunlop and his eccentric habits formed the theme of conversation.

That the Catholics do not always act with hostility towards their Protestant brethren, the following anecdote, which it gives me great pleasure to relate, will sufficiently show: –

In the December of 1840 we had the misfortune to be burnt out, and lost a great part of our furniture, clothing, and winter stores. Poor as we *then* were, this could not be regarded in any other light but as a great calamity. During the confusion occasioned by the fire, and, owing to the negligence of a servant to whose care he was especially confided, my youngest child, a fine boy of two years old, was for some time missing. The agony I endured for about half an hour I shall never forget. The roaring flames, the impending misfortune that hung over us, was forgotten in the terror that shook my mind lest he had become a victim to the flames. He was at length found by a kind neighbour in the kitchen of the burning building, whither he had crept from among the crowd, and was scarcely rescued before the roof fell in.

This circumstance shook my nerves so completely that I gladly accepted the offer of a female friend to leave the exciting scene, and make her house my home until we could procure another.

I was sitting at her parlour window, with the rescued child on my lap, whom I could not bear for a moment out of my sight, watching the smoking brands that had once composed my home, and sadly pondering over our untoward destiny, when Mrs.——'s servant told me that a gentleman wanted to see me in the drawing-room.

With little Johnnie still in my arms I went to receive the visitor; and found the Rev. Father B——, the worthy Catholic priest, waiting to receive me.

At that time I knew very little of Father B——. Calls had been exchanged, and we had been much pleased with his courteous manners and racy Irish wit. I shall never forget the kind, earnest manner in which he condoled with me on our present misfortune. He did not, however, confine his sympathy to words, but offered me the use of his neat cottage until we could provide ourselves with another house.

"You know," he said, with a benevolent smile, "I have no family to be disturbed by the noise of the children; and if you will accept the temporary home I offer you, it is entirely at your service; and," he continued, lowering his voice, "if the sheriff is in want of money to procure necessaries for his family, I can supply him until such time as he is able to repay me."

This was truly noble, and I thanked him with tears in

my eyes. We did not accept the generous offer of this good Samaritan; but we have always felt a grateful remembrance of his kindness. Mr. B—— had been one of the most active among the many gentlemen who did their best in trying to save our property from the flames, a great portion of which was safely conveyed to the street. But here a system of pillage was carried on by the heartless beings, who regard fires and wreck as their especial harvest, which entirely frustrated the efforts of the generous and brave men who had done so much to help us.

How many odd things happen during a fire, which would call up a hearty laugh upon a less serious occasion. I saw one man pitch a handsome chamber-glass out of an upper window into the street, in order to *save* it; while another, at the risk of his life, carried a bottomless china jug, which had long been useless, down the burning staircase, and seemed quite elated with his success; and a carpenter took off the doors, and removed the window-sashes, in order to preserve them, and, by sending a rush of air through the burning edifice, accelerated its destruction.

At that time there was only one fire-engine in the town, and that was not in a state to work. Now they have two excellent engines, worked by an active and energetic body of men.

In all the principal towns and cities in the colony, a large portion of the younger male inhabitants enrol themselves into a company for the suppression of fire. It is a voluntary service, from which they receive no emolument, without an exemption from filling the office of a juryman may be considered as an advantage. These men act upon a principle of mutual safety; and the exertions which are made by them, in the hour of danger, are truly wonderful, and serve to show what can be effected by men when they work in unison together.

To the Canadian fire-companies the public is indebted for the preservation of life and property by a thousand heroic acts; – deeds, that would be recorded as surprising efforts of human courage, if performed upon the battle-field; and which often exhibit an exalted benevolence, when exercised in rescuing helpless women and children from such a dreadful enemy as fire.

The costume adopted by the firemen is rather becoming than otherwise; – a tight-fitting frock-coat of coarse red cloth, and white trousers in summer, which latter portion of their dress is exchanged for dark blue in the winter. They wear a glazed black leather cap, of a military cut, when they assemble to work their engines, or walk in procession; and a leather hat like a sailor's nor'-wester, with a long peak behind, to protect them from injury, when on active duty.

Their members are confined to no particular class. Gen-tlemen and mechanics work side by side in this fraternity, with a zeal and right good will that is truly edifying. Their system appears an excellent one; and I never heard of any dissension among their ranks when their services were required. The sound of the ominous bell calls them to the spot, from the greatest distance; and, during the most stormy nights, whoever skulks in bed, the fireman is sure to be at his post.

Once a year, the different divisions of the company walk in procession through the town. On this occasion their engines are dressed up with flags bearing appropri-ate mottoes; and they are preceded by a band of music. The companies are generally composed of men in the very prime of life, and they make a very imposing appearance. It is always a great gala day in the town, and terminates with a public dinner; that is followed by a ball in the evening, at which the wives and daughters of the members of the company are expected to appear.

Once a month the firemen are called out to practise with the engine in the streets, to the infinite delight of all the boys in the neighbourhood, who follow the engine in crowds, and provoke the operators to turn the hose and play upon their merry ranks: and then what laughing and shouting and scampering in all directions, as the ragged urchins shake their dripping garments, and fly from the ducking they had courted a few minutes before!

The number of wooden buildings that compose the larger portion of Canadian towns renders fire a calamity of very frequent occurrence, and persons cannot be too particular in regard to it. The negligence of one ignorant servant in the disposal of her ashes, may involve the safety of the whole community.

As long as the generality of the houses are roofed with shingles, this liability to fire must exist as a necessary consequence.

The shingle is a very thin pine-board, which is used throughout the colony instead of slate or tiles. After a few years, the heat and rain roughen the outward surface, and give it a woolly appearance, rendering the shingles as inflammable as tinder. A spark from a chimney may be conveyed from a great distance on a windy day, and lighting upon the furry surface of these roofs, is sure to ignite. The danger spreads on all sides, and the roofs of a whole street will be burning before the fire communicates to the walls of the buildings.

So many destructive fires have occurred of late years throughout the colony that a law has been enacted by the municipal councils to prevent the erection of wooden buildings in the large cities. But without the additional precaution of fire-proof roofs, the prohibition will not produce very beneficial effects.

Two other very pretty churches occupy the same hill with the Catholics and Episcopal, – the Scotch Residuary, and the Free Church. The latter is built of dark limestone, quarried in the neighbourhood, and is a remarkably graceful structure. It has been raised by the hearty good-will and free donations of its congregation; and affords another capital illustration of the working of the voluntary principle.

To the soul-fettering doctrines of John Calvin I am myself no convert; nor do I think that the churches established on his views will very long exist in the world. Stern, uncompromising, unloveable and unloved, an object of fear rather than of affection, John Calvin stands out the incarnation of his own Deity; verifying one of the noblest and truest sentences ever penned by man: – "As the man, so his God. God is his idea of excellence, – the compliment of his own being."

The Residuary church is a small neat building of wood, painted white. For several years after the great split in the National Church of Scotland, it was shut up, the few who still adhered to the old way being unable to contribute much to the support of a minister. The church has been reopened within the last two years, and, though the congregation is very small, has a regular pastor.

The large edifice beneath us, in Pinacle-street, leading to the bay, is the Wesleyan Methodist church, or chapel, as it would be termed at home. Thanks to the liberal institutions of the country, such distinctions are unknown in Canada. Every community of Christian worshippers is rightly termed *a church*. *The Church* is only arrogated by one.

The Wesleyans, who have been of infinite use in spreading the Gospel on the North American continent, possess a numerous and highly respectable congregation in this place. Their church is always supplied with good and efficient preachers, and is filled on the Sabbath to overflowing. They have a very fine choir, and lately purchased an organ, which was constructed by one of their own members, a genius in his way, for which they gave the handsome sum of a thousand dollars.

There is also an Episcopal Methodist church, composed of red brick, at the upper end of the town, by the river side, which is well attended.

You can scarcely adopt a better plan of judging of the wealth and prosperity of a town, than by watching, of a Sabbath morning, the congregations of the different denominations going to church.

Belleville weekly presents to the eye of an observing spectator a large body of well-dressed, happy-looking people, – robust, healthy, independent-looking men, and well-formed, handsome women; – an air of content and comfort resting upon their comely faces, – no look of haggard care and pinching want marring the quiet solemnity of the scene.

The dress of the higher class is not only cut in the newest French fashion, imported from New York, but is generally composed of rich and expensive materials. The Canadian lady dresses well and tastefully, and carries herself easily and gracefully. She is not unconscious of the advantages of a pretty face and figure; but her knowledge of the fact is not exhibited in an affected or disagreeable manner. The lower class are not a whit behind their wealthier neighbours in outward adornments. And the poor emigrant, who only a few months previously had landed in rags, is now dressed neatly and respectably. The consciousness of their newly-acquired freedom has raised them in the scale of society, in their own estimation, and in that of their fellows. They feel that they are no longer despised; the ample wages they receive has enabled them to cast off the slough of hopeless poverty, which once threw its deadening influence over them, repressing all their energies, and destroying that self-respect which is so necessary to mental improvement and self-government. The change in their condition is apparent in their smiling, satisfied faces.

This is, indeed, a delightful contrast to the squalid want and poverty which so often meet the eye, and pain the heart of the philanthropist at home. Canada is blessed in the almost total absence of pauperism; for none but the wilfully idle and vicious need starve here, while the wants of the sick and infirm meet with ready help and sympathy from a most charitable public.

The Wesleyan Methodists wisely placed their burying-ground at some distance from the town; and when we first came to reside at Belleville, it was a retired and lovely spot, on the Kingston road, commanding a fine view of the bay. The rapid spread of the village into a town almost embraces in its arms this once solitary spot, and in a few years it will be surrounded with suburban residences.

There is a very large brick field adjoining this cemetery, which employs during the summer months a number of hands.

Turn to the north, and observe that old-fashioned, red-brick house, now tottering to decay, that crowns the precipitous ridge that overlooks the river, and which doubtless at some very distant period once formed its right bank. That house was built by one of the first settlers in Belleville, an officer who drew his lot of wild land on that spot. It was a great house in those days, and he was a great man in the eyes of his poorer neighbours.

This gentleman impoverished himself and his family by supplying from his own means the wants of the poor emigrants in his vicinity during the great Canadian famine, which happened about fifty years ago. The starving creatures promised to repay him at some future period. Plenty again blessed the land; but the generous philanthropist was forgotten by those his bounty had saved. Peace to his memory! Though unrewarded on earth, he has doubtless reaped his reward in heaven.

The river Moira, which runs parallel with the main street of the town, and traverses several fine townships belonging to the county of Hastings in its course to the bay, is a rapid and very picturesque stream. Its rocky banks, which are composed of limestone, are fringed with the graceful cedar, soft maple, and elegant rock elm, that queen of the Canadian forest. It is not navigable, but is one great source of the wealth and prosperity of the place, affording all along its course excellent sites for mills, distilleries, and factories, while it is the main road down which millions of feet of timber are yearly floated, to be rafted at the entrance of the bay.

The spring floods bring down such a vast amount of lumber, that often a jam, as it is technically called, places the two bridges that span the river in a state of blockade.

It is a stirring and amusing scene to watch the French

Canadian lumberers, with their long poles, armed at the end with sharp spikes, leaping from log to log, and freeing a passage for the crowded timbers.

Handsome in person, and lithe and active as wild cats, you would imagine, to watch their careless disregard of danger, that they were born of the waters, and considered death by drowning an impossible casualty in their case. Yet never a season passes without fatal accidents thinning their gay, lighthearted ranks.

These amphibious creatures spend half their lives in and on the waters. They work hard in forming rafts at the entrance of the bay during the day, and in the evening they repair to some favourite tavern, where they spend the greater part of the night in singing and dancing. Their peculiar cries awaken you by day-break, and their joyous shouts and songs are wafted on the evening breeze. Their picturesque dress and shanties, when shown by their red watchfires along the rocky banks of the river at night, add great liveliness, and give a peculiarly romantic character to the water scene.

They appear a happy, harmless set of men, brave and independent; and if drinking and swearing are vices common to their caste and occupation, it can scarcely be wondered at in the wild, reckless, roving life they lead. They never trouble the peaceful inhabitants of the town. Their broils are chiefly confined to their Irish comrades, and seldom go beyond the scene of their mutual labour. It is not often that they find their way into the jail or penitentiary.

A young lady told me an adventure that befell her and her sister, which is rather a droll illustration of the manners of a French Canadian lumberer. They were walking one fine summer evening along the west bank of the Moira, and the narrator, in stooping over the water to gather some wild-flowers that grew in a crevice of the rocks, dropped her parasol into the river. A cry of vexation at the loss of an article of dress, which is expensive, and almost indispensable beneath the rays of a Canadian summer sun, burst from her lips, and attracted the attention of a young man whom she had not before observed, who was swimming at some distance down the river. He immediately turned, and dexterously catching the parasol as it swiftly glided past him, swam towards the ladies with the rescued article, carried dog-fashion, between his teeth.

In his zeal to render this little service, the poor fellow forgot that he was not in a condition to appear before ladies; who, startled at such an extraordinary apparition, made the best of their heels to fly precipitately from the spot.

"I have no doubt," said Miss ——, laughing, "that the good-natured fellow meant well, but I never was so frightened and confounded in my life. The next morning the parasol was returned at the street door, with "Jean Baptiste's compliments to the young ladies." So much for French Canadian gallantry.

It is a pretty sight. A large raft of timber, extending perhaps for a quarter of a mile, gliding down the bay in tow of a steamer, decorated with red flags and green pine boughs, and managed by a set of bold active fellows, whose jovial songs waken up the echoes of the lonely woods. I have seen several of these rafts, containing many thousand pounds worth of timber, taking their downward course in one day.

The centre of the raft is generally occupied by a shanty and cooking apparatus, and at night it presents an imposing spectacle, seen by the red light of their fires, as it glides beneath the shadow of some lofty bank, with its dark overhanging trees. I have often coveted a sail on those picturesque rafts, over those smooth moonlighted waters.

The spring-floods bring with them a great quantity of waste timber and fallen trees from the interior; and it is amusing to watch the poor Irishwomen and children wading to the waist in the water, and drawing out these waifs and strays with hooked sticks, to supply their shanties with fuel. It is astonishing how much an industrious lad can secure in a day of this refuse timber. No gleaner ever

enters a harvest-field in Canada to secure a small portion
of the scattered grain; but the floating treasures which the
waters yield are regarded as a providential supply of fir-
ing, which is always gathered in. These spring-floods are
often productive of great mischief, as they not infre-
quently carry away all the dams and bridges along their
course. This generally happens after an unusually severe
winter, accompanied with very heavy falls of snow.

The melting of the snows in the back country, by filling
all the tributary creeks and streams, converts the larger
rivers into headlong and destructive torrents, that rush
and foam along with "curbless force," carrying huge
blocks of ice and large timbers, like feathers upon their
surface.

It is a grand and beautiful sight, the coming down of the
waters during one of these spring freshets. The river roars
and rages like a chafed lion; and frets and foams against
its rocky barrier, as if determined to overcome every
obstacle that dares to impede its furious course. Great
blocks of ice are seen popping up and down in the boiling
surges; and unwieldy saw-logs perform the most extravagant capers, often starting bolt upright; while their crystal
neighbours, enraged at the uncourteous collision, turn up
their glittering sea-green edges with an air of defiance, and
tumble about in the current like mad monsters of the
deep.

The blocks of ice are sometimes lifted entirely out of the
water by the force of the current, and deposited upon the
top of the bank, where they form an irregular wall of
glass, glittering and melting leisurely in the heat of the
sun.

A stranger who had not witnessed their upheaval,
might well wonder by what gigantic power they had been
placed there.

In March, 1844, a severe winter was terminated by a
very sudden thaw, accompanied by high winds and del-
uges of rain. In a few days the snow was all gone, and
every slope and hill was converted into a drain, down

which the long-imprisoned waters rushed continuously to the river. The roads were almost impassable, and, on the 12th of the month, the river rose to an unusual height, and completely filled its rocky banks. The floods brought down from the interior a great jam of ice, which, accumulating in size and altitude at every bridge and dam it had carried away in its course towards the bay, was at length arrested in its progress at the lower bridge, where the ice, though sunk several feet below the rushing waters, still adhered firmly to the shore. Vast pieces of ice were piled up against the abutments of the bridge, which the mountain of ice threatened to annihilate, as well as to inundate the lower end of the town.

It presented to the eager and excited crowd, who, in spite of the impending danger rushed to the devoted bridge, a curious and formidable spectacle. Imagine, dear reader, a huge mass, composed of blocks of ice, large stones, and drift timber, occupying the centre of the river, and extending back for a great distance; the top on a level with the roofs of the houses. The inhabitants of the town had everything to dread from such a gigantic battering-ram applied to their feeble wooden bridge.

A consultation was held by the men assembled on the bridge, and it was thought that the danger might be averted by sawing asunder the ice, which still held firm, and allowing a free passage for the blocks that impeded the bridge.

The river was soon covered with active men, armed with axes and poles, some freeing the ice at the arch of the bridge, others attempting to push the iceberg nearer to the shore, where, if once stranded, it would melt at leisure. If the huge pile of mischief could have found a voice, it would have laughed at their fruitless endeavours.

While watching the men at their dangerous, and, as it proved afterwards, hopeless work, we witnessed an act of extraordinary courage and presence of mind in two brothers, blacksmiths in the town. One of these young men was busy cutting away the ice just above the bridge, when quite unexpectedly the piece on which he was standing gave way, and he was carried with the speed of thought under the bridge. His death appeared inevitable. But quick as his exit was from the exciting scene, the love in the brother's heart was as quick in taking measures for his safety. As the ice on which the younger lad stood parted, the elder sprang into the hollow box of wood which helped to support the arch of the bridge, and which was filled with great stones. As the torrent swept his brother past him and under the bridge, the drowning youth gave a spring from the ice on which he still stood, and the other bending at the instant from his perch above, caught him by the collar, and lifted him bodily from his perilous situation. All was the work of a moment; yet the spectators held their breath, and wondered as they saw. It was an act of bold daring on the one hand, of cool determined courage on the other. It was a joyful sight to see the rescued lad in his brave brother's arms.

All day we watched from the bridge the hill of ice, wondering when it would take a fresh start, and if it would carry away the bridge when it left its present position. Night came down, and the unwelcome visitant remained stationary. The air was cold and frosty. There was no moon, and the spectators were reluctantly forced to retire to their respective homes. Between the watches of the night we listened to the roaring of the river, and speculated upon the threatened destruction. By daybreak my eager boys were upon the spot, to ascertain the fate of the bridge. All was grim and silent. The ice remained like a giant slumbering upon his post.

So passed the greater part of the day. Curiosity was worn out. The crowd began to disperse, disappointed that the ruin they anticipated had not taken place; just as some persons are sorry when a fire, which has caused much alarm by its central position in a town or city, is extinguished, without burning down a single house. The love of excitement drowns for a time the better feelings of humanity. They don't wish any person to suffer injury; but they give up the grand spectacle they had expected to witness with regret.

At four o'clock in the afternoon most of the wonder-watchers had retired, disgusted with the tardy movements of the ice monster, when a cry arose from the banks of the river, to warn the few persons who still loitered on the bridge, to look out. The ice was in motion. Every one within hearing rushed to the river. We happened to be passing at the time, and, like the rest, hurried to the spot. The vast pile, slowly, almost imperceptibly, began to advance, giving an irresistible impulse to the shore ice, that still held good, and which was instantly communicated to the large pieces that blocked the arch of the bridge, over which the waves now poured in a torrent, pushing before them the great lumps which up to the present moment had been immoveably wedged. There was a hollow, gurgling sound, a sullen roar of waters, a cracking and rending of the shore-bound ice, and the ponderous mass smote the bridge; it parted asunder, and swift as an arrow the crystal mountain glided downwards to the bay, spurning from its base the waves that leaped and foamed around its path, and pouring them in a flood of waters over the west bank of the river.

Beyond the loss of a few old sheds along the shore, very little damage was sustained by the town. The streets near the wharfs were inundated for a few hours, and the cellars filled with water; but after the exit of the iceberg, the river soon subsided into its usual channel.

The winter of 1852 was one of great length and severity. The snow in many of the roads was level with the top rail of the fences, and the spring thaw caused heavy freshets through the colony. In the upper part of the province, particularly on the grand river, the rising of the waters destroyed a large amount of valuable mill property. One mill-owner lost 12,000 saw logs. Our wild, bright Moira was swollen to the brim, and tumbled along with the impetuosity of a mountain torrent. Its course to the bay was unimpeded by ice, which had been all carried out a few days before by a high wind; but vast quantities of saw logs that had broken away from their bosoms in the interior were plunging in the current, sometimes starting bolt upright, or turning over and over, as if endued with the spirit of life, as well as with that of motion.

Several of these heavy timbers had struck the upper bridge, and carried away the centre arch. A poor cow, who was leisurely pacing over to her shed and supper, was suddenly precipitated into the din of waters. Had it been the mayor of the town, the accident could scarcely have produced a greater excitement. The cow belonged to a poor Irishman, and the sympathy of every one was enlisted in her fate. Was it possible that she could escape drowning amid such a mad roar of waves? No human arm could stem for a moment such a current; but fortunately for our heroine, she was not human, but only a stupid quadruped.

The cow for a few seconds seemed bewildered at the strange situation in which she found herself so unexpectedly placed. But she was wise enough and skilful enough to keep her head above water, and she cleared two mill-dams before she became aware of the fact; and she accommodated herself to her critical situation with a stoical indifference which would have done credit to an ancient philosopher. After passing unhurt over the dams, the spectators who crowded the lower bridges to watch the result, began to entertain hopes for her life.

The bridges are in a direct line, and about half a mile apart. On came the cow, making directly for the centre arch of the bridge on which we stood. She certainly neither swam, nor felt her feet, but was borne along by the force of the stream.

"My eyes! I wish I could swim as well as that ere cow," cried an excited boy, leaping upon the top of the bridge.

"I guess you do," said another. "But that's a game cow. There's no boy in the town could beat her."

"She will never pass the arch of the bridge," said a man, sullenly; "she will be killed against the abutment."

"Jolly! she's through the arch!" shouted the first speaker. "Pat has saved his cow!"

"She's not ashore yet," returned the man. "And she begins to flag."

"Not a bit of it," cried the excited boy. "The old daisy-cropper looks as fresh as a rose. Hurrah, boys! let us run down to the wharf, and see what becomes of her."

Off scampered the juveniles; and on floated the cow, calm and self-possessed in the midst of danger. After passing safely through the arch of the bridge, she continued to steer herself out of the current, and nearer to the shore, and finally effected a landing in Front-street, where she quietly walked on shore, to the great admiration of the youngsters, who received her with rapturous shouts of applause. One lad seized her by the tail, another grasped her horns, while a third patted her dripping neck, and wished her joy of her safe landing. Not Venus herself, when she rose from the sea, attracted more enthusiastic admirers than did the poor Irishman's cow. A party, composed of all the boys in the place, led her in triumph through the streets, and restored her to her rightful owner, not forgetting to bestow upon her three hearty cheers at parting.

A little black boy, the only son of a worthy negro, who had been a settler for many years in Belleville, was not so fortunate as the Irishman's cow. He was pushed, it is said accidentally, from the broken bridge, by a white boy of his own age, into that hell of waters, and it was many weeks before his body was found; it had been carried some miles down the bay by the force of the current. Day after day you might see his unhappy father, armed with a long pole, with a hook attached to it, mournfully pacing the banks of the swollen river, in the hope of recovering the remains of his lost child. Once or twice we stopped to speak to him, but his heart was too full to answer. He would turn away, with the tears rolling down his sable cheeks, and resume his melancholy task.

What a dreadful thing is this prejudice against race and

colour! How it hardens the heart, and locks up all the avenues of pity! The premature death of this little negro excited less interest in the breasts of his white companions than the fate of the cow, and was spoken of with as little concern as the drowning of a pup or a kitten.

Alas! this river Moira has caused more tears to flow from the eyes of heart-broken parents than any stream of the like size in the province. Heedless of danger, the children will resort to its shores, and play upon the timbers that during the summer months cover its surface. Often have I seen a fine child of five or six years old, astride of a saw-log, riding down the current, with as much glee as if it were a real steed he bestrode. If the log turns, which is often the case, the child stands a great chance of being drowned.

Oh, agony unspeakable! The writer of this lost a fine talented boy of six years – one to whom her soul clave – in those cruel waters. But I will not dwell upon that dark hour, the saddest and darkest in my sad eventful life. Many years ago, when I was a girl myself, my sympathies were deeply excited by reading an account of the grief of a mother who had lost her only child, under similar circumstances. How prophetic were those lines of all that I suffered during that heavy bereavement! –

THE MOTHER'S LAMENT.

"Oh, cold at my feet thou wert sleeping, my boy,
    And I press on thy pale lips in vain the fond kiss!
Earth opens her arms to receive thee, my joy,
    And all my past sorrows were nothing to this.
The day-star of hope 'neath thine eye-lid is sleeping,
No more to arise at the voice of my weeping.

"Oh, how art thou changed, since the light breath of morning
    Dispersed the soft dewdrops in showers from the tree!
Like a beautiful bud my lone dwelling adorning,
    Thy smiles call'd up feelings of rapture in me:

I thought not the sunbeams all gaily that shone
On thy waking, at night would behold me alone.

"The joy that flash'd out from thy death-shrouded eyes,
    That laugh'd in thy dimples, and brighten'd thy cheek,
Is quench'd – but the smile on thy pale lip that lies,
    Now tells of a joy that no language can speak.
The fountain is seal'd, the young spirit at rest, –
Oh, why should I mourn thee, my lov'd one – my blest!"

The anniversary of that fatal day gave birth to the following lines, with which I will close this long chapter: –

THE EARLY LOST.

"The shade of death upon my threshold lay,
    The sun from thy life's dial had departed;
A cloud came down upon thy early day,
    And left thy hapless mother broken-hearted –
                    My boy – my boy!

"Long weary months have pass'd since that sad day,
    But naught beguiles my bosom of its sorrow;
Since the cold waters took thee for their prey,
    No smiling hope looks forward to the morrow –
                    My boy – my boy!

"The voice of mirth is silenced in my heart,
    Thou wert so dearly loved – so fondly cherish'd;
I cannot yet believe that we must part, –
    That all, save thine immortal soul, has perish'd –
                    My boy – my boy!

"My lovely, laughing, rosy, dimpled, child,
    I call upon thee, when the sun shines clearest;
In the dark lonely night, in accents wild,
    I breathe thy treasured name, my best and dearest –
                    My boy – my boy!

"The hand of God has press'd me very sore –
  Oh, could I clasp thee once more as of yore,
    And kiss thy glowing cheeks' soft velvet bloom,
  I would resign thee to the Almighty Giver
  Without one tear, – would yield thee up for ever,
    And people with bright forms thy silent tomb.
  But hope has faded from my heart – and joy
  Lies buried in thy grave, my darling boy!"

TWO

Local Improvements – Sketches of Society

"Prophet spirit! rise and say,
    What in Fancy's glass you see –
A city crown this lonely bay?"
    "No dream – a bright reality.
Ere half a century has roll'd
    Its waves of light away,
The beauteous vision I behold
    Shall greet the rosy day;
And Belleville view with civic pride
    Her greatness mirror'd in the tide."

S.M.

T HE TOWN of Belleville, in 1840, contained a population of 1,500 souls, or thereabouts. The few streets it then possessed were chiefly composed of frame houses, put up in the most unartistic and irregular fashion, their gable ends or fronts turned to the street, as it suited the whim or convenience of the owner, without the least regard to taste or neatness. At that period there were only two stone houses and two of brick in the place. One of these wonders of the village was the court-house and gaol; the other three were stores. The dwellings of the wealthier portion of the community were distinguished by a coat of white or yellow paint, with green or brown doors and window blinds; while the houses of the poorer class retained the dull grey, which the plain boards always assume after a short exposure to the weather.

In spite of the great beauty of the locality, it was but an insignificant, dirty-looking place. The main street of the town (Front-street, as it is called) was only partially paved with rough slabs of limestone, and these were put so carelessly down that their uneven edges, and the difference in their height and size, was painful to the pedestrian, and destruction to his shoes, leading you to suppose that the paving committee had been composed of shoemakers. In spring and fall the mud was so deep in the centre of the thoroughfare that it required you to look twice before you commenced the difficult task of crossing, lest you might chance to leave your shoes sticking fast in the mud. This I actually saw a lady do one Sunday while crossing the church hill. Belleville had just been incorporated as the metropolitan town of the Victoria District, and my husband presided as Sheriff in the first court ever held in the place.

Twelve brief years have made a wonderful, an almost miraculous, change in the aspect and circumstances of the town. A stranger, who had not visited it during that period, could scarcely recognize it as the same. It has more than doubled its dimensions, and its population has increased to upwards of 4,500 souls. Handsome commodious stores, filled with expensive goods from the mother country and the States, have risen in the place of the small dark frame buildings; and large hotels have jostled into obscurity the low taverns and groceries that once formed the only places of entertainment.

In 1840, a wooded swamp extended almost the whole way from Belleville to Cariff's Mills, a distance of three miles. The road was execrable; and only a few log shanties, or very small frame houses, occurred at intervals along the road-side. Now, Cariff's Mills is as large as Belleville was in 1840, and boasts of a population of upwards of 1000 inhabitants. A fine plank road connects it with the latter place, and the whole distance is one continuous street. Many of the houses by the wayside are pretty ornamental cottages, composed of brick or stone. An immense traffic in flour and lumber is carried on at this place, and the plank road has proved a very lucrative speculation to the shareholders.

In 1840, there was but one bank agency in Belleville, now there are four, three of which do a great business. At that period we had no market, although Saturday was generally looked upon as the market-day; the farmers choosing it as the most convenient to bring to town their farm produce for sale. Our first market-house was erected in 1849; it was built of wood, and very roughly finished. This proved but poor economy in the long run, as it was burnt down the succeeding year. A new and more commodious one of brick has been erected in its place, and it is tolerably supplied with meat and vegetables; but these articles are both dearer and inferior in quality to those offered in Kingston and Toronto. This, perhaps, is owing to the tardiness shown by the farmers in bringing in their produce, which they are obliged to offer first for sale in the market, or be subjected to a trifling fine. There is very little competition, and the butchers and town grocery-keepers have it their own way. A market is always a stirring scene. Here politics, commercial speculations, and the little floating gossip of the village, are freely talked over and discussed. To those who feel an interest in the study of human nature, the market affords an ample field. Imagine a conversation like the following, between two decently dressed mechanics' wives:

"How are you, Mrs. G——?"

"Moderate, I thank you. Did you hear how old P—— was to-day?"

"Mortal bad."

"Why! you don't say. Our folks heard that he was getting quite smart. Is he *dangerous?*"

"The doctor has given him up entirely."

"Well, it will be a bad job for the family if he goes. I've he'rd that there won't be money enough to pay his debts.

But what of this marriage? They do say that Miss A——
is to be married to old Mister B——."

"What are her friends thinking about to let that young
gal marry that old bald-headed man?"

"The money to be sure – they say he's rich."

"If he's rich, he never made his money honestly."

"Ah, he came of a bad set," – with a shake of the head.

And so they go on, talking and chatting over the affairs
of the neighbourhood in succession. It is curious to watch
the traits of character exhibited in buyer and seller. Both
exceed the bounds of truth and honesty. The one, in his
eagerness to sell his goods, bestowing upon them the most
unqualified praise; the other depreciating them below
their real value, in order to obtain them at an unreason-
ably low price.

"Fine beef, ma'am," exclaims an anxious butcher,
watching, with the eye of a hawk, a respectable citizen's
wife, as she paces slowly and irresolutely in front of his
stall, where he has hung out for sale the side of an ox,
neither the youngest nor fattest. "Fine grass-fed beef,
ma'am – none better to be had in the district. What shall I
send you home – sirloin, ribs, a tender steak?"

"It would be a difficult matter to do that," responds the
good wife, with some asperity in look and tone. "It seems
hard and old; some lean cow you have killed, to save her
from dying of the consumption."

"No danger of the fat setting fire to the lum" – suggests
a rival in the trade. "Here's a fine veal, ma'am, fatted
upon the milk of two cows."

"Looks," says the comely dame, passing on to the next
stall, "as if it had been starved upon the milk of one."

Talking of markets puts me in mind of a trick – a
wicked trick – but, perhaps, not the less amusing on that
account, that was played off in Toronto market last year
by a young medical student, name unknown. It was the
Christmas week, and the market was adorned with ever-
greens, and dressed with all possible care. The stalls
groaned beneath the weight of good cheer – fish, flesh,

and fowl, all contributing their share to tempt the appetite and abstract money from the purse. It was a sight to warm the heart of the most fastidious epicure, and give him the nightmare for the next seven nights, only dreaming of that stupendous quantity of food to be masticated by the jaws of man. One butcher had the supreme felicity of possessing a fine fat heifer, that had taken the prize at the provincial agricultural show; and the monster of fat, which was justly considered the pride of the market, was hung up in the most conspicuous place in order to attract the gaze of all beholders.

Dr. C——, a wealthy doctor of laws, was providing good cheer for the entertainment of a few choice friends on Christmas-day, and ordered of the butcher four ribs of the tempting-looking beef. The man, unwilling to cut up the animal until she had enjoyed her full share of admiration, wrote upon a piece of paper, in large characters, "Prize Heifer – four ribs for Dr. C——;" this he pinned upon the carcase of the beast. Shortly after the doctor quitted the market, and a very fat young lady and her mother came up to the stall to make some purchases, our student was leaning carelessly against it, watching with bright eyes the busy scene; and being an uncommonly mischievous fellow, and very fond of practical jokes, a thought suddenly struck him of playing off one upon the stout young lady. Her back was towards him, and dexterously abstracting the aforementioned placard from the side of the heifer, he transferred it to the shawl of his unsuspecting victim, just where its ample folds comfortably encased her broad shoulders.

After a while the ladies left the market, amidst the suppressed titters and outstretched fore-fingers of butchers and hucksters, and all the idle loafers that generally congregate in such places of public resort. All up the length of King-street walked the innocent damsel, marvelling that the public attention appeared exclusively bestowed upon her. Still, as she passed along, bursts of laughter resounded on all sides, and the oft-repeated words, "Prize

Heifer – four ribs for Dr. C——;" it was not until she reached her own dwelling that she became aware of the trick.

The land to the east, north, and west of Belleville, rises to a considerable height, and some of the back townships, like Huntingdon and Hungerford, abound in lofty hills. There is in the former township, on the road leading from Rawdon village to Luke's tavern, a most extraordinary natural phenomenon. The road for several miles runs along the top of a sharp ridge, so narrow that it leaves barely breadth enough for two waggons to pass in safety. This ridge is composed of gravel, and looks as if it had been subjected to the action of water. On either side of this huge embankment there is a sheer descent into a finely wooded level plain below, through which wanders a lonely creek, or small stream. I don't know what the height of this ridge is above the level of the meadow, but it must be very considerable, as you look down upon the tops of the loftiest forest trees as they grow far, far beneath you. The road is well fenced on either side, or it would require some courage to drive young skittish horses along this dangerous pass. The settlers in that vicinity have given to this singular rise the name of the "Ridge road." There is a sharp ridge of limestone at the back of the township of Thurlow, though of far less dimensions, which looks as if it had been thrown up in some convulsion of the earth, as the limestone is shattered in all directions. The same thing occurs on the road to Shannonville, a small but flourishing village on the Kingston road, nine miles east of Belleville. The rock is heaved up in the middle, and divided by deep cracks into innumerable fragments. I put a long stick down one of these deep cracks without reaching the bottom; and as I gathered a lovely bunch of harebells, that were waving their graceful blossoms over the barren rock, I thought what an excellent breeding place for snakes these deep fissures must make.

But to return to Belleville. The west side of the river – a

flat limestone plain, scantily covered with a second growth of dwarf trees and bushes – has not as yet been occupied, although a flourishing village that has sprung up within a few years crowns the ridge above. The plain below is private property, and being very valuable, as affording excellent sites for flour and saw mills, has been reserved in order to obtain a higher price. This circumstance has, doubtless, been a drawback to the growth of the town in that direction; while, shutting out the view of the river by the erection of large buildings, will greatly diminish the natural beauties of this picturesque spot.

The approach to Belleville, both from the east and west, is down a very steep hill, the town lying principally in the valley below. These hills command a beautiful prospect of wood and water, and of a rich, well-cleared, and highly cultivated country. Their sides are adorned with fine trees, which have grown up since the axe first levelled the primeval forests in this part of the colony; a circumstance which, being unusual in Canada round new settlements, forms a most attractive feature in the landscape.

A more delightful summer's evening ride could scarcely be pointed out than along the Trent, or Kingston roads, and it would be a difficult thing to determine which afforded the most varied and pleasing prospect. Residing upon the west hill, we naturally prefer it to the other, but I have some doubts whether it is really the prettiest. I have often imagined a hundred years to have passed away, and the lovely sloping banks of the Bay of Quinte, crowned with rural villages and stately parks and houses, stretching down to these fair waters. What a scene of fertility and beauty rises before my mental vision! My heart swells, and I feel proud that I belong to a race who, in every portion of the globe in which they have planted a colony, have proved themselves worthy to be the sires of a great nation.

The state of society when we first came to this district, was everything but friendly or agreeable. The ferment occasioned by the impotent rebellion of W.L. Mackenzie had hardly subsided. The public mind was in a sore and excited state. Men looked distrustfully upon each other, and the demon of party reigned preeminent, as much in the drawing-room as in the council-chamber.

The town was divided into two fierce political factions; and however moderate your views might be, to belong to the one was to incur the dislike and ill-will of the other. The Tory party, who arrogated the whole loyalty of the colony to themselves, branded, indiscriminately, the large body of Reformers as traitors and rebels. Every conscientious and thinking man, who wished to see a change for the better in the management of public affairs, was confounded with those discontented spirits, who had raised the standard of revolt against the mother country. In justice even to them, it must be said, not without severe provocation; and their disaffection was more towards the colonial government, and the abuses it fostered, than any particular dislike to British supremacy or institutions. Their attempt, whether instigated by patriotism or selfishness – and probably it contained a mixture of both – had failed, and it was but just that they should feel the punishment due to their crime. But the odious term of rebel, applied to some of the most loyal and honourable men in the province, because they could not give up their honest views on the state of the colony, gave rise to bitter and resentful feelings, which were, on all public occasions, to burst into a flame. Even women entered deeply into this party hostility; and those who, from their education and mental advantages, might have been friends and agreeable companions, kept aloof, rarely taking notice of each other, when accidentally thrown together.

The native-born Canadian regarded with a jealous feeling men of talent and respectability who emigrated from the mother country, as most offices of consequence and emolument were given to such persons. The Canadian, naturally enough, considered such preference unjust, and an infringement upon his rights as a native of the colony, and that he had a greater claim, on that account, upon the government, than men who were perfect strangers. This, owing to his limited education, was not always the case; but the preference shown to the British emigrant proved an active source of ill-will and discontent. The favoured occupant of place and power was not at all inclined to conciliate his Canadian rival, or to give up the title to mental superiority which he derived from birth and education; and he too often treated his illiterate, but sagacious political opponent, with a contempt which his practical knowledge and experience did not merit. It was a miserable state of things; and I believe that most large towns in the province bore, in these respects, a striking resemblance to each other. Those who wished to see impartial justice administered to all, had but an uncomfortable time of it, – both parties regarding with mistrust those men who could not go the whole length with them in their political opinions. To gain influence in Canada, and be the leader of a party, a man must, as the Yankees say, "*go the whole hog.*"

The people in the back woods were fortunate in not having their peace disturbed by these political broils. In the depths of the dark forest, they were profoundly ignorant of how the colony was governed; and many did not even know which party was in power, and when the rebellion actually broke out it fell upon them like a thunderclap. But in their ignorance and seclusion there was at least safety, and they were free from that dreadful scourge – "the malicious strife of tongues."

The fever of the "*Clergy Reserves question*" was then at its height. It was never introduced in company but to give offence, and lead to fierce political discussions. All parties were wrong, and nobody was convinced. This vexed political question always brought before my mental vision a ludicrous sort of caricature, which, if I had the artistic skill to delineate, would form no bad illustration of this perplexing subject.

I saw in my mind's eye a group of dogs in the marketplace of a large town, to whom some benevolent individual, with a view to their mutual benefit, had flung a shank of beef, with meat enough upon the upper end to have satisfied the hunger of all, could such an impossible thing as an equal division, among such noisy claimants, have been made.

A strong English bull-dog immediately seized upon the bone, and for some time gnawed away at the best end of it, and contrived to keep all the other dogs at bay. This proceeding was resented by a stout mastiff, who thought that he had as good a right to the beef as the bull-dog, and flung himself tooth and claw upon his opponent. While these two were fighting and wrangling over the bone, a wiry, active Scotch terrier, though but half the size of the other combatants, began tugging at the small end of the shank, snarling and barking with all the strength of his lungs, to gain at least a chance of being heard, even if he did fail in putting in his claims to a share of the meat.

An old cunning greyhound, to whom no share had been offered, and who well knew that it was of no use putting himself against the strength of the bull-dog and mastiff, stood proudly aloof, with quivering ears and tail, regarding the doings of the others with a glance of sovereign contempt; yet, watching with his keen eye for an opportunity of making a successful spring, while they were busily engaged in snarling and biting each other, to carry off the meat, bone and all.

A multitude of nondescript curs, of no weight in themselves, were snapping and snuffling round the bone, eagerly anticipating the few tit bits, which they hoped might fall to their share during the prolonged scuffle among the higher powers: while the figure of Justice, dimly seen in the distance, was poising her scales, and lifting her sword to make an equal division; but her voice failed to be heard, and her august presence regarded, in the universal hubbub. The height to which party feeling was carried in those days, had to be experienced before it could be fully understood.

Happily for the colony, this evil spirit, during the last three years, has greatly diminished. The two rival parties, though they occasionally abuse and villify each other, through the medium of the common safety valve – the public papers – are not so virulent as in 1840. They are more equally matched. The union of the provinces has kept the reform party in the ascendant, and they are very indifferent to the good or ill opinion of their opponents.

The colony has greatly progressed under their administration, and is now in a most prosperous and flourishing state. The municipal and district councils, free schools, and the improvement in the public thoroughfares of the country, are owing to them, and have proved a great blessing to the community. The resources of the country are daily being opened up, and both at home and abroad Canada is rising in public estimation.

As a woman, I cannot enter into the philosophy of these things, nor is it my intention to do so. I leave statistics for wiser and cleverer male heads. But, even as a woman, I cannot help rejoicing in the beneficial effects that these changes have wrought in the land of my adoption. The day of our commercial and national prosperity has dawned, and the rays of the sun already brighten the hill-tops.

To those persons who have been brought up in the old country, and accustomed from infancy to adhere to the conventional rules of society, the mixed society must, for a long time, prove very distasteful. Yet this very freedom, which is so repugnant to all their preconceived notions and prejudices, is by no means so unpleasant as strangers would be led to imagine. A certain mixture of the common and the real, of the absurd and the ridiculous, gives a zest to the cold, tame decencies, to be found in more exclusive and refined circles. Human passions and feelings are exhibited with more fidelity, and you see men and women as they really are. And many kind, good, and noble traits are to be found among those classes, whom at home we regard as our inferiors. The lady and gentleman in Canada are as distinctly marked as elsewhere. There is no mistaking the superiority that mental cultivation bestows; and their mingling in public with their less gifted neighbours, rather adds than takes from their claims to hold the first place. I consider the state of society in a more healthy condition than at home; and people, when they go out for pleasure here, seem to enjoy themselves much more.

The harmony that reigns among the members of a Canadian family is truly delightful. They are not a quarrelsome people in their own homes. No contradicting or disputing, or hateful rivalry, is to be seen between Canadian brothers and sisters. They cling together through good and ill report, like the bundle of sticks in the fable; and I have seldom found a real Canadian ashamed of owning a poor relation. This to me is a beautiful feature in the Canadian character. Perhaps the perfect equality on which children stand in a family, the superior claim of eldership, so much upheld at home, never being enforced, is one great cause of this domestic union of kindred hearts.

Most of the pretence, and affected airs of importance, occasionally met with in Canada, are not the genuine produce of the soil, but importations from the mother country; and, as sure as you hear any one boasting of the rank and consequence they possessed at home, you may be certain that it was quite the reverse. An old Dutch lady, after listening very attentively to a young Irishwoman's account of the grandeur of her father's family at home, said rather drily to the self-exalted damsel, –

"Goodness me, child! if you were so well off, what brought you to a poor country like this? I am sure you had been much wiser had you staid to hum–"

"Yes. But my papa heard such fine commendations of the country, that he sold his estate to come out."

"To pay his debts, perhaps," said the provoking old woman.

"Ah, no, ma'am," she replied, very innocently, "he never paid them. He was told that it was a very fine climate, and he came for the good of our health."

"Why, my dear, you look as if you never had had a day's sickness in your life."

"No more I have," she replied, putting on a very languid air, "but I am very *delicate*."

This term *delicate*, be it known to my readers is a favourite one with young ladies here, but its general application would lead you to imagine it another term for *laziness*. It is quite fashionable to be *delicate*, but horribly vulgar to be considered capable of enjoying such a useless blessing as good health. I knew a lady, when I first came to the colony, who had her children daily washed in water almost hot enough to scald a pig. On being asked why she did so, as it was not only an unhealthy practice, but would rob the little girls of their fine colour, she exclaimed, –

"Oh, that is just what I do it for. I want them to look *delicate*. They have such red faces, and are as coarse and healthy as country girls."

The rosy face of the British emigrant is regarded as no beauty here. The Canadian women, like their neighbours the Americans, have small regular features, but are mostly pale, or their faces are only slightly suffused with a faint flush. During the season of youth this delicate tinting is very beautiful, but a few years deprive them of it, and leave a sickly, sallow pallor in its place. The loss of their teeth, too, is a great drawback to their personal charms, but these can be so well supplied by the dentist that it is not so much felt; the thing is so universal, that it is hardly thought detrimental to an otherwise pretty face.

But, to return to the mere pretenders in society, of which, of course, there are not a few here, as elsewhere. I once met two very stylishly-dressed women at a place of public entertainment. The father of these ladies had followed the lucrative but unaristocratic trade of a tailor in London. One of them began complaining to me of the mixed state of society in Canada, which she considered a dreadful calamity to persons like her and her sister; and ended her lamentations by exclaiming, –

"What would my pa have thought could he have seen us

here to-night? Is it not terrible for ladies to have to dance in the same room with storekeepers and their clerks?"

Another lady of the same stamp, the daughter of a tavern-keeper, was indignant at being introduced to a gentleman, whose father had followed the same calling.

Such persons seem to forget, that as long as people retain their natural manners, and remain true to the dignity of their humanity, they cannot with any justice be called vulgar; for vulgarity consists in presumptuously affecting to be what we are not, and in claiming distinctions which we do not deserve, and which no one else would admit.

The farmer, in his homespun, may possess the real essentials which make the gentleman – good feeling, and respect for the feelings of others. The homely dress, weather-beaten face, and hard hands, could not deprive him of the honest independence and genial benevolence he derived from nature. No real gentleman would treat such a man, however humble his circumstances, with insolence or contempt. But place the same man out of his class, dress him in the height of fashion, and let him attempt to imitate the manners of the great, and the whole world would laugh at the counterfeit.

Uneducated, ignorant people often rise by their industry to great wealth in the colony; to such the preference shown to the educated man always seems a puzzle. Their ideas of gentility consist in being the owners of fine clothes, fine houses, splendid furniture, expensive equipages, and plenty of money. They have all these, yet even the most ignorant feel that something else is required. They cannot comprehend the mysterious ascendancy of mind over mere animal enjoyments; yet they have sense enough, by bestowing a liberal education on their children, to endeavour, at least in their case, to remedy the evil.

The affectation of wishing people to think that you had been better off in the mother country than in Canada, is not confined to the higher class of emigrants. The very poorest are the most remarked for this ridiculous boasting. A servant girl of mine told me, with a very grand toss of the head, "that she did not choose to *demane* hersel' by scrubbing a floor; that she belonged to the *ra'al gintry* in the ould counthry, and her papa and mamma niver brought her up to hard work."

This interesting scion of the aristocracy was one of the coarsest specimens of female humanity I ever beheld. If I called her to bring a piece of wood for the parlour fire, she would thrust her tangled, uncombed red head in at the door, and shout at the top of her voice, "Did yer holler?"

One of our working men, wishing to impress me with the dignity of his wife's connexions, said with all becoming solemnity of look and manner –

"Doubtless, ma'am, you have heard in the ould counthry of Connor's racers: Margaret's father kept those racers."

When I recalled the person of the individual whose fame was so widely spread at home, and thought of the racers, I could hardly keep a "straight face," as an American friend terms laughing, when you are bound to look grave.

One want is greatly felt here; but it is to be hoped that a more liberal system of education and higher moral culture will remedy the evil. There is a great deficiency among our professional men and wealthy traders of that nice sense of honour that marks the conduct and dealings of the same class at home. Of course many bright exceptions are to be found in the colony, but too many of the Canadians think it no disgrace to take every advantage of the ignorance and inexperience of strangers.

If you are not smart enough to drive a close bargain, they consider it only fair to take you in. A man loses very little in the public estimation by making over all his property to some convenient friend, in order to defraud his creditors, while he retains a competency for himself.

Women, whose husbands have been detained on the limits for years for debt, will give large parties and dress in

the most expensive style. This would be thought dishonourable at home, but is considered no disgrace here.

"Honour is all very well in an old country like England," said a lady, with whom I had been arguing on the
subject; "but, Mrs. M——, it won't do in a new country
like this. You may as well cheat as be cheated. For my
part, I never lose an advantage by indulging in such foolish notions."

I have no doubt that a person who entertained such
principles would not fail to reduce them to practice.

The idea that some country people form of an author is
highly amusing. One of my boys was tauntingly told by
another lad at school, "that his ma' said that Mrs. M——
invented lies, and got money for them." This was her
estimation of works of mere fiction.

Once I was driven by a young Irish friend to call upon
the wife of a rich farmer in the country. We were shewn by
the master of the house into a very handsomely furnished
room, in which there was no lack of substantial comfort,
and even of some elegancies, in the shape of books, pictures,
and a piano. The good man left us to inform his wife of our
arrival, and for some minutes we remained in solemn state,
until the mistress of the house made her appearance.

She had been called from the washtub, and, like a sensible woman, was not ashamed of her domestic occupation.
She came in wiping the suds from her hands on her apron,
and gave us a very hearty and friendly welcome. She was a
short, stout, middle-aged woman, with a very pleasing
countenance; and though only in her coloured flannel
working-dress, with a nightcap on her head, and spec-
tacled nose, there was something in her frank good-
natured face that greatly prepossessed us in her favour.

After giving us the common compliments of the day,
she drew her chair just in front of me, and, resting her
elbows on her knees, and dropping her chin between her
hands, she sat regarding me with such a fixed gaze that it
became very embarrassing.

"So," says she, at last, "you are Mrs. M——?"

"Yes."

"The woman that writes?"

"The same."

She drew back her chair for a few paces, with a deep-drawn sigh, in which disappointment and surprise seemed strangely to mingle. "Well, I have he'rd a great deal about you, and I wanted to see you bad for a long time; but you are only a humly person like myself after all. Why I do think, if I had on my best gown and cap, I should look a great deal younger and better than you."

I told her that I had no doubt of the fact.

"And pray," continued she, with the same provoking scrutiny, "how old do you call yourself?"

I told her my exact age.

"Humph!" quoth she, as if she rather doubted my word, "two years younger nor me! you look a great deal older nor that."

After a long pause, and another searching gaze, "Do you call those teeth your own?"

"Yes," said I, laughing; for I could retain my gravity no longer; "in the very truest sense of the word they are mine, as God gave them to me."

"You luckier than your neighbours," said she. "But airn't you greatly troubled with headaches?"

"No," said I, rather startled at this fresh interrogatory.

"My!" exclaimed she, "I thought you must be, your eyes are so sunk in your head. Well, well, so you are Mrs. M—— of Belleville, the woman that writes. You are but a humly body after all."

While this curious colloquy was going on, my poor Irish friend sat on thorns, and tried, by throwing in a little judicious blarney, to soften the thrusts of the home truths to which he had unwittingly exposed me. Between every pause in the conversation, he broke in with – "I am sure Mrs. M—— is a fine-looking woman – a very young-looking woman for her age. Any person might know at a glance that those teeth were her own. They look too natural to be false."

Now, I am certain that the poor little woman never meant to wound my feelings, nor give me offence. She literally spoke her thoughts, and I was too much amused with the whole scene to feel the least irritated by her honest bluntness. She expected to find in an author something quite out of the common way, and I did not come up at all to her expectations.

Her opinion of me was not more absurd than the remarks of two ladies who, after calling upon me for the first time, communicated the result of their observations to a mutual friend.

"We have seen Mrs. M——, and we were so surprised to find her just like other people!"

"What did you expect to see in her?"

"Oh, something very different. We were very much disappointed."

"That she was not sitting upon her head," said my friend, smiling; "I like Mrs. M——, because she is in every respect like other people; and I should not have taken her for a blue-stocking at all."

The sin of authorship meets with little toleration in a new country. Several persons of this class, finding few minds that could sympathise with them, and enter into their literary pursuits, have yielded to despondency, or fallen victims to that insidious enemy of souls, *Canadian whisky*. Such a spirit was the unfortunate Dr. Huskins, late of Frankfort on the river Trent. The fate of this gentleman, who was a learned and accomplished man of genius, left a very sad impression on my mind. Like too many of that highly-gifted, but unhappy fraternity, he struggled through his brief life, overwhelmed with the weight of undeserved calumny, and his peace of mind embittered with the most galling neglect and poverty.

The want of sympathy experienced by him from men of his own class, pressed sorely upon the heart of the sensitive man of talent and refinement; he found very few who could appreciate or understand his mental superiority, which was pronounced as folly and madness by the ignorant persons about him. A new country, where all are rushing eagerly forward in order to secure the common necessaries of life, is not a favourable soil in which to nourish the bright fancies and delusive dreams of the poet. Dr. Huskins perceived his error too late, when he no longer retained the means to remove to a more favourable spot, – and his was not a mind which could meet and combat successfully with the ills of life. He endeavoured to bear proudly the evils of his situation, but he had neither the energy nor the courage to surmount them. He withdrew himself from society, and passed the remainder of his days in a solitary, comfortless, log hut on the borders of the wilderness. Here he drooped and died, as too many like him have died, heartbroken and alone. A sad mystery involves the last hours of his life: it is said that he and Dr. Sutor, another talented but very dissipated man, had entered into a compact to drink until they both died. Whether this statement is true cannot now be positively ascertained. It is certain, however, that Dr. Sutor was found dead upon the floor of the miserable shanty occupied by his friend, and that Dr. Huskins was lying on his bed in the agonies of death. Could the many fine poems, composed by Dr. Huskins in his solitary exile, be collected and published, we feel assured that posterity would do him justice, and that his name would rank high among the bards of the green isle.

TO THE MEMORY OF DR. HUSKINS.

"Neglected son of genius! thou hast pass'd
    In broken-hearted loneliness away;
And one who prized thy talents, fain would cast
    The cypress-wreath above thy nameless clay.
    Ah, could she yet thy spirit's flight delay,
'Till the cold world, relenting from its scorn,
The fadeless laurel round thy brows should twine,
    Crowning the innate majesty of mind,
By crushing poverty and sorrow torn.

Peace to thy mould'ring ashes, till revive
Bright memories of thee in deathless song!
True to the dead, Time shall relenting give
The meed of fame deserved – delayed too long,
And in immortal verse the Bard again shall live!"

Alas! this frightful vice of drinking prevails throughout the colony to an alarming extent. Professional gentlemen are not ashamed of being seen issuing from the bar-room of a tavern early in the morning, or of being caught reeling home from the same sink of iniquity late at night. No sense of shame seems to deter them from the pursuit of their darling sin. I have heard that some of these regular topers place brandy beside their beds that, should they awake during the night, they may have within their reach the fiery potion for which they are bartering body and soul. Some of these persons, after having been warned of their danger by repeated fits of *delirium tremens*, have joined the tee-totallers; but their abstinence only lasted until the re-establishment of their health enabled them to return to their old haunts, and become more hardened in their vile habits than before. It is to be questioned whether the signing of any pledge is likely to prove a permanent remedy for this great moral evil. If an appeal to the heart and conscience, and the fear of incurring the displeasure of an offended God, are not sufficient to deter a man from becoming an active instrument in the ruin of himself and family, no forcible restraint upon his animal desires will be likely to effect a real reformation. It appears to me that the temperance people begin at the wrong end of the matter, by restraining the animal propensities before they have convinced the mind. If a man abstain from drink only as long as the accursed thing is placed beyond his reach, it is after all but a negative virtue, to be overcome by the first strong temptation. Were incurable drunkards treated as lunatics, and a proper asylum provided for them in every large town, and the management of their affairs committed to their wives or adult children, the bare idea of being confined under such a plea would operate more forcibly upon them than by signing a pledge, which they can break or resume according to the caprice of the moment.

A drunkard, while under the influence of liquor, is a madman in every sense of the word, and his mental aberration is often of the most dangerous kind. Place him and the confirmed maniac side by side, and it would be difficult for a stranger to determine which was the most irrational of the two.

A friend related to me the following anecdote of a physician in his native town: – This man, who was eminent in his profession, and highly respected by all who knew him, secretly indulged in the pernicious habit of dram-drinking, and after a while bade fair to sink into a hopeless drunkard. At the earnest solicitations of his weeping wife and daughter he consented to sign the pledge, and not only ardent spirits but every sort of intoxicating beverage was banished from the house.

The use of alcohol is allowed in cases of sickness to the most rigid disciplinarians, and our doctor began to find that keeping his pledge was a more difficult matter than he had at first imagined. Still, for *example's sake*, of course, a man of his standing in society had only joined for *example's sake*; he did not like openly to break it. He therefore feigned violent toothache, and sent the servant girl over to a friend's house to borrow a small phial of brandy.

The brandy was sent, with many kind wishes for the doctor's speedy recovery. The phial now came every night to be refilled; and the doctor's toothache seemed likely to become a case of incurable *tic douloureux*. His friend took the alarm. He found it both expensive and inconvenient, providing the doctor with his nightly dose; and wishing to see how matters really stood, he followed the maid and the brandy one evening to the doctor's house.

He entered unannounced. It was as he suspected. The

doctor was lounging in his easy chair before the fire, indulging in a hearty fit of laughter over some paragraph in a newspaper, which he held in his hand.

"Ah, my dear J——, I am so glad to find you so well. I thought by your sending for the brandy, that you were dying with the toothache."

The doctor, rather confounded – "Why, yes; I have been sadly troubled with it of late. It does not come on, however, before eight o'clock, and if I cannot get a mouthful of brandy, I never can get a wink of sleep all night."

"Did you ever have it before you took the pledge?"

"Never," said the doctor emphatically.

"Perhaps the cold water does not agree with you?"

The doctor began to smell a rat, and fell vigorously to minding the fire.

"I tell you what it is, J——," said the other; "the toothache is a *nervous affection*. It is the *brandy* that is the *disease*. It may cure you of an imaginary toothache; but I assure you, that it gives your wife and daughter an *incurable heartache*."

The doctor felt at that moment a strange palpitation at his own. The scales fell suddenly from his eyes, and for the first time his conduct appeared in its true light. Returning the bottle to his friend, he said, very humbly – "Take it out of my sight; I feel my error now. I will cure their heartache by curing myself of this beastly vice."

The doctor, from that hour, became a temperate man. He soon regained his failing practice, and the esteem of his friends. The appeal of his better feelings effected a permanent change in his habits, which signing the pledge had not been able to do. To keep up an appearance of consistency he had had recourse to a mean subterfuge, while touching his heart produced a lasting reform.

Drinking is the curse of Canada, and the very low price of whisky places the temptation constantly in every one's reach. But it is not by adopting by main force the Maine Liquor law, that our legislators will be able to remedy the evil. Men naturally resist any oppressive measures that infringe upon their private rights, even though such measures are adopted solely for their benefit. It is not wise to thrust temperance down a man's throat; and the surest way to make him a drunkard is to insist upon his being sober. The zealous advocates of this measure (and there are many in Canada) know little of their own, or the nature of others. It would be the fruitful parent of hypocrisy, and lay the foundation of crimes still greater than the one it is expected to cure.

To wean a fellow-creature from the indulgence of a gross sensual propensity, as I said before, we must first convince the mind: the reform must commence there. Merely withdrawing the means of gratification, and treating a rational being like a child, will never achieve a great moral conquest.

In pagan countries, the missionaries can only rely upon the sincerity of the converts, who are educated when children in their schools; and if we wish to see drunkenness banished from our towns and cities, we must prepare our children from their earliest infancy to resist the growing evil.

Show your boy a drunkard wallowing in the streets, like some unclean animal in the mire. Every side walk, on a market-day, will furnish you with examples. Point out to him the immorality of such a degrading position; make him fully sensible of all its disgusting horrors. Tell him that God has threatened in words of unmistakable import, that he will exclude such from his heavenly kingdom. Convince him that such loathsome impurity must totally unfit the soul for communion with its God – that such a state may truly be looked upon as the second death – the foul corruption and decay of both body and soul. Teach the child to pray against drunkenness, as he would against murder, lying, and theft; shew him that all these crimes are often comprised in this one, which in too many cases has been the fruitful parent of them all.

When the boy grows to be a man, and mingles in the world of men, he will not easily forget the lesson impressed on his young heart. He will remember his early prayers against this terrible vice – will recall that disgusting spectacle – and will naturally shrink from the same contamination. Should he be overcome by temptation, the voice of conscience will plead with him in such decided tones that she will be heard, and he will be ashamed of becoming the idiot thing he once feared and loathed.

THE DRUNKARD'S RETURN.

"Oh! ask not of my morn of life,
　　How dark and dull it gloom'd o'er me;
Sharp words and fierce domestic strife,
　　Robb'd my young heart of all its glee, –
The sobs of one heart-broken wife,
　　Low, stifled moans of agony,
That fell upon my shrinking ear,
In hollow tones of woe and fear;
As crouching, weeping, at her side,
　　I felt my soul with sorrow swell,
In pity begg'd her not to hide
　　The cause of grief I knew too well;
Then wept afresh to hear her pray
That death might take us both away!

"Away from whom? – Alas! what ill
　　Press'd the warm life-hopes from her heart?
Was she not young and lovely still?
　　What made the frequent tear-drops start
From eyes, whose light of love could fill
　　My inmost soul, and bade me part
　　From noisy comrades in the street,
To kiss her cheek, so cold and pale,
　　To clasp her neck, and hold her hand,
And list the oft-repeated tale
　　Of woes I could not understand;
Yet felt their force, as, day by day,
I watch'd her fade from life away.

"And *he*, the cause of all this woe,
    Her mate – the father of her child,
In dread I saw him come and go,
    With many an awful oath reviled;
And from harsh word, and harsher blow,
    (In answer to her pleadings mild,)
I shrank in terror, till I caught
From her meek eyes th' unwhisper'd thought –
    'Bear it, my Edward, for thy mother's sake!
He cares not, in his sullen mood,
    If this poor heart with anguish break.'
That look was felt, and understood
    By her young son, thus school'd to bear
    His wrongs, to soothe her deep despair.

"Oh, how I loath'd him! – how I scorn'd
    His idiot laugh, or demon frown, –
His features bloated and deform'd;
    The jests with which he sought to drown
The consciousness of sin, or storm'd,
    To put reproof or anger down.
Oh, 'tis a fearful thing to feel
Stern, sullen hate, the bosom steel
    'Gainst one whom nature bids us prize
The first link in her mystic chain;
    Which binds in strong and tender ties
The heart, while reason rules the brain,
    And mingling love with holy fear,
    Renders the parent doubly dear.

"I cannot bear to think how deep
    The hatred was I bore him then;
But he has slept his last long sleep,
    And I have trod the haunts of men;
Have felt the tide of passion sweep
    Through manhood's fiery heart, and when
By strong temptation toss'd and tried,
I thought how that lost father died;

Unwept, unpitied, in his sin;
Then tears of burning shame would rise,
    And stern remorse awake within
A host of mental agonies.
    He fell – by one dark vice defiled;
    Was I more pure – his erring child?

"Yes – erring child; – but to my tale.
    My mother loved that lost one still,
From the deep fount which could not fail
    (Through changes dark, from good to ill,)
Her woman's heart – and sad and pale,
    She yielded to his stubborn will;
Perchance she felt remonstrance vain, –
The effort to resist gave pain.
    But carefully she hid her grief
From him, the idol of her youth;
And fondly hoped, against belief,
    That her deep love and stedfast truth
Would touch his heart, and win him back
From Folly's dark and devious track.

"Vain hope! the drunkard's heart is hard as stone,
    No grief disturbs his selfish, sensual joy;
His wife may weep, his starving children groan,
    And Poverty with cruel gripe annoy:
He neither hears, nor heeds their famish'd moan,
    The glorious wine-cup owns no base alloy.
Surrounded by a low, degraded train,
His fiendish laugh defiance bids to pain;
    He hugs the cup – more dear than friends to him –
Nor sees stern ruin from the goblet rise,
    Nor flames of hell careering o'er the brim, –
The lava flood that glads his bloodshot eyes
    Poisons alike his body and his soul,
    Till reason lies self-murder'd in the bowl.

"It was a dark and fearful winter night,
    Loud roar'd the tempest round our hovel home;

Cold, hungry, wet, and weary was our plight,
    And still we listen'd for his step to come.
My poor sick mother! – 'twas a piteous sight
    To see her shrink and shiver, as our dome
Shook to the rattling blast; and to the door
She crept, to look along the bleak, black moor.
    He comes – he comes! – and, quivering all with dread,
She spoke kind welcome to that sinful man.
    His sole reply, – 'Get supper – give me bread!'
Then, with a sneer, he tauntingly began
    To mock the want that stared him in the face,
    Her bitter sorrow, and his own disgrace.

" 'I have no money to procure you food,
    No wood, no coal, to raise a cheerful fire;
The madd'ning cup may warm your frozen blood –
    We die, for lack of that which you desire!'
She ceased, – erect one moment there he stood,
    The foam upon his lip; with fiendish ire
He seized a knife which glitter'd in his way,
And rush'd with fury on his helpless prey.
    Then from a dusky nook I fiercely sprung,
The strength of manhood in that single bound:
    Around his bloated form I tightly clung,
And headlong brought the murderer to the ground.
    We fell – his temples struck the cold hearth-stone,
    The blood gush'd forth – he died without a moan!

"Yes – by my hand he died! one frantic cry
    Of mortal anguish thrill'd my madden'd brain,
Recalling sense and mem'ry. Desperately
    I strove to raise my fallen sire again,
And call'd upon my mother; but her eye
    Was closed alike to sorrow, want, and pain.
Oh, what a night was that! – when all alone
I watch'd my dead beside the cold hearth-stone.
    I thought myself a monster, – that the deed
To save my mother was too promptly done.
    I could not see her gentle bosom bleed,

And quite forgot the father, in the son;
  For her I mourn'd – for her, through bitter years,
  Pour'd forth my soul in unavailing tears.

"The world approved the act; but on my soul
  There lay a gnawing consciousness of guilt,
A biting sense of crime, beyond control:
  By my rash hand a father's blood was spilt,
And I abjured for aye the death-drugg'd bowl.
  This is my tale of woe; and if thou wilt
Be warn'd by me, the sparkling cup resign;
A serpent lurks within the ruby wine,
  Guileful and strong as him who erst betray'd
The world's first parents in their bowers of joy.
  Let not the tempting draught your soul pervade;
It shines to kill, and sparkles to destroy.
  The drunkard's sentence has been seal'd above, –
  Exiled for ever from the heaven of love!"

THREE

Free Schools – Thoughts on Education

> "Truth, Wisdom, Virtue – the eternal three,
> Great moral agents of the universe –
> Shall yet reform and beautify the world,
> And render it fit residence for Him
> In whom these glorious attributes combined,
> To render perfect manhood one with God!"
>
> S.M.

THERE IS no calculating the immense benefit which the colony will derive from the present liberal provision made for the education of the rising generation.

A few years ago schools were so far apart, and the tuition of children so expensive, that none but the very better class could scrape money enough together to send their children to be instructed. Under the present system, every idle ragged child in the streets, by washing his face and hands, and presenting himself to the free school of his ward, can receive the same benefit as the rest.

What an inestimable blessing is this, and how greatly will this education of her population tend to increase the wealth and prosperity of the province! It is a certain means of a calling out and making available all the talent in the colony; and as, thanks be to God, genius never was confined to any class, the poor will be more benefited by this wise and munificent arrangement than the rich.

These schools are supported by a district tax, which falls upon the property of persons well able to pay it; but avarice and bigotry are already at work, to endeavour to deprive the young of his new-found blessing. Persons grumble at having to pay this additional tax. They say, "If poor people want their children taught, let them pay for it: their instruction has no right to be forced from our earnings."

What a narrow prejudice is this – what miserable, short-sighted policy! The education of these neglected children, by making them better citizens, will in the long run prove a great protection both to life and property.

Then the priests of different persuasions lift up their voices because no particular creed is allowed to be taught in the seminaries, and exclaim – "The children will be infidels. These schools are godless and immoral in the extreme." Yes; children will be taught to love each other without any such paltry distinctions as party and creed. The rich and the poor will meet together to learn the sweet courtesies of a common humanity, and prejudice and avarice and bigotry cannot bear that.

There is a spirit abroad in the world – and an evil spirit it is – which through all ages has instigated the rich to look down with contemptuous feelings of superiority on the humble occupations and inferior circumstances of the poor. Now, that this spirit is diametrically opposed to the benevolent precepts of Christianity, the fact of our blessed Lord performing his painful mission on earth in no higher capacity than that of a working mechanic, ought sufficiently to show. What divine benevolence – what god-like humility was displayed in this heroic act! Of all the wonderful events in his wonderful history, is there one more astonishing than this –

> "That Heaven's high Majesty his court should keep
> In a clay cottage, by each blast controll'd, –
> That Glory's self should serve our hopes and fears,
> And free Eternity submit to years?"

What a noble triumph was this, over the cruel and unjust prejudices of mankind! It might truly be termed the divine philosophy of virtue. This condescension on the part of the great Creator of the universe, ought to have been sufficient to have rendered labour honourable in the minds of his followers; and we still indulge the hope, that the moral and intellectual improvement of mankind will one day restore labour to her proper pedestal in the temple of virtue.

The chosen disciples of our Great Master – those to whom he entrusted the precious code of moral laws that was destined to overthrow the kingdom of Satan, and reform a degraded world – were poor uneducated men. The most brilliant gems are often enclosed in the rudest incrustations; and He who formed the bodies and souls of men, well knew that the most powerful intellects are often concealed amidst the darkness and rubbish of uneducated minds. Such minds, enlightened and purified by his wonder-working Spirit, He sent forth to publish his message of glad tidings through the earth.

The want of education and moral training is the only *real* barrier that exists between the different classes of men. Nature, reason, and Christianity, recognise no other. Pride may say nay; but pride was always a liar, and a great hater of the truth. Wealth, in a hard, abstract point of view, can never make any. Take away the wealth from an ignorant man, and he remains just the same being he was before he possessed it, and is no way bettered from the mere circumstance of his having once been rich. But let that wealth procure for him the only true and imperishable riches – knowledge, and with it the power to do good to himself and others, which is the great end of moral and religious training – and a mighty structure is raised which death itself is unable to destroy. The man has indeed changed his nature, and is fast regaining the resemblance he once bore to his Creator.

The soul of man is no rank, sex, or colour. It claims a distinction far above all these; and shall we behold its

glorious energies imprisoned in the obscene den of ignorance and want, without making the least effort to
enlighten its hideous darkness?

It is painful to reflect upon the vast barren wilderness of
human intellect which on every side stretches around us –
to know that thousands of powerful minds are condemned
by the hopeless degradation of their circumstances to
struggle on in obscurity, without one gleam of light. What
a high and noble privilege has the Almighty conferred
upon the wealthy and well-educated portion of mankind,
in giving them the means of reclaiming and cultivating
those barren minds, and of lifting them from the mire of
ignorance in which they at present wallow, to share with
them the moral dignity of thinking men!

A small portion of the wealth that is at present
bestowed upon mere articles of luxury, or in scenes of riot
and dissipation, would more than effect this great purpose. The education of the poorer classes must add greatly
to the well-being and happiness of the world, and tend to
diminish the awful amount of crimes and misery, which
up to the present moment has rendered it a vale of tears.

The ignorance of the masses must, while it remains, for
ever separate them from their more fortunate brethren.
Remove this stumbling block out of the way, and the hard
line of demarcation which now divides them will soften,
and gradually melt away. Their supposed inferiority lies in
their situation alone. Turn to the history of those great
men whom education has rescued from the very lowest
walks of life, and you will find a mighty host, who were in
their age and day the companions, the advisers, the
friends of princes – men who have written their names
with the pen and sword upon the pillars of time, and, if
immortality can exist in a world of constant change, have
been rendered immortal by their words or deeds.

Let poverty and bigotry do their utmost to keep such
spirits, while living, in the shades of obscurity, death, the
great equalizer, always restores to its possessors the rights
of mind, and bids them triumph for ever over the low

prejudices of their fellow-men, who, when reading the works of Burns, or gazing on the paintings of Raphael, reproach them with the lowliness of their origin; yea, the proudest who have taste to appreciate their glorious creations, rejoice that genius could thus triumph over temporary obstacles.

It has often been asserted by the rich and nobly-born, that if the poorer classes were as well educated as themselves, it would render them familiar and presumptuous, and they would no longer pay to their superiors in station that deference which must exist for the well-being of society. We view the subject with far other eyes, and conclude from analogy, that that which has conferred such incalculable benefits on the rich, and helped mainly to place them in the position they now hold, could not be detrimental to the poor. The man who knows his duty, is more likely to perform it well than the ignorant man, whose services are compulsory, and whose actions are influenced by the moral responsibility which a right knowledge must give.

My earnest wish for universal education involves no dislike to royal rule, or for those distinctions of birth and wealth which I consider necessary for the well-being of society. It little matters by what name we call them; men of talent and education will exert a certain influence over the minds of their fellow-men, which will always be felt and acknowledged in the world if mankind were equalized to-morrow. Perfect, unadulterated republicanism, is a beautiful but fallacious chimera which never has existed upon the earth, and which, if the Bible be true, (and we have no doubts on the subject,) we are told never will exist in heaven. Still we consider that it would be true wisdom and policy in those who possess a large share of the good things of this world, to make labour honourable, by exalting the poor operative into an intelligent moral agent. Surely it is no small privilege to be able to bind up his bruised and broken heart – to wipe the dust from his brow, and the tears from his eyes – and bid him once more stand erect in his Maker's image. This is, indeed, to become the benefactor both of his soul and body; for the mind, once convinced of its own real worth and native dignity, is less prone to fall into low and degrading vices, than when struggling with ignorance and the galling chain of despised poverty.

It is impossible for the most depraved votary of wealth and fashion *really* to despise a poor, honest, well-informed man. There is an aristocracy of virtue as well as of wealth; and the rich man who dares to cast undeserved contempt upon his poor, but high-minded brother, hears a voice within him which, in tones which cannot be misunderstood, reproves him for blaspheming his Maker's image. A glorious mission is conferred on you who are rich and nobly born, which, if well and conscientiously performed, will make the glad arch of heaven ring with songs of joy. Nor deem that you will be worse served because your servant is a religious, well-educated man, or that you will be treated with less respect and attention by one who knows that your station entitles you to it, than by the rude, ignorant slave, who hates you in his heart, and performs his appointed services with an envious, discontented spirit.

When we consider that ignorance is the fruitful parent of crime, we should unite with heart and voice to banish it from the earth. We should devote what means we can spare, and the talents with which God has endowed us, in furthering every national and benevolent institution set on foot for this purpose; and though the progress of improvement may at first appear slow, this should not discourage any one from endeavouring to effect a great and noble purpose. Many months must intervene, after sowing a crop, before the husbandman can expect to reap the harvest. The winter snows must cover, the spring rains vivify and nourish, and the summer sun ripen, before the autumn arrives for the ingathering of his labour, and then the increase, after all his toil and watching, must be with God.

During the time of our blessed Lord's sojourn upon

earth, he proclaimed the harvest to be plenteous and the labourers few; and he instructed his disciples to pray to the Lord of the harvest to send more labourers into the field. Does it not, therefore, behove those who live in a more enlightened age – when the truth of the Gospel, which he sealed with his blood, has been preached in almost every country – to pray the Father of Spirits to proportion the labourers to the wants of his people, so that Christian kindness, brotherly love, and moral improvement, may go hand in hand, and keep pace with increasing literary and scientific knowledge?

A new country like Canada cannot value the education of her people too highly. The development of all the talent within the province will in the end prove her real worth, for from this source every blessing and improvement must flow. The greatness of a nation can more truly be estimated by the wisdom and intelligence of her people, than by the mere amount of specie she may possess in her treasury. The money, under the bad management of ignorant rulers, would add but little to the well-being of the community, while the intelligence which could make a smaller sum available in contributing to the general good, is in itself an inexhaustible mine of wealth.

If a few enlightened minds are able to add so much strength and importance to the country to which they belong, how much greater must that country become if all her people possessed this intelligence! How impossible it would be to conquer a country, if she could rely upon the united wisdom of an educated people to assist her in her hour of need! The force of arms could never subdue a nation thus held together by the strong hands of intellectual fellowship.

To the wisdom of her educated men, Britain owes the present position she holds among the nations. The power of mind has subdued all the natural obstacles that impeded her course, and has placed her above all her competitors. She did not owe her greatness to extent of territory. Look at the position she occupies upon the map

– a mere speck, when compared with several European nations. It was not to her superior courage, great as that is acknowledged to be; the French, the Germans, the Spaniards, are as brave, as far as mere courage is concerned, are as ready to attack and as slow to yield, as the lion-hearted king himself. No, it is to the moral power of her educated classes that she owes her superiority. It is more difficult to overcome mind than matter. To contend with the former, is to contend with God himself, for all true knowledge is derived from him; to contend with the latter, is to fight with the grosser elements of the earth, which being corruptible in their nature, are more easily overcome. From her educated men have sprung all those wonderful discoveries in science, which have extended the commerce of Great Britain, enlarged her capacity for usefulness, and rendered her the general benefactress of mankind.

If education has accomplished these miracles – for they would have been regarded as such in a more remote period of the world's history – think of what importance it is to Canada to bestow this inestimable gift upon her children.

Yet I should be sorry to see the sons of the poor emigrant wasting their valuable time in acquiring Latin and Greek. A man may be highly educated, may possess the most lofty and comprehensive mind, without knowing one syllable of either. The best years of a boy's life are often thrown away in acquiring the Latin language, which often proves of little use to him in after life, and which, for the want of practice, becomes to him a dead letter, as well as a dead language. Let the boy be taught to think, to know the meaning thoroughly of what he learns, and, by the right use of his reflective faculties, be enabled to communicate the knowledge thus acquired to others. A comprehensive knowledge of the arts and sciences, of history, geography, chemistry, and mathematics, together with a deep and unbigoted belief in the great truths of Christianity, would render a man or woman a highly intellectual and rational companion, without going beyond the pale of plain English. – "Light! give me more light!" were the dying words of Goëthe; and this should be the constant prayer of all rational souls to the Father of light. More crimes are committed through ignorance than through the influence of bad and malignant passions. An ignorant man is incapable of judging correctly, however anxious he may be to do so. He gropes in the dark, like a blind man; and if he should happen to stumble on the right path, it is more by accident than from any correct idea which has been formed in his mind respecting it.

The mind which once begins to feel a relish for acquiring knowledge is not easily satisfied. The more it knows, the less it thinks of its own acquirements, and the more anxious it becomes to arrive at the truth; and finding that perfection is not a growth of earth, it carries its earnest longings beyond this world, and seeks it in communion with the Deity. If the young could once be fully persuaded that there was no disgrace in labour, in honest, honourable poverty, but a deep and lasting disgrace in ignorance and immorality, their education would be conducted on the most enlightened plan, and produce the most beneficial results.

The poor man who could have recourse to a book for amusement, instead of wasting a leisure hour in the barroom of a tavern, would be more likely to promote the comfort and respectability of his family. Why should the labourer be debarred from sharing with the rich the great world of the past, and be able to rank amongst his best friends the distinguished men of all creeds and countries, and to feel for these dead worthies (who, thanks to the immortal art of printing, still live in their works) the warmest gratitude and admiration? The very mention of some names awaken in the mind the most lively emotion. We recall their beautiful thoughts to memory, and repeat them with as much earnestness as though the dead spake again through our lips.

Of all the heaven-inspired inventions of man, there are

none to which we are so greatly indebted as to the art of printing. To it we shall yet owe the emancipation of the larger portion of mankind from a state of mental and physical slavery. What floods of light have dawned upon the world since that silent orator, the press, set at liberty the imprisoned thoughts of men, and poured the wealth of mind among the famishing sons of earth! Formerly few could read, because manuscript books, the labours of the pen, were sold at such an enormous price that only men of rank or great wealth could afford to purchase them. The peasant, and the landholder who employed him, were alike ignorant; they could not obtain books, and therefore learning to read might well be considered in those dark ages a waste of time. This profound ignorance gave rise to all those superstitions which in the present enlightened age are regarded with such astonishment by thinking minds.

"How could sensible, good men, condemn poor old women to death for being witches?" was a question once asked me by my nephew, a fine, intelligent boy, of eight years of age.

Now this boy had read a good deal, young as he was, and thought more, and was wiser in his day and generation than these same pious bigots. And why? The boy had read the works of more enlightened men, and, making a right use of his reason, he felt convinced that these men were in error (although he had been born and brought up in the backwoods of Canada) – a fact which the great Mathew Hale was taught by bitter experience.

I have said more on this subject than I at first intended, but I feel deeply impressed with the importance of it; and, though I confess myself wholly inadequate to do it the justice it deserves, I hope the observations I have made will attract the attention of my Canadian readers, and lead them to study it more profoundly for themselves. Thanks be to God! Canada is a free country; a land of plenty; a land exempt from pauperism, burdensome taxation, and all the ills which crush and finally sink in ruin older communities. While the vigour of young life is yet hers, and she has before her the experience of all other nations, it becomes an act of duty and real *patriotism* to give to her children the best education that lies in her power.

THE POET.

"Who can read the Poet's dream,
Shadow forth his glorious theme,
And in written language tell
The workings of the potent spell,
Whose mysterious tones impart
Life and vigour to his heart?
'Tis an emanation bright,
Shooting from the fount of light;
Flowing in upon the mind,
Like sudden dayspring on the blind;
Gilding with immortal dyes
Scenes unknown to common eyes;
Revealing to the mental sight
Visions of untold delight.
'Tis the key by Fancy brought,
That opens up the world of thought;
A sense of power, a pleasing madness,
A hope in grief, a joy in sadness,
A taste for beauty unalloyed,
A love of nature never cloyed;
The upward soaring of a soul
Unfetter'd by the world's control,
Onward, heavenward ever tending,
Its essence with the Eternal blending;
Till, from "mortal coil" shook free,
It shares the seraph's ecstacy."

FOUR

Amusements

"Life hath its pleasures, stern Death hath its fears,
   Joy hath gay laughter, and Grief bitter tears;
   Rejoice with the one, nor shrink from the other, –
   Yon cloud hides the sun, and death is life's brother!
   As the beam to the day, so the shade to the night –
   Be certain that Heaven orders all for the right."

S.M.

M Y DEAR reader, before we proceed further on our journey, it may be as well to give you some idea of how the Canadian people in towns spend their time. I will endeavour to describe to you the various sources from whence they derive pleasure and amusement.

In large cities, like Montreal and Toronto, the higher classes are as refined and intellectual as ladies and gentlemen at home, and spend their lives much in the same manner. Their houses abound in all the elegancies and luxuries of life, and to step into their drawing-rooms you would imagine yourself still in England. They drive handsome carriages, and ride fine spirited horses; and if they are encumbered with fewer domestic pests in the shape of pampered servants, they have, in this respect, a decided advantage over their European friends. They dress well and expensively, and are very particular to have their clothes cut in the newest fashion. Men and women adopt the reigning mode so universally, that they look all dressed alike. The moment a fashion becomes at all obsolete, the articles of dress made to suit it are discarded. In England, a lady may please herself in the choice of colours, and in adopting as much of a fashion as suits her style of person and taste, but in Canada they carry this imitation of the fashions of the day to extremes. If green was the prevailing colour, every lady would adopt it, whether it suited her complexion or no; and, if she was ever so stout, that circumstance would not prevent her from wearing half-a-dozen more skirts than was necessary, because that absurd and unhealthy practice has for a long period prevailed. Music is taught very generally. Though very few attain any great perfection in the science, a great many perform well enough to gratify their friends, and contribute to the enjoyment of a social evening. You will find a piano in every wealthy Canadian's house, and even in the dwellings of most of the respectable mechanics.

I never met with a Canadian girl who could not dance, and dance well. It seems born in them, and it is their favourite amusement. Polkas, waltzes, and quadrilles, are the dances most approved in their private and public assemblies. The eight Scotch reel has, however, its admirers, and most parties end with this lively romping dance.

Balls given on public days, such as the Queen's birthday, and by societies, such as the Freemasons', the Odd Fellows', and the Firemen's, are composed of very mixed company, and the highest and lowest are seen in the same room. They generally contrive to keep to their own set – dancing alternately – rarely occupying the floor together. It is surprising the goodwill and harmony that presides in these mixed assemblies. As long as they are treated with civility, the lower classes shew no lack of courtesy to the higher. To be a spectator at one of these public balls is very amusing. The country girls carry themselves with such an easy freedom, that it is quite entertaining to look at and listen to them. At a freemasons' ball, some years ago, a very amusing thing took place. A young handsome woman, still in her girlhood, had brought her baby, which she carried with her into the ball-room. On being asked to dance, she was rather puzzled what to do with the child; but, seeing a young lawyer, one of the *elite* of the town, standing with folded arms looking on, she ran across the room, and putting the baby into his arms, exclaimed – "You are not dancing, sir; pray hold my baby for me, till the next quadrille is over." Away she skipped back to her partner, and left the gentleman overwhelmed with confusion, while the room shook with peals of laughter. Making the best of it, he danced the baby to the music, and kept it in high good humour till its mother returned.

"I guess," she said, "that you are a married man?"

"Yes," said he, returning the child, "and a mason."

"Well, I thought as much any how, by the way you acted with the baby."

"My conduct was not quite free from selfishness – I expect a reward."

"As how?"

"That you will give the baby to your husband, and dance the next set with me."

"With all my heart. Let us go a-head."

If legs did not do their duty, it was no fault of their pretty owner, for she danced with all her strength, greatly to the amusement of her aristocratic partner.

When we first came to Belleville, evening parties commenced at the primitive and *rational* hour of six o'clock, but now invitations are issued for eight; the company, however, seldom assemble before nine, and those who wish to be very fashionable don't make their appearance before ten. This is rather absurd in a country, but Folly, as well as Wisdom, is justified of her children. Evening parties always include dancing and music, while cards are provided for those gentlemen who prefer whist to the society of the ladies. The evening generally closes with a splendid supper, in which there is no lack of the good things which the season affords. The ladies are always served first, the gentlemen waiting upon them at supper; and they never sit down to the table, when the company is large, until after the ladies have returned to the drawing-room. This custom would not be very agreeable to some English epicures, but it is an universal one with Canadian gentlemen, whose politeness and attention to the other sex is one of the most pleasing traits in their character.

The opportunities of visiting the theatre occur very seldom, and only can be enjoyed by those who reside in the *cities* of Canada. The young men of the place sometimes get up an amateur performance, in which they act the part of both ladies and gentlemen, greatly to the delight and amusement of their audience. I must say that I have enjoyed a play in one of these private houses more than ever I did at Drury Lane or Covent Garden. The lads act with their whole hearts, and I have seen them shed real tears over the sorrows they were called upon to pourtray. They did not feign – they really felt the part. Of course, there was little artistic skill, but a good deal of truth and nature.

In the summer, riding and boating parties take the place of dancing. These are always regular pic-nics, each party contributing their share of eatables and drinkables to the general stock. They commonly select some pretty island in the bay, or shady retired spot on the main land, for the general rendezvous, where they light a fire, boil their kettles, and cook the vegetables to eat with their cold prog, which usually consists of hams, fowls, meat pies, cold joints of meat, and abundance of tarts and cakes, while the luxury of ice is conveyed in a blanket at the bottom of one of the boats.

These water parties are very delightful. The ladies stroll about and gather wild fruit and flowers, while the gentlemen fish. The weather at that season of the year is sure to be fine, and the water scenery beautiful in the extreme. Those who possess good voices sing, and the young folks dance on the greensward. A day spent thus happily with nature in her green domain, is one of pure and innocent enjoyment. There is always a reunion, in the evening, of the party, at the house of one of the married ladies who were present at the pic-nic.

In a riding party, some place is selected in the country, and those who are invited meet at a fixed hour on the appointed ground. The Oakhill pond, near the village of Rawdon, and about sixteen miles from Belleville, is a very favourite spot, and is one of singular beauty. This Oakhill pond is a small, clear, and very deep lake, on the summit of a high hill. It is about two miles in circumference, and being almost circular, must nearly be as broad as it is long. The waters are intensely blue, the back-ground is filled up with groves of dark pine, while the woods in front are composed of the dwarf oaks and firs, which are generally found on these table lands, interspersed with low bushes – the sandy soil abounding with every Canadian variety of wild fruits and flowers.

There is an excellent plank road all the way from Belleville to Rawdon. The Oakhills lie a little to the left, and you approach them by a very steep ascent, from the summit of which you obtain as fine a prospect as I have seen in this part of Canada. A vast country lies stretched beneath your feet, and you look down upon an immense forest, whose tree-tops, moved by the wind, cause it to undulate like a green ocean. From this spot you may trace the four windings of the bay, to its junction with the blue waters of the Ontario. The last time I gazed from the top of this hill a thunder-storm was frowning over the woods, and the dense black clouds gave an awful grandeur to the noble picture.

The village of Rawdon lies on the other side of this table land, quite in a valley. A bright, brisk little stream runs through it, and turns several large mills. It is a very pretty rural place, and is fast rising towards the dignity of a town. When we first came to Belleville, the spot on which Rawdon now stands belonged principally, if not altogether, to an enterprising Orkney man, Edward Fidlar, Esq., to whose energy and industry it mainly owes its existence. Mr. Fidlar, might truly be termed the father of the village. A witty friend suggested, that instead of Rawdon, it ought more properly to be called "Fidlar's Green."

There is a clean country inn just at the foot of the long hill leading to the Oakhill pond, kept by a respectable widow-woman of the name of Fairman. If the pic-nic party does not wish to be troubled with carrying baskets of provisions so far, they send word to Mrs. Fairman the day previous, to prepare dinner for so many guests. This she always does in the best possible country style, at the moderate charge of half-a-dollar per head.

A dinner in the country in Canada, taken at the house of some substantial yeoman, is a very different affair from a dinner in the town. The table literally groans with good cheer; and you cannot offer a greater affront to your hostess, than to eat sparingly of the dainties set before you.

They like to have several days' warning of your intended visit, that they may go "*to trouble*," as they most truly term making such magnificent preparations for a few guests. I have sat down to a table of this kind in the country, with only Mr. M. and myself as guests, and we have been served with a dinner that would have amply fed twenty people. Fowls of several sorts, ham, and joints of roast and boiled meat, besides quantities of pies, puddings, custards, and cakes. Cheese is invariably offered to you with apple pie; and several little glass dishes are ranged round your plate, for preserves, honey, and apple sauce, which latter dainty is never wanting at a country feast. The mistress of the house constantly presses you to partake of all these things, and sometimes the accumulation of rich food on one plate, which it is impossible for you to consume, is everything but agreeable.

Two ladies, friends of mine, went to spend the day at one of these too hospitable entertainers. The weather was intensely hot. They had driven a long way in the sun, and both ladies had a headache, and very little appetite in consequence. The mistress of the house went "*to trouble*," and prepared a great feast for her guests; but, finding that

they partook very sparingly of her good cheer, her pride was greatly hurt, and rising suddenly from her seat, and turning to them with a stern brow, she exclaimed, –
"I should like to know what ails my victuals, that you don't choose to eat."

The poor ladies explained the reason of their appetites having failed them; but they found it a difficult matter to soothe their irritated hostess, who declared that she would never go "*to trouble*" for them again. It is of no use arguing against this amiable weakness, for as eating to uneducated people is one of the greatest enjoyments of life, they cannot imagine how they could make you more comfortable, by offering you less food, and of a more simple kind.

Large farmers in an old cleared country live remarkably well, and enjoy within themselves all the substantial comforts of life. Many of them keep carriages, and drive splendid horses. The contrast between the pork and potato diet, (and sometimes of potatoes alone without the pork), in the backwoods, is really striking. Before a gentleman from the old country concludes to settle in the bush, let him first visit these comfortable abodes of peace and plenty.

The Hon. R.B.——, when canvassing the county, paid a round of visits to his principal political supporters, and they literally almost killed him with kindness. Every house provided a feast in honour of their distinguished guest, and he was obliged to *eat* at all.

Coming to spend a quiet evening at our house, the first words he uttered were – "If you have any regard for me, Mrs. M——, pray don't ask me to eat. I am sick of the sight of food."

I can well imagine the amount of "*trouble*" each good wife had taken upon herself on this great occasion.

One of the most popular public exhibitions is the circus, a sort of travelling Astley's theatre, which belongs to a company in New York. This show visits all the large towns once during the summer season. The performance consists of feats of horsemanship, gymnastics, dancing on the tight and slack rope, and wonderful feats of agility and strength; and to those who have taste and nerve enough to admire such sights, it possesses great attractions. The company is a large one, often exceeding forty persons; it is provided with good performers, and an excellent brass band. The arrival of the circus is commonly announced several weeks before it makes its actual *entrée*, in the public papers; and large handbills are posted up in the taverns, containing coarse woodcuts of the most exciting scenes in the performance. These ugly pictures draw round them crowds of little boys, who know the whole of the programme by heart, long before the caravans containing the tents and scenery arrive. Hundreds of these little chaps are up before day-break on the expected morning of the show, and walk out to Shannonville, a distance of nine miles, to meet it.

However the farmers may grumble over bad times and low prices, the circus never lacks its quantum of visitors; and there are plenty of half-dollars to be had to pay for tickets for themselves and their families.

The Indians are particularly fond of this exhibition, and the town is always full of them the day the circus comes in.

A large tent is pitched on the open space between the Scotch church and the old hospital, big enough to contain at least a thousand people, besides a wide area for the performance and the pit. An amphitheatre of seats rise tier above tier, to within a few feet of the eaves of the tent, for the accommodation of the spectators; and the whole space is lighted by a large chandelier, composed of tin holders, filled with very bad, greasy, tallow candles, that in the close crowded place emit a very disagreeable odour.

The show of horses and feats of horsemanship are always well worth seeing, but the rest grows very tiresome on frequent repetition. Persons must be very fond of this sort of thing who can twice visit the circus, as year after year the clown repeats the same stale jests, and shows up the same style of performers.

The last time I went, in order to please my youngest son, I was more amused by the antics of a man who carried about bull's-eyes and lemonade, than by any of the actors. Whenever he offered his tray of sweets to the ladies, it was with such an affectedly graceful bend; and throwing into his voice the utmost persuasion, he contrived to glance down on the bulls'-eyes with half an eye, and to gaze up at the ladies he addressed with all that remained of the powers of vision, exclaiming, with his hand on his heart, – "How sweet they a-r-e!" combining a recommendation of his bulls'-eyes with a compliment to the fair sex.

The show opens at two o'clock, P.M., and again at half-past seven in the evening. The people from a distance, and the young children, visit the exciting scene during the day; the town's-people at night, as it is less crowded, cooler, and the company more select. Persons of all ranks are there; and the variety of faces and characters that nature exhibits gratis, are far more amusing to watch than the feats of the Athletes.

Then there is Barnham's travelling menagerie of wild animals, and of tame darkie melodists, who occupy a tent by themselves, and a *white nigger* whom the boys look upon with the same wonder they would do at a white rat or mouse. Everybody goes to see the wild beasts, and to poke fun at the elephants. One man who, born and brought up in the Backwoods, had never seen an elephant before, nor even a picture of one, ran half frightened home to his master, exclaiming as he bolted into the room, "Oh, sir! sir! you must let the childer go to the munjery. Shure there's six huge critters to be seen, with no eyes, and a tail before and behind."

The celebrated General Tom Thumb paid the town a visit last summer. His presence was hailed with enthusiastic delight, and people crowded from the most remote settlements to gaze upon the tiny man. One poor Irishwoman insisted "that he was not a human crathur, but a fairy changeling, and that he would vanish away some day, and never be heard of again." Signor Blitz, the great conjuror, occasionally pays us a visit, but his visits are like angel visits, few and far between. His performance never fails in filling the large room in the court-house for several successive nights, and his own purse. Then we have lecturers from the United States on all subjects, who commonly content themselves with hiring the room belonging to the Mechanics' Institute, where they hold forth, for the moderate sum of a York shilling a head, on mesmerism, phrenology, biology, phonography, spiritual communications, &c.

These wandering lectures are often very well attended, and their performance is highly entertaining. Imagine a tall, thin, bearded American, exhibiting himself at a small wooden desk between two dingy tallow candles, and holding forth in the *genuine* nasal twang on these half-supernatural sciences on which so much is advanced, and of which so little is at present understood. Our lecturer, however, expresses no doubts upon the subject of which he treats. He proves on the persons of his audience the truth of phrenology, biology, and mesmerism, and the individuals he pitches upon to illustrate his facts perform their parts remarkably well, and often leave the spectators in a maze of doubt, astonishment, and admiration.

I remember, about three years ago, going with my husband to hear the lecturers of a person who called himself Professor R——. He had been lecturing for some nights running at the Mechanics' Institute for nothing, and had drawn together a great number of persons to hear him, and witness the strange things he effected by mesmerism on the persons of such of the audience who wished to test his skill. This would have been but a poor way of getting his living. But these American adventurers never give their time and labour for nothing. He obtained two dollars for examining a head phrenologically, and drawing out a chart; and as his lectures seldom closed without securing him a great many heads for inspection, our disinterested professor contrived to pocket a great deal of money, and to find his cheap lectures an uncommonly profitable speculation.

We had heard a great deal of his curing a blacksmith of *tic-douloureux* by mesmerizing him. The blacksmith, though a big, burly man, had turned out an admirable clairvoyant, and by touching particular bumps in his cranium, the professor could make him sing, dance, and fight all in a breath, or transport him to California, and set him to picking gold. I was very curious to witness this man's conduct under his alleged mesmeric state, and went accordingly. After a long lecture, during which the professor put into a deep sleep a Kentuckian giant, who travelled with him, the blacksmith was called upon to satisfy the curiosity of the spectators. I happened to sit near this individual, and as he rose to comply with the vociferous demands of the audience, I shall never forget the sidelong knowing glance he cast across the bench to a friend of his own; it was, without exception, the most intelligent telegraphic despatch that it was possible for one human eye to convey to another, and said more plainly than words could – "You shall see how I can humbug them all." That look opened my eyes completely to the farce that was acting before me, and entering into the spirit of the scene, I must own that I enjoyed it amazingly. The blacksmith was mesmerised by a *look* alone, and for half an hour went on in a most funny manner, keeping the spectators with their eyes open, and in convulsions of laughter. After a while, the professor left him to enjoy his mesmeric nap, and chose another subject, in the person of a man who had lectured a few nights before on the science of mnemonics, and had been disappointed in a very scanty attendance.

After a decent time had elapsed, the new subject yielded very easily to the professor's magic passes, and fell into a profound sleep. The mesmerizer then led him, with his eyes shut, to the front of the stage, and pointed out to the spectators the phrenological development of his head; he then touched the bump of language, and set the seeming automaton talking. But here the professor was caught in his own trap. After once setting him going, he of the mnemonics refused to hold his tongue until he had given, to his weary listeners, the whole lecture he had delivered a few nights before. He pranced to and fro on the platform, declaiming in the most pedantic voice, and kept us for one blessed hour before he would suffer the professor to deprive him of the unexpected opportunity thus afforded him of being heard. It was a droll scene: the sly blacksmith in a profound fox's sleep – the declaimer pretending to be asleep, and wide awake all the time – and the thin, long-faced American, too wise to betray his colleagues, but evidently annoyed beyond measure at the trick they had played him.

I once went to hear a lecture at the Mechanics' Institute, delivered by a very eccentric person, who styled himself the Hon. James Spencer Lidstone – *the Great Orator of the West*. My astonishment may be guessed better than described, when he gave out for the subject of his lecture – "Great women, from Eve down to Mrs. M——." Not wishing to make myself a laughing-stock to a pretty numerous audience, I left the room. Going up the street next morning, a venerable white-haired old man ran after me, and pulling me by the shawl, said, "Mrs. M——, why did you leave us last night? He did you justice – indeed he did. You should have stayed and heard all the fine things he said of you."

Besides scientific lecturers, Canada is visited by singers and musicians of every country, and of every age and sex – from the celebrated Jenny Lind, and the once celebrated Braham, down to pretenders who can neither sing nor play, worth paying a York shilling to hear. Some of these wandering musicians play with considerable skill, and are persons of talent. Their life is one of strange vicissitudes and adventure, and they have an opportunity of making the acquaintance of many odd characters. In illustration of this, I will give you a few of the trials of a travelling musician, which I took down from the dictation of a young friend, since dead, who earned a precarious living by his profession. He had the faculty of telling his adventures without the power of committing them to paper; and, from the simplicity and truthfulness of his character, I have no doubt of the variety of all the amusing anecdotes he told. But he shall speak for himself in the next chapter.

A MAY-DAY CAROL.

"There's not a little bird that wings
    Its airy flight on high,
In forest bowers, that sweetly sings
    So blithe in spring as I.
I love the fields, the budding flowers,
    The trees and gushing streams;
I bathe my brow in balmy showers,
    And bask in sunny beams.

"The wanton wind that fans my cheek,
    In fancy has a voice,
In thrilling tones that gently speak –
    Rejoice with me, rejoice!
The bursting of the ocean-floods,
    The silver tinkling rills,
The whispering of the waving woods,
    My inmost bosom fills.

"The moss for me a carpet weaves
    Of patterns rich and care;
And meekly through her sheltering leaves
    The violet nestles there.
The violet! –oh, what tales of love,
    Of youth's sweet spring are thine!
And lovers still in field and grove,
    Of thee will chaplets twine.

"Mine are the treasures Nature strews
    With lavish hand around;

My precious gems are sparkling dews,
   My wealth the verdant ground.
Mine are the songs that freely gush
   From hedge, and bush, and tree;
The soaring lark and speckled thrush
   Discourse rich melody.

"A cloud comes floating o'er the sun,
   The woods' green glories fade;
But hark! the blackbird has begun
   His wild lay in the shade.
He hails with joy the threaten'd shower,
   And plumes his glossy wing;
While pattering on his leafy bower,
   I hear the big drops ring.

"Slowly at first, but quicker now,
   The rushing rain descends;
And to each spray and leafy bough
   A crown of diamonds lends.
Oh, what a splendid sight appears!
   The sun bursts forth again;
And, smiling through sweet Nature's tears,
   Lights up the hill and plain.

"And tears are trembling in my eyes,
   Tears of intense delight;
Whilst gazing upward to the skies,
   My heart o'erflows my sight.
Great God of nature! may thy grace
   Pervade my inmost soul;
And in her beauties may I trace
   The love that form'd the whole!"

FIVE

Trials of a Travelling Musician

"The man that hath not music in his soul."

I WILL SAY no more. The quotation, though but too true, is too well known; but it will serve as the best illustration I can give to the various annoyances which beset the path of him who is musically inclined, and whose soul is in unison with sweet sounds. This was my case. I loved music with all my heart and soul, and in order to give myself wholly up to my passion, and claim a sort of moral right to enjoy it, I made it a profession.

Few people have a better opportunity of becoming acquainted with the world than the travelling musician; yet such is the absorbing nature of his calling, that few make use of it less. His nature is open, easy, and unsuspecting; pleased with his profession, he hopes always to convey the same pleasure to his hearers; and though doubts will sometimes cross his mind, and the fear of ridicule make him awkward and nervous, yet, upon the whole, he is generally sure of making a favourable impression on the simple-hearted and generous among his hearers.

The musician moves among his fellow-men as a sort of privileged person; for who ever suspects him of being a rogue? His first attempt to deceive would defeat its own object, and prove him to be a mere pretender. His hand and voice must answer for his skill, and form the only true test of his abilities. If tuneless and bad, the public will not fail to condemn him.

The adventures of the troubadours of old, if they were more full of sentiment and romance than the every-day occurrences that beset the path of the modern minstrel, were not more replete with odd chances and ludicrous incident. Take the following for an example of the many droll things which have happened to me during my travels.

In the summer of 1846 I was making a professional tour through the United States, and had advertised a concert for the ensuing evening at the small town of –, and was busy making the necessary arrangements, when I was suddenly accosted, as I left the hotel, by a tall, thin, lack-a-daisical looking man, of a most unmusical and unprepossessing appearance: "How-do-ye-do? I'm highly tickled to see you. I s'pose you are going to give an extra sing here – ain't you?"

"Yes; I intend giving a concert here this evening."

"Hem! How much dew you ax to come in? That is – I want to say – what are you goin' to chearge a ticket?"

"Half a dollar – the usual price."

"How?" inclining his ear towards me, as if he doubted the soundness of the organ.

"Half a dollar?" repeated I, carelessly.

"Tis tew much. You had better chearge twenty-five cents. If you dew, you'll have a pretty good house. If you make it twelve and a half cents, you'll have a *smasher*. If, mister, you'll lower that agin to six and a quarter cents, you'll have to take a field, – there ain't a house would hold 'em." After a pause, scratching his head, and shuffling with his feet, "I s'pose you ginnerally give the profession tickets?"

"Sometimes."

"I'm a *leetle* in your line myself. Although I'm a shoemaker by trade, I leads the first Presbyterian choir upon the hill. I should like to have you come up, if you stay long enough."

"As that is the case, perhaps you can tell me if I am likely to have a good house to-night?"

"I kind a reckon as how you will; that is, if you don't chearge tew much."

"Where shall I get the best room?"

"Well, I guess, you had better try the old meetin' house."

"Thank you. Allow me, sir, to present you with a ticket." I now thought that I had got rid of him, and amply paid him for the information I had received. The ticket was for a single admission. He took it, turned it slowly round, held it close to his eyes, spelt it carefully over, and then stared at me. "What next?" thought I.

"There's my wife. Well – I s'pose she'd like to come in."

"You wish me to give you a double ticket?"

"I don't care if you dew," again turning the new ticket in his hand; and, scratching his head more earnestly, he said, "I've one of the smartest boys you ever seed; he's a fust-rate ear for music; he can whistle any tune he hears right straight off. Then there's my wife's sister a-staying with us jist now; she's very fond of music tew."

"Perhaps," said I, losing all patience, "you would prefer a family ticket?"

"Well; I'd be obliged. It don't cost you any, mister; and if we don't use it, I'll return it tomorrow."

The stranger left me, and I saw no more of him, until I spied him in the concert-room, with a small family of ten or twelve. Presently, another man and a dog arrived. Says he to the doorkeeper, "What's a-goin on here?"

"It's a concert, – admission, half-a-dollar."

"I'm not a-goin' to give half-a-dollar to go in here. I hire a pew in this here church by the year, and I've a right to go in whenever the door's open." So in he went with his dog.

The evening turned out very wet, and these people happened to form all my audience; and as I did not feel at all inclined to sing for their especial benefit, I returned to my lodgings. I learned from my doorkeeper the next morning, that my friends waited for an hour and a half for my re-appearance, which could not reasonably have been expected under existing circumstances.

I thought I had got rid of the musical shoemaker for ever, but no such good luck. Before I was out of my bed, he paid me a visit.

"You will excuse my calling so early," says he, "but I was anxious to see you before you left the town."

Wishing him at the bottom of the Mississippi, I put on my dressing gown, and slipped from my bed, whilst he continued his introductory address.

"I was very sorry that you had not a better attendance last night; and I s'pose that accounted for your leaving us as you did. We were all kinder disappointed. You'd have had a better house, only the people thought there was a *leetle* humbug about this," and he handed me one of my programmes.

It is well known to most of my readers, that in writing these bills the name of the composer generally follows the song, particularly in any very popular compositions, such as

Grand Introduction to Pianoforte . . . . Henry Hertz.
Life on the Ocean Wave . . . . Henry Russell.
Old English Gentleman . . . . Melody by Mart. Luther.

"Humbug!" said I, attempting to take the bill, in order to see that no mistake had originated in the printing, but my tormentor held it fast. "Look," said he; "Now where is Henry Hertz; and Henry Russell, where is he? And the Old English Gentleman, Martin Luther, what has become of him? The folks said that he was dead, but I didn't believe that, for I didn't think that you would have had the face to put his name in your bill if he was."

Thus ended my acquaintance with the enlightened shoe-maker of the Mississippi. I was travelling in one of the western canal boats the same summer, and was sauntering to and fro upon the deck, admiring the beauty of the country through which we were passing, when I observed a very tall, thin-faced, sharp looking man, regarding me with very fixed attention. Not knowing who or what he was, I was at last a little annoyed by the pertinacity of this steady stare. It was evident that he meditated an attack upon me in some shape or other. Suddenly he came up to me, and extending his hand, exclaimed, –

"Why, Mister H——, is this you? I have not seen you since you gave your *consort* at N——; it seems a tarnation long while ago. I thought, perhaps, you had got blowed up in one of those exploded steam-boats. But here you are as large as life – and that's not over large neither, (glancing at the slight dimensions of my figure,) and as ready to raise the wind as ever. I am highly gratified to meet with you, as I have one of the greatest songs you ever he'rd to show you. If you can but set it to music, and sing it in New York city, it will immortalize you, and immortalize me tew."

Amused at the earnestness with which the fellow spoke, I inquired the subject of his song.

"Oh, 'tis des-crip-tive; 'tis tre-men-dous. It will make a sensation all over the Union."

"But what is it about? – Have you got it with you?"

"No – no, mister; I never puts these things down on paper, lest other folk should find them and steal them. But I'll give you some *idee* of what it is. Look you, mister. I was going from Syracuse to Rochester, on the canal-boat. We met on our way a tre-men-dous storm. The wind blew, and the rain came down like old sixty, and everything looked as black as my hat; and the passengers got scared and wanted to get off, but the captain sung out, 'Whew – let 'em go, Jem!' and away we went at the rate of tew miles an hour, and they could not stop. By and by we struck a rock, and down we went."

"Indeed!" said I, "that's very unusual in a canal-boat; were any lives lost?"

"No, but we were all dreadfully sceared and covered

with mud. I sat down by the *en-gine* till I got dry, and then I wrote my pome. I will repeat what I can to you, and what I can't I will write right off when I gets hum. – Hold on – hold on –" he continued, beating his forehead with the back of his hand, as if to awaken the powers of memory –

"I have it now – I have it now, – 'tis tre-men-dous –'"

> "Oh Lord, who know'st the wants of men,
>   Guide my hand, and guide my pen,
>   And help me bring the truth to light,
>   Of that dread scene and awful night,
>   Ri, tu, ri, tu, ri, tu.
> There was Mister Cadoga in years a-bud,
> Was found next morning in tew feet mud;
> He strove – he strove, – but all in vain,
> The more he got up, he fell down again.
>   Ri, tu, ri, tu, ri, tu."

The poet paused for a moment to gain breath, evidently overcome by the recollection of the awful scene. "Is not that bee-u-tiful?" he exclaimed. "What a fine effect you could give to that on the pee-a-ne, humouring the keys to imitate his squabbling about in the mud. Let me tell you, mister, it would beat Russell's 'Ship on Fire' all hollow."

Wiping the perspiration from his face, he recommenced, –

> "The passengers rushed unto the spot,
>   Together with the crew;
> We got him safe out of the mud,
>   But he had lost his shoe.
>   Ri, tu, ri, tu, ri, tu."

I could not listen to another line of this sublime effusion, the passengers who had gathered around us drowning his nasal drawl in a complete roar of laughter. Seeing that I was as much infected as the rest, the poet turned to me, with an air of offended dignity, –

"I don't take the trouble, mister, to repeat any more of

my *pomes* to you; nor do I take it kind at all, your laughing at me in that ere way. But the truth is, you can't comprehend nor appreciate anything that is sublime, or out of the common way. Besides, I don't think you could set it to music; it is not in you, and you can't fix it nohow."

This singular address renewed our mirth; and, finding myself unable to control my inclination to laugh, and not wishing to hurt his feelings, I was about to leave him, when the man at the helm sung out, "Bridge!"

The passengers lowered their heads to ensure their safety – all but my friend the poet, who was too much excited to notice the signal before he came in contact with the bridge, which sent him sprawling down the gangway. He picked himself up, clambered up the stairs, and began striding up and down the deck at a tremendous rate, casting from time to time indignant glances at me.

I thought, for my part, that the man was not in his right senses, or that the blow he had received had so dulled his bump of caution, that he could no longer take care of himself; for the next moment he stumbled over a little child, and would have been hurt severely if I had not broken his fall, by catching his arm before he again measured his length on the deck. My timely assistance mollified his anger, and he once more became friendly and confidential.

"Here, take this piece of poetry, Mister H——, and see if you can set *it* to music. Mind you, it is none of mine; but though not *quite* so good, it is som'at in my style. I cut it out of a newspaper down East. You are welcome to it," he continued, with a patronizing nod, "that is, if you are able to do justice to the subject."

I took the piece of dirty crumpled newspaper from his hand; and, struck with the droll quizzing humour of the lines, I have preserved them ever since. As I have never seen them before or since, I will give you them here.

TO THE FALLS OF NIAGARA.

"I wonder how long you've been roarin'
　　At this infernal rate;
　I wonder if all you've been pourin'
　　Could be cipher'd on a slate.

"I wonder how such a thunderin' sounded
　　When all New York was woods, –
　'Spose likely some Injins have been drownded,
　　When the rains have raised your floods.

"I wonder if wild stags and buffaloes
　　Have stood where now I stand;
　Well – s'pose being scared at first, they stubb'd their toes;
　　I wonder where they'd land.

"I wonder if that rainbow has been shinin'
　　Since sun-rise at creation;
　And this waterfall been underminin'
　　With constant spatteration.

"That Moses never mention'd ye – I've wonder'd,
　　While other things describin'; –
　My conscience! – how ye must have foam'd and thunder'd
　　When the deluge was subsidin'!

"My thoughts are strange, magnificent, and deep,
　　When I look down on thee; –
　Oh, what a glorious place for washing sheep
　　Niagara would be!

"And oh, what a tremendous water power
　　Is wash'd over its edge;
　One man might furnish all the world with flour,
　　With a single privilege.

"I wonder how many times the lakes have all
  Been emptied over here;
Why Clinton did not feed the grand Canal
  Up here – I think is queer.

"The thoughts are very strange that crowd my brain,
  When I look up to thee;
Such thoughts I never expect to have again,
  To all eternity."

After reading the lines, I begged my friend to excuse
me, as I wanted to go below and take a nap. I had not
been long in the cabin before he followed me. To get rid of
him I pretended to be asleep. After passing me two or
three times, and leaning over me in the most inquisitive
manner, until his long nose nearly went into my eye; and
humming a bow-wow tune in my ear to ascertain if I were
really napping, he turned from me with a dissatisfied
grunt, flung himself into a settee, and not long after was
puffing and blowing like a porpoise. I was glad of this
opportunity to go on deck again, and "I left him alone in
his glory." But, while I was congratulating myself on my
good fortune, I found him once more at my side.

Good heavens! how I wished him at the bottom of the
canal, when he commenced telling me some *awful* dream
he had had. I was too much annoyed at being pestered
with his company to listen to him, a circumstance I now
rather regret, for had his dreams been equal to his poetry,
they certainly must have possessed the rare merit of origi-
nality; and I could have gratified my readers with something entirely out of the common way.

Turning abruptly from him, I entered into conversation
with another gentleman, and quite forgot my eccentric
friend until I retired for the night, when I found him
waiting for me in the cabin.

Ho, ho, mister, – is that you? I was afear'd we had put
you ashore. What berth are you goin' to take?"

I pointed to No. 4.

"Then," said he, "would you have any objection to my locating in the one above you, as I feel a *leetle afear'd*? It is so awful dark out-doors, and the clouds look tre-men-dous black, as if they'd be a-pourin' all night. The reason why I prefer the upper berth is this," he continued confidentially; "if we should fall in with a storm, and all go to the bottom, I should have a better chance of saving myself. But mind you, if she should sink I will give you half of my berth, if you'll come up."

I thanked him for his offer, and not being at all apprehensive, I told him that I preferred staying where I was. Soon after I retired, hoping to sleep, but I had not calculated on the powers of annoyance possessed by my quondam friend. I had just laid myself comfortably down, when I felt one of his huge feet on the side of my berth. Looking out, I espied him crawling up on all-fours to his place of security for the night. His head had scarcely touched the pillow before he commenced telling me some long yarn; but I begged him, in no very gentle tone, to hold on till the morning, as I had a very severe headache, and wanted to go to sleep.

I had fallen into a sort of doze, when I thought I heard some one talking in a low voice close to my ear. I started into a sitting posture, and listened a moment. It was pitch dark; I could see nothing. I soon, however, discovered that the mysterious sounds proceeded from the berth above me. It was my friend reciting, either for my amusement or his own, the poem he had favoured me with in the morning. He was apparently nearly asleep, and he drawled the half-uttered sentences through his nose in the most ludicrous manner. He was recapitulating the disastrous condition of Mr. Cadoza: –

"There was Mister Ca-do-za – in years a-bud –
Next morning – tew – feet – mud –
He strove – he – but – in vain;
The more he fell – down – he got up – a-g-a-in
                    Ri – tu – ri – tu."

Here followed a tremendous snore, and I burst into a prolonged fit of laughter, which fortunately did not put a stop to the sonorous bass of my companion overhead, whose snoring I considered far more tolerable than his conversation.

Just at this moment the boat struck the bank, which it frequently does of a very dark night, which gave the vessel such a shock, that it broke the cords that secured the poet's bed to the beam above, and down he came, head foremost, to the floor. This accident occasioned me no small discomfort, as he nearly took my berth with him. It was fortunate for me that I was awake, or he might have killed me in his descent; as it was, I had only time to throw myself back, when he rushed past me with the speed of an avalanche, carrying bed and bed-clothes with him in one confused heap; and there he lay upon the floor, rolling and roaring like some wild beast caught in a net.

"Oh, dear! oh, dear! I wonder where I is; what a tre-men-dous storm – what a dreadful night – not a soul can be saved, – I knew it – I dreampt it all. Oh Lord! we shall all go to the bottom, and find eternity there. – Captain – captain – where be we?"

Here a child belonging to one of the passengers, awakened by his bellowing, began to cry.

"Oh, dear! Some one else sinking. – Captain – captain – confound him! I s'pose he's drownded, like the rest. Thank heaven! here's something to hold on to, to keep me from sinking;" and, clutching at the table in the dark, he upset it, and broke the large lamp that had been left upon it. Down came the broken glass upon him in a shower which, doubtless, he took for the waves breaking over him, for he raised such a clatter with his hands and feet, and uttered such doleful screams, that the passengers started simultaneously from their sleep, –

"What's the matter? is that man mad or drunk?" exclaimed several voices.

The gentleman beneath the bed-clothes again groaned

forth, – "We are all lost. If I once get upon dry land, you'll never catch me in a canal-boat agin."

Pitying his distress I got up, groped my way to the steward's berth, and succeeded in procuring a light. When I returned to the cabin, I found the poet lying on the floor, with the table upon him, and he holding it fast with both hands, crying vehemently, "I will never let go. I will hang on to the last."

"You are dreaming," said I; "come, get up. The cords of your bed were not strong enough to hold you, and you have got a tumble on to the floor; nothing else is the matter with you."

As I ceased speaking the vessel again struck the bank, and my friend, in his eagerness to save himself, upset me, light and all. I again upset all the small pieces of furniture in my reach, to the great amusement of the passengers, who were sitting up in their berths listening to, and laughing at our conversation. We were all once more in the dark, and I can assure my readers that my situation was everything but comfortable, as the eccentric gentleman had hold of both my legs.

"You foolish fellow," cried I, kicking with all my might to free myself. "There is no harm done; the boat has only struck again upon the bank."

"Where is the bank?" said he, still labouring under the delusion that he was in the water. "Give me a hold on it. If I can only get on the bank I shall be safe."

Finding it impossible to convince him how matters really stood, I left him to unrol himself to his full dimensions on the floor, and groping my way to a sofa, laid myself down once more to sleep.

When the passengers met at the breakfast-table, the poor poet and his misfortunes during the night gave rise to much quizzing and merriment, particularly when he made his appearance with a black eye, and the skin rubbed off the tip of his nose.

One gentleman, who was most active in teasing him,

cried out to me, – "Mr. H——, do try and set last night's adventures to music, and sing them this evening at your concert. They would make a *tre–men–dous sensation*, I assure you."

The poet looked daggers at us, and seizing his carpet-bag, sprang to the deck, and from the deck to the shore, which he fortunately reached in safety, without casting a parting glance at his tormentors.

THE MOUNTAIN AIR.

"Rave not to me of your sparkling wine;
  Bid not for me the goblet shine;
  My soul is athirst for a draught more rare,
  A gush of the pure, fresh mountain air!

"It wafts on its currents the rich perfume
  Of the purple heath, and the honied broom;
  The golden furze, and the hawthorn fair,
  Shed all their sweets to the mountain air.

"It plays round the bank and the mossy stone,
  Where the violet droops like a nun alone;
  Shrouding her eyes from the noon-tide glare,
  But breathing her soul to the mountain-air.

"It gives to my spirits a tone of mirth –
  I bound with joy o'er the new-dress'd earth,
  When spring has scatter'd her blossoms there,
  And laden with balm the mountain air.

"From nature's fountain my nectar flows,
  'Tis the essence of each sweet bud that blows;
  Then come, and with me the banquet share,
  Let us breathe together the mountain air!"

SIX

The Singing Master

Trials of a Travelling Musician

THE SINGING SCHOOL.

"Conceit's an excellent great-coat, and sticks
　　Close to the wearer for his mortal life;
　　It has no spot nor wrinkle in his eyes,
　　And quite cuts out the coats of other men."

　　　　　　　　　　　　　　　　　　　　　　S.M.

"He had a fiddle sadly out of tune,
　　A voice as husky as a raven croaking,
Or owlet hooting to the clouded moon,
　　Or bloated bull-frog in some mud-hole choking."

DURING my professional journies through the country,
I have often had the curiosity to visit the singing
schools in the small towns and villages through which I
passed. These are often taught by persons who are perfectly ignorant of the common rules of music – men who
have followed the plough all their lives, and know about as
much of the divine science they pretend to teach as one of
their oxen.

I have often been amused at their manner of explaining
the principles of their art to their pupils, who profit so
little by their instructions, that they are as wise at the end
of their quarter as when they began. The master usually

endeavours to impress upon them the importance of making themselves heard, and calls him the smartest fellow who is able to make the most noise. The constant vibration they keep up through their noses gives you the idea that their teacher has been in the habit of raising sheep, and had caught many of their peculiar notes. This style he very kindly imparts to his pupils; and as apt scholars generally try to imitate their master, choirs taught by these individuals resemble a flock of sheep going bahing one after another over a wall.

I will give you a specimen of one of these schools, that I happened to visit during my stay in the town of W——, in the western states. I do not mean to say that all music masters are like the one I am about to describe, but he bears a very close resemblance to a great many of the same calling, who practise their profession in remote settlements, where they are not likely to find many to criticise their performance.

I had advertised a concert for the 2d of January, 1848, to be given in the town of W——. I arrived on the day appointed, and fortunately made the acquaintance of several gentlemen amateurs, who happened to be boarding at the hotel to which I had been recommended. They kindly manifested a lively interest in my success, and promised to do all in their power to procure me a good house.

While seated at dinner, one of my new friends received a note, which he said came from a singing master residing in a small village a few miles back of W——. After reading the epistle, and laughing heartily over its contents, he gave it to me. To my great astonishment it ran as follows: –

"MY DEAR ROBERTS,

"How do you do? I hope you will excuse me for troubling you on this occasion; but I want to ax you a partic'lar question. Is you acquainted with the man who is a-goin' to give a sing in your town to-night? If you be, jist say to him, from me, that if he will come over here, we will get him up a house. If he will – or won't cum – please let me know. I am teaching a singing school over here, and I can do a great deal for him, if he will only cum.

> "Yours, most respectfully,
> "JOHN BROWNE."

"You had better go, Mr. H——," said Roberts. "This John Browne is a queer chap, and I promise you lots of fun. If you decide upon going we will all accompany you, and help to fill your house."

"By all means," said I. "You will do me a great favour to return an answer to the professional gentleman to that effect. I will send him some of my programmes, and if he can get a tolerable piano, I will go over and give them a concert next Saturday evening."

The note and the bills of performance were duly despatched to –, and the next morning we received an answer from the singing master to say that all was right, and that Mr. Browne would be happy to give Mr. H—— his valuable assistance; but, if possible, he wished that I could come out on Friday, instead of Saturday, as his school met on that evening at six o'clock, and he would like me to witness the performance of his scholars, which would only last from five in the evening till six, and consequently need not interfere at all with my concert, which was to commence at eight.

We ordered a conveyance immediately, and as it was the very day signified in the note, we started off for the village of ——. On our arrival we were met at the door of the only hotel in the place, by the man a "*leetle* in my line."

"Is this you, Mr. Thing-a-my. I can't for the life of me think of your name. But no matter. Ain't you the chap as is a-goin' to give us the con-sort this evening?"

I answered in the affirmative, and he continued –

"What a *leetle* fellow you be. Now I stand six feet four inches in my boots, and my voice is high in proportion. But I s'pose you can sing. Small fellows allers make a great noise. A bantam roaster allers crows as loud as an old game crower, to make folks believe that the dung-hill is his'n."

I was very much amused at his comparing me to a bantam cock, and felt almost inclined to clap my wings and crow.

"I have sent all your bills about town," continued the odd man, "and invited all the tip-tops to cum and hear you. I have engaged a good room, and a forty pound pee-a-ne. I s'pose it's worth as much, for 'tis a terrible smart one. It belongs to Deacon S——; and his two daughters are the prettiest galls hereabouts. They play 'Old Dan Tucker,' and all manner of tunes. I found it deuced hard to get the old woman's consent; but I knew she wouldn't refuse me, as she is looking out to cotch me for one of the daughters. She made many objections – said that she would rather the cheese-press and the cook-stove, and all the rest of the furniture went out of the house than the pee-a-ne, as she afear'd that the strings would break, and all the keys spill out by the way. The strings are rusty, and keys loose enough already. I told the old missus that I would take good care that the right side was kept upper-most; and that if any harm happened to the instrument, you could set it all right agin."

"I am sorry," said I, "to hear such a poor account of the instrument. It is impossible to sing well to a bad piano –"

"Phoo, phoo, man! there's nobody here that ever he'rd a better. Bad or good, it's the only one in the village. I play on this pee-a-ne a *leetle* myself, and that *ought* to be some encouragement to you. I am goin' to do a consider-able business in the singing line here. I have stirred up all the *leetle* girls and boys in the place, and set them whist-ling an' playing on the Jew's harp. Then I goes to the old 'uns, and says to them, what genuses for music these young 'uns be! it is your duty to improve a talent that providence has bestowed on your children. I puts on a long face, like a parson, when I talks of providence and the like o'that, and you don't know how amazingly it takes with the old folks. They think that providence is allers on the look out to do them some good turn. –

" 'What do you charge, Mr. Browne?' says they, instanter.

"Oh, a mere trifle, say I, instanter. Jist half-a-dollar a quarter – part in cash, part in *produce*.

" ' 'Tis cheap,' says they agin.

"Tew little, says I, by half.

" 'Well, the children shall go,' says the old man. 'Missus, you see to it.'

"The children like to hear themselves called genuses, and they go into it like smoke. When I am tuning my voice at my lodgings in the evening, just by way of recreation, the *leetle* boys all gets round my winder to listen to my singing. They are so fond of it I can't get them away. They make such a confounded noise, in trying to imitate my splendid style. But I'll leave you to judge of that for yourself. 'Spose you'll be up with me to the singing-school, and then you will hear what I can do."

"I shall be most happy to attend you."

"You see, Mr. Thing-a-my, this is my first lesson, and you must make all allowances, if there should be any trouble, or that all should not go right. You see one seldom gets the hang of it the first night, no how. I have been farming most of my life, but I quits that about five weeks ago, and have been studying hard for my profession ever since. I have got a large school here, another at A——, and another at L——; and before the winter is over, I shall be qualified to teach at W——. I play the big bass fiddle and the violin right off, and –"

Here a little boy came running up to say that his father's sheep had got out of the yard, and had gone down to Deacon S——; and, said he, "The folks have sent for you, Mister Browne, to cum and turn 'em out."

"A merciful intervention of providence," thought I, who was already heartily weary of my new acquaintance, and began to be afraid that I never should get rid of him.

To tell the truth, I was so tired of looking up at him, that I felt that I could not converse much longer with him without endangering the elasticity of my neck, and he would have been affronted if I had asked him to walk in and sit down.

He was not very well pleased with Deacon S——'s message.

"That comes of borrowing, mister. If I had not asked the loan of the pee-a-ne, they never would have sent for me to look arter their darned sheep. I must go, however. I hope you'll be able to keep yourself alive in my absence. I have got to string up the old fiddle for to-night. The singing-school is about a mile from this. I will come down with my old mare arter you, when its just time to be a-goin'. So good-bye."

Away he strode at the rate of six miles an hour; his long legs accomplishing at one step what would have taken a man of my dimensions three to compass. I then went into the hotel to order dinner for my friends, as he had allowed me no opportunity to do so. The conceited fellow had kept me standing a foot deep in snow for the last hour, while listening to his intolerably dull conversation. My disgust and disappointment afforded great amusement to my friends; but in spite of all my entreaties, they could not be induced to leave their punch and a warm fire to accompany me in my pilgrimage to the singing-school.

We took dinner at four o'clock, and the cloth was scarcely drawn, when my musical friend made his appearance with the old mare, to take me along to the school.

Our turn-out was everything but prepossessing. A large unwieldy cutter of home manufacture, the boards of which it was composed unplained and unpainted, with rope harness, and an undressed bull's hide by way of buffalo's, formed our equipage. But no description that I could give you would do justice to the old mare. A sorry beast she was – thick legged, rough coated, and of a dirty yellow-white. Her eyes, over one of which a film was spread, were dull as the eyes of a stale fish, and her temples so hollow, that she looked as if she had been worn out by dragging the last two generations to their graves. I was ashamed of adding one more to the many burdens she must have borne in her day, and I almost wished that she had realized in her own person the well-known verse in the Scotch song –

> "The auld man's mare's dead,
> A mile ayont Dundee,"

before I ever had set my eyes upon her.

"Can she carry us?" said I, pausing irresolutely, with my foot on the rough heavy runner of the cutter.

"I guess she can," quoth he. "She will skim like a bird over the snow; so get into the sleigh, and we will go straight off to the singing-school."

It was intensely cold. I drew the collar of my great coat over my ears, and wrapped my half of the bull's hide well round my feet, and we started. The old mare went better than could have been expected from such a skeleton of a beast. To be sure, she had no weight of flesh to encumber her motions, and we were getting on pretty well, when the music master drove too near a stump, which suddenly upset us both, and tumbled him head foremost into a bank of snow. I fortunately rolled out a-top of him, and soon extricated myself from the difficulty; but I found it no easy matter to drag my ponderous companion from beneath the snow, and the old bull's hide in which he was completely enveloped.

The old mare stood perfectly still, gazing with her one eye intently on the mischief she had done, as if she never had been guilty of such a breach of manners before. After shaking the snow from our garments, and getting all right for a second start, my companion exclaimed in an agonized tone –

"My fiddle! Where, where is my fiddle? I can do nothing without my fiddle."

We immediately went in search of it; but we did not succeed in finding it for some time. I had given it up in despair, and, half-frozen with cold, was stepping into the cutter to take the benefit of the old bull's hide, when, fortunately for the music-master, one of the strings of the lost instrument snapped with the cold. We followed the direction of the sound, and soon beheld the poor fiddle sticking in a snowbank, and concealed by a projecting stump. The instrument had sustained no other injury than the loss of three of the strings.

"Well, arn't that too bad?" says he. "I have no more catgut without sending to W——. That's done for, at least for to-night."

"It's very cold," I cried, impatiently, seeing that he was in no hurry to move on. "Do let us be going. You can examine your instrument better in the house than standing up to your knees in the snow."

"I was born in the Backwoods," say he; "I don't feel the cold." Then jumping into the cutter, he gave me the fiddle to take care of, and pointing with the right finger of his catskin gloves to a solitary house on the top of a bleak hill, nearly a mile a-head, he said, – "That white building is the place where the school is held."

We soon reached the spot. "This is the old Methodist church, mister, and a capital place for the voice. There is no furniture or hangings to interrupt the sound. Go right in, while I hitch the mare; I will be arter you in a brace of shakes."

I soon found myself in the body of the old dilapidated church, and subjected to the stare of a number of very unmusical-looking girls and boys, who, certainly from their appearance, would never have led you to suppose that they ever could belong to a Philharmonic society. Presently, Mr. Browne made his *début*.

Assuming an air of great importance as he approached his pupils, he said – "Ladies and gentlemen, allow me to introduce to your notice Mr. H——, the celebrated vocalist. He has cum all the way from New York on purpose to hear you sing."

The boys grinned at me and twirled their thumbs, the

girls nudged one another's elbows and giggled, while their eloquent teacher continued –

"I don't know as how we shall be able to do much to-night; we upset, and that spilt my fiddle into the snow. You see," – holding it up – "it's right full of it, and that busted the strings. A dropsical fiddle is no good, no how. Jist look at the water dripping out of her."

Again the boys laughed, and the girls giggled. Said he –

"Hold on, don't laugh; it's no laughing matter, as you'll find."

After a long pause, in which the youngsters tried their best to look grave, he went on –

"Now all of you, girls and boys, give your attention to my instructions this evening. I'm goin' to introduce a new style, for your special benefit, called the Pest-a-lazy (Pestalozzi) system, now all the fashion. If you are all ready, produce your books. Hold them up. One – two – three! Three books for forty pupils? That will never do! We can't sing to-night; well, never mind. You see that black board; I will give you a lesson to-night upon that. Who's got a piece of chalk?"

A negative shake of the head from all. To me "Chalk's scarce in these diggings." To the boys: "What, nobody got a piece of chalk? That's unlucky; a piece of charcoal out of the stove will do as well."

"No 'ar won't," roared out a boy with a very ragged coat. "They be both the same colour."

"True, Jenkins, for you; go out and get a lump of snow. Its darnation strange if I can't fix it somehow."

"Now," thought I, "what is this clever fellow going to do?"

The boys winked at each other, and a murmur of suppressed laughter ran through the old church. Jenkins ran out, and soon returned with a lump of snow.

Mr. Browne took a small piece, and squeezing it tight, stuck it upon the board. "Now, boys, that is Do, and that is Re, and that is Do again, and that is Mi, this Do, and that Fa; and that, boys, is a part of what we call a *scale*."

Then turning to a tall, thin, shabby-looking man, very much out at the elbows, whom I had not seen before, he said – "Mr. Smith, how is your *base viol*? Hav'nt you got it tuned up yet?"

"Well, squire, I guess it's complete."

"Hold on; let me see," and taking a tuning-fork from his pocket, and giving it a sharp thump upon the stove, he cried out in a still louder key – "Now, that's A; jist tune up to A."

After Mr. Smith had succeeded in tuning his instrument, the teacher proceeded with his lucid explanations: – "Now, boys, start fair; give a grand chord. What sort of a noise do you call that? (giving a luckless boy a thump over the head with his fiddle-stick). You bray through your nose like a jackass. I tell you to quit; I don't want discord." The boy slunk out of the class, and stood blubbering behind the door.

"Tune up again, young shavers! Sing the notes as I have made them on the board, – Do, re-do, mi, do-fa. Now, when I count four commence. One–two–three–four. Sing! Hold on! – hold on! Don't you see that all the notes are running off, and you can't sing running notes yet."

Here he was interrupted by the noise of some one forcing their way into the church, in a very strange and unceremonious manner, and

> "The chorister's song, that late was so strong,
>   Grew a quaver of consternation."

The door burst open, and a ghastly head was protruded through the aperture. "A ghost! – a ghost!" shrieked out all the children in a breath; and jumping over the forms, they huddled around the stove, upsetting the solitary tallow candle, the desk, and the bass viol, in their flight. One lad sprang right upon the unfortunate instrument, which broke to pieces with a terrible crash. We were now left in the dark. The girls screamed, and clung round me for protection, while the ghastly apparition continued to stare upon us through the gloom, with its large, hollow eyes. I must confess that I felt rather queer; but I wisely kept my fears to myself, while I got as far from the door as I possibly could. Just as our terror had reached a climax, the grizzly phantom uttered a low, whining neigh.

"It's the old mare! I'll be darned if it isn't!" cried one of the older boys, at the top of his voice. This restored confidence to the rest; and one rather bolder than his comrades at length ventured to relight the fallen candle at the stove, and holding it up, displayed to our view the old white mare, standing in the doorway. The poor beast had forced her way into the porch to protect herself from the cold; and she looked at her master, as much as to say, "I have a standing account against you." No doubt she would have been highly tickled, could she have known that her sudden intrusion had been the means of shortening her term of probation by at least half an hour, and of bringing the singing-school to a close. She had been the innocent cause of disabling both the musical instruments, and Mr. Browne could not raise a correct note without them. Turning to his pupils, with a very rueful countenance, and speaking in a very unmusical voice, but very expressive withal, he said – "Chore (meaning choir), you are dismissed. But, hold on! – don't be in such a darnation hurry to be off. I was a-going to tell you, this ere gentleman, Mr. H—— (my name, for a wonder, popping into his head at that minute) is to give a *con-sort* to-morrow night. It was to have been to-night; but he changed his mind, that he might have the pleasure of hearing you. I shall assist Mr. H—— in the singing department; so you must all be sure to cum. Tickets for boys over ten years, twenty-five cents; under ten, twelve and a half cents. So you *leetle* chaps will know what to do. The next time the school meets will be when the fiddles are fixed. Now scamper." The children were not long in obeying the order. In the twinkling of an eye they were off, and we heard them shouting and skylarking in the lane.

"Cum, Mr. H——," said the music-master, buttoning his great-coat up to his chin, "let us be a-goin'."

On reaching the spot where we had left the cutter, to our great disappointment, we found only one-half of it remaining; the other half, broken to pieces, strewed the ground. Mr. Browne detained me for another half-hour, in gathering together the fragments. "Now you, Mr. Smith, you take care of the crippled fiddles, while I take care of the bag of oats. The old mare has been trying to hook them out of the cutter, which has been the cause of all the trouble. You, Mr. H——, mount up on the old jade, and take along the bull's hide, and we will follow on foot."

"Yes," said I, "and glad of the chance, for I am cold and tired."

Not knowing a step of the way, I let Mr. Browne and his companion go a-head; and making a sort of pack-saddle of the old hide, I curled myself up on the back of the old mare, and left her to her own pace, which, however, was a pretty round trot, until we reached the out-skirts of the town, where, dismounting, I thanked my companions, very insincerely I'm afraid, for my evening's amusement, and joined my friends at the hotel, who were never tired of hearing me recount my adventures at the singing-school.

I had been obliged to postpone my own concert until the next evening, for I found the borrowed piano such a poor one, and so miserably out of tune, that it took me several hours rendering it at all fit for service. Before I had concluded my task, I was favoured with the company of Mr. Browne, who stuck to me closer than a brother, never allowing me out of his sight for a moment. This persevering attention, so little in unison with my feelings, caused me the most insufferable annoyance. A thousand times I was on the point of dismissing him very unceremoniously, by informing him that I thought him a most conceited, impertinent puppy; but for the sake of my friend Roberts, who was in some way related to the fellow, I contrived to master my anger. About four o'clock he jumped up from the table, at which he had been lounging and sipping hot punch at my expense for the last hour, exclaiming –

"I guess it's time for me to see the pee-a-ne carried up to the con-sort room."

"It's all ready," said I. "Perhaps, Mr. Browne, you will oblige me by singing a song before the company arrives, that I may judge how far your style and mine will agree;" for I began to have some horrible misgivings on the subject. "If you will step up stairs, I will accompany you on the piano. I had no opportunity of hearing you sing last night."

"No, no," said he, with a conceited laugh; "I mean to astonish you by and by. I'm not one of your common amateurs, no how. I shall produce quite a sensation upon your audience."

So saying, he darted through the door, and left me to finish my arrangements for the night.

The hour appointed for the concert at length arrived. It was a clear, frosty night, the moon shining as bright as day. A great number of persons were collected about the doors of the hotel, and I had every reason to expect a full house. I was giving some directions to my door-keeper, when I heard a double sleigh approaching at an uncommon rate; and looking up the road, I saw an old-fashioned, high-backed vehicle, drawn by two shabby-looking horses, coming towards the hotel at full gallop. The passengers evidently thought that they were too late, and were making up for lost time.

The driver was an old farmer, and dressed in the cloth of the country, with a large capote of the same material drawn over his head and weather-beaten face, which left his sharp black eyes, red nose, and wide mouth alone visible. He flourished in his hand a large whip of raw hide, which ever and anon descended upon the backs of his raw-boned cattle like the strokes of a flail.

"Get up – go along – waye," cried he, suddenly drawing up at the door of the hotel. "Well, here we be at last, and

jist in time for the con-sort." Then hitching the horses to
the post, and flinging the buffalo robes over them, he left
the three females he was driving in the sleigh, and ran
directly up to me, – "Arn't you the con-sort man? I guess
you be, by them ere black pants and Sunday-goin' gear."

I nodded assent.

"What's the damage?"

"Half a dollar."

"Half a dollar? You don't mean to say that!"

"Not a cent less."

"Well, it will be *expensive*. There's my wife and two
darters, and myself; and the galls never seed a con-sort."

"Well," said I, "as there are four of you, you may come
in at a dollar and a half."

"How; a dollar and a harf! I will go and have a talk with
the old woman, and hear what she says to it."

He returned to the sleigh, and after chatting for a few
minutes with the women, he helped them out, and the four
followed me into the common reception room of the inn.
The farmer placed a pail of butter on the table, and said
with a shrewd curl of his long nose, and a wink from one
of his cunning black eyes, "There's some pretty good butter, mister."

I was amused at the idea, and replied, "*Pretty good
butter!* What is that to me? I do not buy butter."

"Not buy butter! Why you don't say! It is the very best
article in the market jist now."

For a bit of fun I said, – "Never mind; I will take your
butter. What is it worth?"

"It was worth ten cents last week, mister; I don't know
what it's worth now. It can't have fallen, no-how."

I took my knife from my pocket, and in a very business-
like manner proceeded to taste the article. "Why," said I,
"this butter is not good."

Here a sharp-faced woman stepped briskly up, and
poking her head between us, said, at the highest pitch of
her cracked voice, – "Yes, it is good; it was made this
morning *express-ly* for the *con-sort*."

"I beg your pardon, madam. I am not in the habit of buying butter. To oblige you, I will take this. How much is there of it?"

"I don't know. Where are your steelyards?"

"Oh," said I, laughing, "I don't carry such things with me. I will take it at your own valuation, and you may go in with your family."

" 'Tis a bargain," says she. "Go in, galls, and fix yourselves for the *consort*."

As the room was fast filling, I thought it time to present myself to the company, and made my entrance, accompanied by that incorrigible pest, the singing master, who, without the least embarrassment, took his seat by the piano. After singing several of my best songs, I invited him to try his skill.

"Oh, certainly," said he; "to tell you the truth, I am a *leetle* surprised that you did not ask me to lead off."

"I would have done so; but I could not alter the arrangement of the programme."

"Ah, well, I excuse you this time, but it was not very polite, to say the least of it." Then, taking my seat at the piano with as much confidence as Braham ever had, he run his hand over the keys, exclaiming "What shall I sing? I will give you one of Russell's songs; they suit my voice best. Ladies and gentlemen, I am going to favour you by singing Henry Russell's celebrated song, '*I love to roam*,' and accompany myself upon the pee-a-ne-forty."

This song is so well known to most of my readers, that I can describe his manner of singing it without repeating the whole of the words. He struck the instrument in playing with such violence that it shook his whole body, and produced the following ludicrous effect: –

"Some love to ro-o-o-a-me
　O'er the dark sea fo-o-ome,
　　Where the shill winds whistle fre-e-e-e;
　But a cho-o-sen ba-a-and in a mountain la-a-a-and,
　　And life in the woo-o-ds for me-e-e."

This performance was drowned in an uproar of laughter, which brought our vocalist to a sudden stop.

"I won't sing another line if you keep up that infernal noise," he roared at the top of his voice. "When a fellow does his best, he expects his audience to appreciate his performance; but I allers he'rd as how the folks at W—— knew nothing about music."

"Oh, do stop," exclaimed an old woman, rising from her seat, and shaking her fist at the unruly company, – "can't yee's; he do sing *butiful*; and his voice in the winds do sound so *natural*, I could almost hear them 'an owling. It minds me of old times, it dew."

This voluntary tribute to his genius seemed to console and re-assure the singing master, and, stemming with his stentorian voice the torrent of mistimed mirth, he sang his song triumphantly to the end; and the clapping of hands, stamping of feet, and knocking of benches, were truly deafening.

"What will you have now?" cried he. "I thought you would comprehend good singing at last."

"Give them a comic song," said I, in a whisper.

"*A comic song!* (aloud) Do you think that I would waste *my* talents in singing trash that any jackass could bray? No, sirra, my style is purely *sentimental*. I will give the ladies and gentlemen the '*Ivy Green*.'"

He sang this beautiful original song, which is decidedly Russell's best, much in the same style as the former one; but, getting a little used to his eccentricities, we contrived to keep our gravity until he came to the chorus, "Creeping, creeping, creeping," for which he substituted, "crawling, crawling, crawling," when he was again interrupted by such a burst of merriment that he was unable to crawl any further.

"Well," said he, rising; "if you won't behave, I will leave the instrument to Mr. H——, and make one of the audience."

He had scarcely taken his seat, when the farmer from whom I had bought the butter forced his way up to the piano. Says he, "There's that pail; it is worth ten cents and a half. You must either pay the money, or give me back the pail. – (Hitching up his nether garments) – "I s'pose you'll do the thing that's right."

"Oh, certainly, there are twelve and a half cents."

"I hav'nt change," said he, with a knowing look.

"So much the better; keep the difference."

"Then we're square, mister," and he sank back into his place.

"Did he pay you the money?" I heard the wife ask in an anxious tone.

"Yes, yes; more than the old pail was worth by a long chalk. I'd like to deal with that chap allers."

I now proceeded with the concert. The song of the drowning child saved by the Newfoundland dog, drew down thunders of applause. When the clamour had a little subsided, a tall man rose from his seat at the upper end of the room, and, after clearing his throat with several loud hems, he thus addressed me, – "How do you do, Mr. H——? I am glad, sir, to make your acquaintance. This is my friend, Mr. Derby," drawing another tall man conspicuously forward before all the spectators. "He, tew, is very happy to make your acquaintance. We both want to know if that dog you have been singing about belongs to you. If so, we should be glad to buy a pup." He gravely took his seat, amid perfect yells of applause. It was impossible to be heard in such a riot, and I closed the adventures of the evening by giving out " 'Hail, Columbia,' to be sung by all present." This *finale* gave universal satisfaction, and the voice of my friend the singing-master might be heard far above the rest.

I was forced, in common politeness, to invite Mr. Browne, to partake of the oyster supper I had provided for my friends from W——. "Will you join our party this evening, Mr. Browne?"

"Oh, by all manner of means," said he, rubbing his hands together in a sort of ecstasy of anticipation; "I knew that you would do the thing handsome at last. I have not tasted an i'ster since I sang at Niblo's in New York. But did we not come on famously at the *con-sort*? Confess, now, that I beat you holler. You sing *pretty* well, but you want confidence. You don't give expression enough to your voice. The applause which followed my first song was tremendous."

"I never heard anything like it, Mr. Browne. I never expect to merit such marks of public approbation."

"All in good time, my *leetle* friend," returned he, clapping me familiarly on the shoulder. "Rome was not built in a day, and you are a young man – a very young man – and very *small* for your age. Your voice will never have the volume and compass of mine. But I smell the i'sters: let's in, for I'm tarnation hungry."

Gentle reader! you would have thought so to have seen him eat. My companions looked rather disconcerted at the rapidity with which they disappeared within his capacious jaws. After satisfying his enormous appetite, he washed down the oysters with long draughts of porter, until his brain becoming affected, he swung his huge body back in his chair, and, placing his feet on the supper-table, began singing in good earnest, – not one song in particular, but a mixture of all that had appeared in the most popular Yankee song books for the last ten years.

I wish I could give you a specimen of the sublime and the ridiculous, thus unceremoniously huddled together. The effect was so irresistible, when contrasted with the grave exterior of the man, that we laughed until our sides ached at his absurdities. Exhausted by his constant vociferations, the musician at length dropped from his chair in a drunken sleep upon the floor, and we carried him into the next room and put him to bed; and, after talking over the events of the evening, we retired about midnight to our respective chambers, which all opened into the great room in which I held the concert.

About two o'clock in the morning my sleep was disturbed by the most dismal cries and groans, which appeared to issue from the adjoining apartment. I rubbed my eyes, and sat up in the bed and listened, when I recognized the well-known voice of the singing master, exclaiming in tones of agony and fear – "Landlord! landlord! cum quick. Somebody cum. Landlord! landlord! there's a man under my bed. Oh, Lord! I shall be murdered! a man under my bed!"

As I am not fond of such nocturnal visitors myself, not being much gifted with physical strength or courage, I listened a moment to hear if any one was coming. The sound of approaching footsteps along the passage greatly aided the desperate effort I made to leave my comfortable pillow, and proceed to the scene of action. At the chamber door I met the landlord, armed with the fire-tongs and a light.

"What's all this noise about?" he cried in an angry tone.

I assured him that I was as ignorant as himself of the cause of the disturbance. Here the singing master again sung out –

"Landlord! landlord! there's a *man* under the *bed*. Cum! somebody cum!"

We immediately entered his room, and were joined by two of my friends from W——. Seeing our party strengthened to four, our courage rose amazingly, and we talked loudly of making mincemeat of the intruder, kicking him down stairs, and torturing him in every way we could devise. We found the singing master sitting bolt upright in his bed, his small-clothes gathered up under his arm ready for a start; his face as pale as a sheet, his teeth chattering, and his whole appearance indicative of the most abject fear. We certainly did hear very mysterious sounds issuing from beneath the bed, which caused the boldest of us to draw back.

"He is right," said Roberts; "there is some one under the bed."

"What a set of confounded cowards you are!" cried the landlord; "can't you lift the valence and see what it is?"

He made no effort himself to ascertain the cause of the

alarm. Roberts, who, after all, was the boldest man of the party, seized the tongs from the landlord, and, kneeling cautiously down, slowly raised the drapery that surrounded the bed. "Hold the light here, landlord." He did so, but at arm's length. Roberts peeped timidly into the dark void beyond, dropped the valance, and looked up with a comical, quizzing expression, and began to laugh.

"What is it?" we all cried in a breath.

"Landlord! landlord!" he cried, imitating the voice of the singing master, "cum quick! Somebody cum! There's a dog under the bed! He will bite me! Oh, dear! oh, dear! I shall die of hydrophobia. I shall be smothered in a feather-bed!"

"A dog!" said the landlord.

"A dog!" cried we all.

"Aye, a black dog."

"You don't say!" cried the singing master, springing from his bed. "Where is he? I'm able for *him* any how." And seizing a corn broom that stood in a corner of the room, he began to poke at the poor animal, and belabour him in the most unmerciful manner.

The dog, who belonged to a drover who penned his cattle in the inn-yard for the night, wishing to find a comfortable domicile, had taken a private survey of the premises when the people were out of the way, and made his quarters under Mr. Browne's bed. When that worthy commenced snoring, the dog, to signify his approbation at finding himself in the company of some one, amused himself by hosting his tail up and down; now striking the sacking of the bed, and now tapping audibly against the floor. These mysterious salutations became, at length, so frequent and vehement that they awoke the sleeper, who, not daring to ascertain the cause of the alarm, aroused the whole house with his clamours.

Mr. Browne finding himself unable to thrash the poor brute out of his retreat, and having become all of a sudden very brave, crawled under the bed and dragged the dog out by his hind legs.

"You see I'm enough for him; give me the poker, and I'll beat out his brains."

"You'll do no such thing, sir," said the landlord, turning the animal down the stairs. "The dog belongs to a quiet decent fellow, and a good customer, and he shall meet with no ill usage here. "Your mountain, Mr. Browne, has brought forth a mouse."

"A dog sir," quoth the singing master, not in the least abashed by the reproof. "If the brute had cut up such a dido under your bed, you would have been as 'turnal sceared as I was."

"Perhaps, Mr. Browne," said I, "you took it for the ghost of the old mare?".

"Ghost or no ghost," returned the landlord, "he has given us a great deal of trouble, and nearly frightened himself into fits."

"The fear was not all on my side," said the indignant vocalist; "and I look upon you as the cause of the whole trouble."

"As how?"

"If the dog had not cum to your house, he never would have found his way under my bed. When I pay for my night's lodging, I don't expect to have to share it with a strange dog – no how."

So saying he retreated, grumbling, back to his bed, and we gladly followed his example.

I rose early in the morning to accompany my friends to W——. At the door of the hotel I was accosted by Mr. Browne –

"Why, you arn't goin' to start without bidding me good-bye? Besides, you have not paid me for my assistance at the *con-sort*."

I literally started with surprise at this unexpected demand. "Do you expect a professional price for your services?"

"Well, I guess the *con-sort* would have been nothing without my help; but I won't be hard upon you, as you are a young beginner, and not likely to make your fortune in that line any how. There's that pail of butter; if you don't mean to take it along, I'll take that; we wants butter to hum. Is it a bargain?"

"Oh, yes; if you are satisfied, I am well pleased." (I could have added, to get rid of you at any price.) "You will find it on the table in the hall."

"Not exactly; I took it hum this morning – I thought how it would end. Good-bye to you, Mr. H——. If ever you come this way again, I shall be happy to lend you my assistance."

I never visited that part of the countryside since, but I have no doubt that Mr. Browne is busy in his vocation, and flattering himself that he is one of the first vocalists in the Union. I think he should change his residence, and settle down for life in *New Harmony*.

TO ADELAIDE,*
A Beautiful Young Canadian Lady.

"Yes, thou art young, and passing fair;
    But time, that bids all blossoms fade,
Will rob thee of the rich and rare;
    Then list to me, sweet Adelaide.
He steals the snow from polish'd brow,
    From soft bewitching eyes the blue,
From smiling lips their ruby glow,
    From velvet cheeks their rosy hue.

"Oh, who shall check the spoiler's power! –
    'Tis more than conquering love may dare;
He flutters round youth's summer bower,
    And reigns o'er hearts like summer fair.
He basks himself in sunny eyes,
    Hides 'mid bright locks, and dimpled smiles;
From age he spreads his wings and flies, –
    Forgets soft vows, and pretty wiles.

*The daughter of Colonel Coleman, of Belleville; now Mrs. Easton.

"The charms of mind are ever young,
　　Their beauty never owns decay;
The fairest form by poet sung,
　　Before their power must fade away.
The mind immortal wins from time
　　Fresh beauties as its years advance;
Its flowers bloom fresh in every clime –
　　They cannot yield to change and chance.

"E'en over love's capricious boy
　　They hold an undiminish'd sway;
For chill and storm can ne'er destroy
　　The blossoms of eternal day.
Then deem these charms, sweet Adelaide,
　　The brightest gems in beauty's zone:
Make these thine own, – all others fade;
　　They live when youth and grace are flown."

SEVEN

Camp Meetings

"On – on! – for ever brightly on,
   Thy lucid waves are flowing:
Thy waters sparkle as they run,
   Their long, long journey going."
S.M.

WE HAVE rounded Ox Point, and Belleville is no longer in sight. The steamboat has struck into mid channel, and the bold shores of the Prince Edward District are before us. Calmly we glide on, and islands and headlands seem to recede from us as we advance; and now they are far in the distance, half seen through the warm purple haze that rests so dreamily upon woods and waters. Heaven is above us, and another heaven – more soft, and not less beautiful – lies mirrored beneath; and within that heaven are traced exquisite forms of earth – trees, and flowers, and verdant slopes, and bold hills, and barren rugged rocks. The scene is one of surpassing loveliness, and we open our hearts to receive its sweet influences, while our eyes rest upon it with intense delight, and the inner voice of the soul whispers – God is here! Dost thou not catch the reflection of his glory in this superb picture of Nature's own painting, while the harmony that surrounds his throne is faintly echoed by the warm balmy wind that stirs the lofty branches of the woods, and the waves that swell and break in gentle undulation against these rocky isles?

> "So smiled the heavens upon the vestal earth,
>   The morn she rose exulting from her birth;
>   A living harmony, a perfect plan
>   Of power and beauty, ere the rebel man
>   Defiled with sin, and stain'd with kindred blood,
>   The paradise his God pronounced as good."

That rugged point to the left contains a fine quarry of limestone, which supplies excellent building materials. The stones are brought by the means of a scow, a very broad flat-bottomed boat, to Belleville, where they are sawn into square blocks, and dressed for doors sills and facings of houses. A little further on, the Salmon river discharges its waters into the bay, and on its shores the village of Shannonville has risen, as if by magic, within a very few years. Three schooners are just now anchored at its mouth, receiving cargoes of sawn lumber to carry over to Asmego. The timber is supplied from the large mill, the din of whose machinery can be heard distinctly at this distance. Lumber forms, at present, the chief article of export from this place. Upwards of one million of sawn lumber was shipped from this embryo town during the past year.

Shannonville owes its present flourishing prospects to the energy and enterprise of a few individuals, who saw at a glance its capabilities, and purchased for a few hundred pounds the site of a town which is now worth as many thousands. The steamboats do not touch at Shannonville, in their trips to and from Kingston. The mouth of the river is too narrow to admit a larger vessel than a schooner, but as the place increases, wharfs will be built at its entrance into the bay.

On the road leading from Belleville to this place, which is in the direct route to Kingston, there is a large tract of plain land which is still uncultivated. The soil is sandy, and the trees are low and far apart, a natural growth of

short grass and flowering shrubs giving it very much the
appearance of a park. Clumps of butternut, and hiccory
trees, form picturesque groups; and herds of cattle,
belonging to the settlers in the vicinity, roam at large over
these plains that sweep down to the water's edge. This is a
very favourite resort of summer parties, as you can drive
light carriages in all directions over this elevated platform.
It used formerly to be a chosen spot for camp-meetings,
and all the piously disposed came hither to listen to the
preachers, and "*get religion*."

I never witnessed one of these meetings, but an old lady
gave me a very graphic description of one of them that
was held on this spot some thirty years ago. There were no
churches in Belleville then, and the travelling Methodist
ministers used to pitch their tents on these plains, and
preach night and day to all goers and comers. A pulpit,
formed of rough slabs of wood, was erected in a conveniently open space among the trees, and they took it by
turns to read, exhort, and pray, to the dwellers in the
wilderness. At night they kindled large fires, which served
both for light and warmth, and enabled the pilgrims to
this sylvan shrine to cook their food, and attend to the
wants of their little ones. Large booths, made of the
boughs of trees, sheltered the worshippers from the heat
of the sun during the day, or from the occasional showers
produced by some passing thunder cloud at night.

"Our bush farm," said my friend, "happened to be near
the spot, and I went with a young girl, a friend and neighbour, partly out of curiosity and partly out of fun, to hear
the preaching. It was the middle of July, but the weather
was unusually wet for that time of year, and every tent and
booth was crowded with men, women, and children, all
huddled together to keep out of the rain. Most of these
tents exhibited some extraordinary scene of fanaticism
and religious enthusiasm; the noise and confusion were
deafening. Men were preaching at the very top of their
voice; women were shrieking and groaning, beating their
breasts and tearing their hair, while others were uttering

the most frantic outcries, which they called *ejaculatory prayers*. One thought possessed me all the time, that the whole assembly were mad, and that they imagined God to be deaf, and that he could not hear them without their making this shocking noise. It would appear to you like the grossest blasphemy were I to repeat to you some of their exclamations; but one or two were so absurdly ridiculous, that I cannot help giving them as I heard them.

"One young woman, after lying foaming and writhing upon the ground, like a creature possessed, sprang up several feet into the air, exclaiming, 'I have got it! I have got it! I have got it!' To which others responded – 'Keep it! keep it! keep it!' I asked a bystander what she meant. He replied, 'she has got religion. It is the Spirit that is speaking in her.' I felt too much shocked to laugh out, yet could scarcely retain my gravity.

"Passing by one of the tents, I saw a very fat woman lying upon a bench on her face, uttering the most dismal groans, while two well-fed, sleek-looking ministers, in rusty black coats and very dirty-looking white chokers, were drumming upon her fat back with their fists, exclaiming – 'Here's glory! here's glory, my friends! Satan is departing out of this woman. Hallelujah!' This spectacle was too shocking to provoke a smile.

"There was a young lady dressed in a very nice silk gown. Silk was a very scarce and expensive article in those days. The poor girl got dreadfully excited, and was about to fling herself down upon the wet grass, to show the depth of her humility and contrition, when she suddenly remembered the precious silk dress, and taking a shawl of less value from her shoulders, carefully spread it over the wet ground.

"Ah, my dear friend," continued the old lady, "one had a deal to learn at that camp-meeting. A number of those people knew no more what they were about than persons in a dream. They worked themselves up to a pitch of frenzy, because they saw others carried away by the same spirit; and they seemed to try which could make the most noise, and throw themselves into the most unnatural positions. Few of them carried the religious zeal they manifested in such a strange way at that meeting, into their own homes. Before the party broke up it was forgotten, and they were laughing and chatting about their worldly affairs. The young lads were sparking the girls, and the girls laughing and flirting with them. I remarked to an old farmer, who was reckoned a very pious man, 'that such conduct, in persons who had just been in a state of despair about their sins, was very inconsistent, to say the least of it;' and he replied, with a sanctimonious smile – 'It is only the Lord's lambs, playing with each other."

These camp-meetings seldom take place near large towns, where the people have the benefit of a resident minister, but they still occur on the borders of civilization, and present the same disorderly mixture of fanaticism and vanity.

More persons go for a frolic than to obtain any spiritual benefit. In illustration of this, I will tell you a story which a very beautiful young married lady told to me with much glee, for the thing happened to herself, and she was the principal actor in the scene.

"I had an aunt, the wife of a very wealthy yeoman, who lived in one of the back townships of C——, on the St. Lawrence. She was a very pious and hospitable woman, and none knew it better than the travelling ministers, who were always well fed and well lodged at her house, particularly when they assembled to hold a camp-meeting, which took place once in several years in that neighbourhood.

"I was a girl of fifteen, and was staying with my aunt for the benefit of the country-air, when one of these great gatherings took place. Having heard a great deal about their strange doings at these meetings, I begged very hard to be allowed to make one of the spectators. My aunt, who knew what a merry, light-hearted creature I was, demurred for some time before she granted my request.

"If the child does not *get religion*,' she said, 'she will

turn it all into fun, and it will do her more harm than good.'

"Aunt was right enough in her conjunctures; but still she entertained a latent hope, that the zeal of the preachers, the excitement of the scene, and the powerful influence produced by the example of the pious, might have a beneficial effect on my young mind, and lead to my conversion. Aunt had herself been reclaimed from a state of careless indifference by attending one of these meetings, and at last it was determined that I was to go.

"First came the ministers, and then the grand feed my aunt had prepared for them, before they opened the campaign. Never shall I forget how those holy men devoured the good things set before them. I stood gazing upon them in utter astonishment, wondering when their meal would come to an end. They none wore whiskers, and their broad fat faces literally shone with high feeding. When I laughed at their being such excellent knife and fork men, aunt gravely reproved my levity, by saying, 'that the labourer was worthy of his hire; and that it would be a great sin to muzzle the ox that treadeth out the corn; that field preaching was a very exhausting thing, and that these pious men required a great deal of nourishment to keep up their strength for the performance of good work.'

"After they were gone, I dressed and accompanied my aunt to the scene of action.

"It was a lovely spot, about a mile from the house. The land rose in a gentle slope from the river, and was surrounded on three sides by lofty woods. The front gave us a fine view of the St. Lawrence, rushing along in its strength, the distant murmur of the waves mingling with the sigh of the summer breeze, that swept the dense foliage of the forest trees. The place had been cleared many years before, and was quite free from stumps and fallen timber, the ground carpeted with soft moss and verdant fresh looking turf.

"The area allotted for the meeting was fenced around

with the long thin trunks of sapling trees, that were tied together with strips of bass-wood. In the centre of the enclosure was the platform for the preachers, constructed of rough slabs, and directly behind this rural pulpit was a large tent connected with it by a flight of board steps. Here the preachers retired, after delivering their lectures, to rest and refresh themselves. Fronting the platform was a sort of amphitheatre of booths, constructed of branches of trees, and containing benches of boards supported at either end by a round log laid lengthwise at the sides of the tent. Behind these rough benches persons had placed mattrasses, which they had brought with them in their waggons, that such as came from a distance might not want for a bed during their stay – some of these meetings lasting over a week.

"The space without the enclosure was occupied by a double line of carts, waggons, light carriages, and ox sleds, while the animals undivested of their harness were browsing peacefully among the trees. The inner space was crowded with persons of all classes, but the poorer certainly predominated. Well dressed, respectable people, however, were not wanting; and though I came there to see and to be seen, to laugh and to make others laugh, I must confess that I was greatly struck with the imposing and picturesque scene before me, particularly when a number of voices joined in singing the hymn with which the service commenced."

There is something very touching in this blending of human voices in the open air – this choral song of praise borne upwards from the earth, and ascending through the clear atmosphere to heaven. Leaving my friend and her curious narrative for a few minutes, I must remark here the powerful effect produced upon my mind by hearing "God save the King," sung by the thousands of London on the proclamation of William IV. It was impossible to distinguish good or bad voices in such a mighty volume of sound, which rolled through the air like a peal of solemn thunder. It thrilled through my heart, and paled my cheek. It seemed to me the united voice of a whole nation rising to the throne of God, and it was the grandest combination of sound and sentiment that ever burst upon human ears. Long, long may that thrilling anthem rise from the heart of England, in strains of loyal thanksgiving and praise, to the throne of that Eternal Potentate in whose hand is the fate of princes!

"There were numbers of persons who, like myself, came there for amusement, and who seemed to enjoy themselves quite as much as I did. The preaching at length commenced with a long prayer, followed by an admonitory address, urging those present to see their danger, repent of their sins, and flee from the wrath to come.

"Towards the middle of his discourse, the speaker wrought himself up into such a religious fury that it became infectious, and cries and groans resounded on all sides; and the prayers poured out by repentant sinners for mercy and pardon were heart-rending. The speaker at length became speechless from exhaustion, and stopping suddenly in the midst of his too eloquent harangue, he tied a red cotton handkerchief round his head, and hastily descended the steps, and disappeared in the tent provided for the accommodation of the ministers. His place was instantly supplied by a tall, dark, melancholy looking man, who, improving upon his reverend brother's suggestions, drew such an awful picture of the torments endured by the damned, that several women fainted, while others were shrieking in violent hysterics.

"I had listened to the former speaker with attention and respect, but this man's violent denunciations rather tended to harden my heart, and make me resist any religious feeling that had been growing up in my breast. I began to tire of the whole thing, and commenced looking about for some object that might divert my thoughts into a less gloomy channel.

"The bench on which I, together with a number of persons, was sitting, was so insecurely placed on the round rolling logs that supported it, that I perceived that the least motion given to it at my end would capsize it, and bring all the dear groaning creatures who were sitting upon it, with their eyes turned up to the preacher, sprawling on the ground.

"'Would it not be glorious fun?' whispered the spirit of mischief – perhaps the old one himself – in my ears. 'I can *do it*, and I *will do it* – so here goes!' As I sat next to the round log that supported my end of the plank, I had only to turn my face that way, and apply my foot like a lever to the round trunk, on which the end of the bench had the slightest possible hold, and the contemplated downfall became a certainty. No sooner thought than done. The next moment old and young, fat and lean, women and children, lay sprawling together on the ground, in the most original attitudes and picturesque confusion. I, for my part, was lying very comfortably on one of the mattrasses, laughing until real tears, but not of contrition, streamed down my face.

"Never shall I forget a fat old farmer, who used to visit at my aunt's, as he crawled out of the human heap on all fours, and shook his head at me –

"'You wicked young sinner, this is all your doings.'

"Before the storm could burst upon me, I got up and ran laughing out of the tent, and hid myself among the trees to enjoy my wicked thoughts alone. Here I remained for a long time, watching, at a safe distance, the mad gesticulations of the preacher, who was capering up and down on the platform, and using the most violent and extravagant language, until at length, overcome by his vehemence, he too tied the invariable red handkerchief round his head, and tumbled back into the tent, to be succeeded by another and another.

"Night, with all her stars, was now stealing upon us; but the light from a huge pile of burning logs, and from torches composed of fat pine, and stuck in iron grates supported on poles in different parts of the plain, scattered the darkness back to the woods, and made it as light as noon-day.

"The scene was now wild in the extreme: the red light streamed upon the moving mass of human beings who pressed around the pulpit, glaring upon clenched fists and upturned faces, while the preacher standing above them, and thrown into strong relief, with his head held back and his hands raised towards heaven, looked like some inspired prophet of old, calling down fire from heaven to consume the ungodly. It was a spectacle to inspire both fear and awe, but I could only view it in the most absurd light, and laugh at it.

"At length I was determined to know what became of the preachers, after tying the red handkerchief round their heads and retreating to their tents. I crept carefully round to the back of this holy of holies, and applying my eyes to a little aperture in the canvas, I saw by the light of a solitary candle several men lying upon mattrasses fast asleep, their noses making anything but a musical response to the hymns and prayers without. While I was gazing upon these prostrate forms, thus soundly sleeping after the hubbub and excitement their discourse had occasioned among their congregation, the last speaker hastily entered the tent, and flinging himself on to the floor, exclaimed, in a sort of ecstacy of gratitude – 'Well, thank God my task is ended for the night; and now for a good sleep!'

"While I was yet pondering these things in my heart, I felt the grasp of a hand upon my shoulder. I turned with a shriek; it was my aunt seeking me. 'What are you doing here?' she said, rather angrily.

" 'Studying my lesson, aunt,' said I, gravely, pointing to the sleepers. 'Do these men preach for their own honour and glory, or for the glory of God? I have tried to find out, but I can't tell.'

" 'The night's grown chilly, child,' said my aunt, avoiding the answer I expected; 'it is time you were in bed.'

"We went home. I got a sound lecture for the trick I had played, and I never went to a camp-meeting again; yet, in spite of my bad conduct as a child, I believe they often do good, and are the means of making careless people think of the state of their souls."

Though the steamboats do not stop at Shannonville, they never fail to do so at the pretty town of Northport, on the other side of the bay, in order to take in freight and passengers.

Northport rises with a very steep slope from the water's edge, and the steamer runs into the wharf which projects but a few feet from the shore. Down the long hill which leads to the main street, men and boys are running to catch a sight of the steamboat, and hear the news. All is bustle and confusion. Barrels of flour are being rolled into the boat, and sheep and cattle are led off – men hurry on board with trunks and carpet bags – and women, with children in their arms or led by the hand, hasten on board; while our passengers, descending to the wharf, are shaking hands with merchants and farmers, and talking over the current prices of grain and merchandise at their respective towns. The bell rings – the cable that bound us to the friendly wharf is cast off and flung on the deck – the steamer opens her deep lungs, and we are once more stemming our way towards Kingston.

While we sail up that romantic part of the Bay of Quinté, called the "Long Reach," at the head of which stands the beautiful town of Picton, I will give you a few reminiscences of Northport. It is a most quiet and primitive village, and one might truly exclaim with Moore –

> "And I said if there's peace to be found on the earth,
>   The heart that is humble might hope for it here."

No gentler picture of society in a new country could be found, than the one exhibited by the inhabitants of Northport. The distinctions, unavoidable among persons of wealth and education, are hardly felt or recognised here. Every one is a neighbour in the strictest sense of the word, and high and low meet occasionally at each other's houses. Even the domestics are removed by such a narrow line of demarcation, that they appear like members of one family.

The Prince Edward district, one of the wealthiest rural districts in Upper Canada, was settled about sixty years ago by U.E. loyalists; and its inhabitants are mainly composed of the descendants of Dutch and American families. They have among them a large sprinkling of Quakers, who are a happy, hospitable community, living in peace and brotherly kindness with all men.

The soil of this district is of the best quality for agricultural purposes; and though the march of improvement has been slow, when compared with the rapid advance of other places that possessed fewer local advantages, it has gone on steadily progressing, and the surface of a fine undulating country is dotted over with large well-cleared farms, and neat farmhouses.

One of the oldest and wealthiest inhabitants of Northport, Captain ——, is a fine specimen of the old school of Canadian settlers; one of nature's gentlemen, a man respected and beloved by all who know him, whose wise head, and keen organs of observation, have rendered him a highly intelligent and intellectual man, without having received the benefit of a college education. His house is always open for the reception of friends, neighbours, and strangers. He has no children of his own, but has adopted several orphan children, on whom he has bestowed all the affection and care of a real parent.

This system of adopting children in Canada is one of great benevolence, which cannot be too highly eulogized. Many an orphan child, who would be cast utterly friendless upon the world, finds a comfortable home with some good neighbour, and is treated with more consideration, and enjoys greater privileges, than if his own parents had lived. No difference if made between the adopted child and the young ones of the family; it is clothed, boarded, and educated with the same care, and a stranger would find it difficult to determine which was the real, which the transplanted scion of the house.

Captain —— seldom dines alone; some one is always going and coming, stepping in and taking pot-luck, by accident or invitation. But the Captain can afford it. Sociable, talkative, and the soul of hospitality, he entertains his guests like a prince. "Is he not a glorious old fellow?" said our beloved and excellent chief-justice Robinson; "Captain —— is a credit to the country." We echoed this sentiment with our whole heart. It is quite a treat to make one of his uninvited guests, and share the good-humoured sociability of his bountiful table.

You meet there men of all grades and conditions, of every party and creed, – the well-educated, well-dressed clergymen of the Establishment, and the travelling dispensers of gospel truths, with shabbier coats and less pretensions. No one is deemed an intruder – all find excellent cheer, and a hearty welcome.

Northport does not want its native poet, though the money-making merchants and farmers regard him with a suspicious and pitying eye. The manner in which they speak of his unhappy malady reminds me of what an old Quaker said to me regarding his nephew, Bernard Barton – "Friend Susanna, it is a great pity, but my nephew Bernard is sadly addicted to literature."

So Isaac N——, gentleman farmer of the township of Ameliasburgh, is sadly gifted with the genuine elements of poetry, and, like Burns, composes verses at the ploughtail. I have read with great pleasure some sweet lines by this rural Canadian bard; and were he now beside me, instead of "Big bay" lying so provokingly between, I would beg from him a specimen of his rhyming powers, just to prove to my readers that the genuine children of song are distinguished by the same unmistakeable characteristics in every clime.

I remember being greatly struck by an overcoat, worn by a clergyman I had the pleasure of meeting many years ago at this village, which seemed to me a pretty good substitute for the miraculous purse of Fortunatus. The garment to which I allude was long and wide, and cut round somewhat in the shape of a spencer. The inside lining formed one capacious pocket, into which the reverend gentleman could conveniently stow away newspapers, books, and sermons, and, on a pinch, a fat fowl, a bottle of wine, or a homebaked loaf of bread. On the present occasion, the kind mistress of the house took care that the owner should not travel with it empty; so, to keep him fairly balanced on his horse, she stowed away into this convenient garment such an assortment of good things, that I sat and watched the operation in curious amazement.

Some time after I happened to dine with a dissenting minister at Mr. ——'s house. The man had a very repulsive and animal expression; he ate so long and lustily of a very fat goose, that he began to look very uncomfortable, and complained very much of being troubled with *dyspepsy* after his meals. He was a great teetotaller, or professed to be one, but certainly had forgotten the text, "Be ye moderate in all things;" for he by no means applied the temperance system to the substantial creature comforts, of which he partook in a most immoderately voracious manner.

"I know what would cure you, Mr. R——," said my friend, who seemed to guess at a glance the real character of his visitor; "but then I know that you would never consent to make use of such a remedy."

"I would take anything that would do me good," said black-coat with a sigh.

"What think you of a small wine-glass of brandy just before taking dinner?"

"Against my principles, Sir; it would never do," with a lugubrious shake of the head.

"There is nothing on earth so good for your complaint."

."Do you *reely* think it would serve me?" with a sudden twinkle of his heavy fishy eyes.

"Not a doubt of the fact" (*pouring out a pretty large dram*); "it will kill the heartburn, and do away with that uncomfortable feeling you experience after eating rich food. And as to principles, your pledge allows it in case of disease."

"True," said black-coat, coquetting with the glass; "still I should be sorry to try an *alcoholic* remedy while another could be found."

"Perhaps you would prefer *eating less*," said my friend slyly, "which, I have been told by a medical man, is generally a certain cure if persevered in."

"Oh, ah, yes. But, Sir, my constitution would never stand that. I think for *once* I will try the effect of your first prescription; but, remember, it is only *medicinally*."

The next moment the glass was returned to the table empty, and the good man took his leave.

"Now, Mr.——, was it not too bad of you to make that man break his pledge?" observed a person at table.

"My dear Sir, that man requires very little temptation to do that. The total abstinence of a glutton is entirely for the public."

The houses built by the Dutch settlers have very little privacy, as one bed-chamber invariably opens into another. In some cases, the sleeping apartments all open into a common sitting-room occupied by the family. To English people, this is both an uncomfortable and very unpleasant arrangement.

I slept for two nights at Mr.——'s house, with my husband, and our dormitory had no egress but through another bed-chamber; and as that happened to be occupied on the first night by a clergyman, I had to wait for an hour, after my husband was up and down stairs rejoicing in the fresh air of a lovely summer morning, before I could escape from my chamber, – my neighbour, who was young and very comely, taking a long time for his prayers, as the business of the toilet.

My husband laughed very heartily at my imprisonment, as he termed it; but the next day I had the laugh against him, for our sleeping neighbours happened to be a middle-aged Quaker, with a very sickly delicate wife. I, of course, was forced to go to bed when she did, or be obliged to pass through her chamber after brother Jonathan had retired for the night. This being by no means desirable, I left a very interesting argument, in which my husband, the Quaker, and the poet were fighting an animated battle on reform principles, against the clergyman and my very much respected Tory host. How they got on I don't know, for the debate was at its height when I was obliged to beat my retreat to bed.

After an hour or so I heard Jonathan tumble upstairs to bed, and while undressing he made the following very innocent remark to his wife, – "Truly, Hannah, I fear that I have used *too* many words tonight. My uncle is a man of many words, and one is apt to forget the rules of prudence when arguing with him."

If the use of many words was looked upon as a serious transgression by honest Jonathan, my husband, my friend, and the poet, must have been very guilty men, for they continued their argument until the "sma' hours ayont the twal."

My husband had to pass through the room occupied by the Friends, in order to reach mine, but he put a bold face upon the matter, and plunged at once through the difficulty, the Quaker's nose giving unmistakeable notice that he was in the land of Nod. The pale sickly woman just opened her dreamy black eyes, but hid them instantly beneath the bed-clothes, and the passage, not of arms, but of the bed-chamber, was won.

The next morning we had to rise early to take the boat, and Jonathan was up by the dawn of day; so that I went through as bold as a lion, and was busily employed in discussing an excellent breakfast, while my poor partner was sitting impatiently nursing his appetite at the foot of his bed, and wishing the pale Quakeress across the bay. The steamer was in sight before he was able to join us at the breakfast-table. I had now my revenge, and teased him all the way home on being kept a prisoner, with only a sickly woman for a jailor.

A young lady gave me an account of a funeral she

witnessed in this primitive village, which may not be uninteresting to my English readers, as a picture of some of the customs of a new country.

The deceased was an old and very respectable resident in the township; and as the Canadians delight in large funerals, he was followed to his last home by nearly all the residents for miles round.

The use of the hearse is not known in rural districts, and, indeed, is seldom used in towns or cities here. The corpse is generally carried to the grave, the bearers being chosen from among the gentlemen of most note in the neighbourhood, who, to the honour of the country be it spoken, never refuse to act on these mournful occasions. These walking funerals are far more imposing and affecting spectacles than the hearse with its funeral plumes; and the simple fact of friends and neighbours conveying a departed brother to his long home, has a more solemn and touching effect upon the mind, than the train of hired mourners and empty state-carriages.

When a body is brought from a distance for interment, it is conveyed in a waggon, if in summer, spring, or autumn, and on a sleigh during the winter season, and is attended to the grave by all the respectable yeomen in the township.

I cannot resist the strong temptation of digressing from my present subject, in order to relate a very affecting instance I witnessed at one of these funerals of the attachment of a dog to his deceased master, which drew tears from my eyes, and from the eyes of my children.

The body of a farmer had been brought in a waggon from one of the back townships, a distance of twenty or thirty miles, and was, as usual in such cases, attended by a long train of country equipages. My house fronted the churchyard, and from the windows you could witness the whole of the funeral ceremonial, and hear the service pronounced over the grave. When the coffin was lifted by the stalwart sons of the deceased from the waggon, and the procession formed to carry it into the church, I observed a

large, buff Flemish dog fall into the ranks of the
mourners, and follow them into the sacred edifice, keeping
as near the coffin as those about it would permit him.
After the service in the church was ended, the creature
persevered in following the beloved remains to the grave.
When the crowd dispersed, the faithful animal retired to
some distance, and laid himself quietly down upon a
grave, until the sexton had finished his mournful task, and
the last sod was placed upon the fresh heap that had
closed for ever over the form he loved.

When the man retired, the dog proceeded to the spot,
walked carefully round it, smelt the earth, lifted his head,
and uttered the most unearthly howls. He then endeavoured to disinter the body, by digging a large hole at one
end of the grave; but finding that he could not effect his
purpose, he stretched himself at full length over it, as if to
guard the spot, with his head buried between his fore-
paws, his whole appearance betokening the most intense
dejection.

All that day and night, and the next day and night, he
never quitted his post for an instant, at intervals smelling
the earth, and uttering those mournful, heart-rending
cries. My boys took him bread and meat, and tried to
coax him from the grave; but he rejected the food and
their caresses. The creature appeared wasted and heart-
broken with grief. Towards noon of the third day, the
eldest son of his late master came in search of him; and the
young man seemed deeply affected by this instance of the
dog's attachment to his father. Even *his* well-known voice
failed to entice him from the grave, and he was obliged to
bring a collar and chain, and lift him by force into his
waggon, to get him from his post.

Oh, human love! is thy memory and thy faith greater
than the attachment of this poor, and, as we term him,
unreasoning brute, to his dead master? His grief made an
impression on my mind, and on that of my children,
which will never be forgotten.

But to return to the village funeral. The body in this

case was borne to the church by the near relatives of the deceased; and a clergyman of the establishment delivered a funeral sermon, in which he enumerated the good qualities of the departed, his long residence among them, and described the trials and hardships he had encountered as a first settler in that district, while it was yet in the wilderness. He extolled his conduct as a good citizen, and faithful Christian, and a public-spirited man. His sermon was a very complete piece of rural biography, very curious and graphic in its way, and was listened to with the deepest attention by the persons assembled.

When the discourse was concluded, and the blessing pronounced, one of the sons of the deceased rose and informed the persons present, that if any one wished to take a last look of the dear old man, now was the time.

He then led the way to the aisle, in which the coffin stood upon the tressels, and opening a small lid in the top, revealed to the astonishment of my young friend the pale, ghastly face of the dead. Almost every person present touched either the face, hands, or brow of the deceased; and after their curiosity had been fully satisfied, the procession followed the remains to their last resting-place. This part of the ceremony concluded, the indifferent spectators dispersed to their respective homes, while the friends and relations of the dead man returned to dine at the house of one of his sons, my friend making one of the party.

In solemn state the mourners discussed the merits of an excellent dinner, – the important business of eating being occasionally interrupted by remarks upon the appearance of the corpse, his age, the disease of which he died, the probable division of his property, and the merits of the funeral discourse. This was done in such a business-like, matter-of-fact manner, that my friend was astonished how the blood relations of the deceased could join in these remarks.

After the great business of eating was concluded the spirits of the party began to flag. The master of the house perceiving how matters were going, left the room, and soon returned with a servant bearing a tray with plates and fork, and a large dish of hiccory nuts. The mourners dried their tears, and set seriously to work to discuss the nuts, and while deeply engaged with their mouse-like employment, forgot for awhile their sorrow for the dead, continuing to keep up their spirits until the announcement of tea turned their thoughts into a new channel. By the time all the rich pies, cakes, and preserves were eaten, their feelings seemed to have subsided into their accustomed everyday routine.

It is certain that death is looked upon by many Canadians more as a matter of business, and a change of property into other hands, than as a real domestic calamity. I have heard people talk of the approaching dissolution of their nearest ties with a calm philosophy which I never could comprehend. "Mother is old and delicate; we can't expect her to last long," says one. "My brother's death has been looked for these several months past; you know he's in the consumption." My husband asked the son of a respectable farmer, for whom he entertained an esteem, how his father was, for he had not seen him for some time? "I guess," was the reply, "that the old man's fixing for the other world." Another young man, being asked by my friend, Captain ——, to spend the evening at his house, replied – "No, can't – much obliged; but I'm afear'd that grandfather will give the last kicks while I'm away."

Canadians flock in crowds to visit the dying, and to gaze upon the dead. A doctor told me that being called into the country to visit a very sick man, he was surprised on finding the wife of his patient sitting alone before the fire in the lower room, smoking a pipe. He naturally inquired if her husband was better?

"Oh, no, sir, far from that; he is dying!"

"Dying! and *you* here?"

"I can't help that, sir. The room is so crowded with the neighbours, that I can't get in to wait upon him."

"Follow me," said the doctor. "I'll soon make a clearance for you."

On ascending the stairs that led to the apartment of the sick man, he found them crowded with people struggling to get in, to take a peep at the poor man. It was only by telling them that he was the doctor, that he forced his way to the bedside. He found his patient in a high fever, greatly augmented by the bustle, confusion, and heat, occasioned by so many people round him. With great difficulty he cleared the room of these intruders, and told the brother of his patient to keep every one but the sick man's wife out of the house. The brother followed the doctor's advice, and the man cheated the curiosity of the death-seekers, and recovered.

The Canadians spend a great deal of money upon their dead. An old lady told me that her nephew, a very large farmer, who had the misfortune to lose his wife in childbed, had laid out a great deal of money – a little fortune she termed it – on her grave-clothes. "Oh, my dear," she said, "it is a thousand pities that you did not go and see her before she was buried. She was dressed so expensively, and she made such a beautiful corpse! Her cap was of real thread lace, trimmed with white French ribbons, and her linen the finest that could be bought in the country."

The more ostentatious the display of grief for the dead, the less I have always found of the reality. I heard two young ladies, who had recently lost a mother, not more than sixteen years older than the eldest of the twain, lamenting most pathetically that they could not go to a public ball, because they were in mourning for ma'! Oh, what a pitiful farce is this, of wearing mourning for the dead! But as I have a good deal to say to sensible people on that subject, I will defer my long lecture until the next chapter.

RANDOM THOUGHTS.

"When is Youth's gay heart the lightest? –
When the torch of health burns brightest,

And the soul's rich banquet lies
In air and ocean, earth and skies;
Till the honied cup of pleasure
Overflows with mental treasure.

"When is Love's sweet dream the sweetest? –
When a kindred heart thou meetest,
Unpolluted with the strife,
The selfish aims that tarnish life;
Ere the scowl of care has faded
The shining chaplet Fancy braided,
And emotions pure and high
Swell the heart and fill the eye;
Rich revealings of a mind
Within a loving breast enshrined,
To thine own fond bosom plighted,
In affection's bonds united:
The sober joys of after years
Are nothing to those smiles and fears.

"When is Sorrow's sting the strongest? –
When friends grow cold we've loved the longest,
And the bankrupt heart would borrow
Treacherous hopes to cheat the morrow;
Dreams of bliss by reason banish'd,
Early joys that quickly vanish'd,
And the treasured past appears
Only to augment our tears;
When, within itself retreating,
The spirit owns life's joys are fleeting,
Yet, racked with anxious doubts and fears,
Trusts, blindly trusts to future years.

"Oh, this is grief, the preacher saith, –
The world's dark woe that worketh death!
Yet, oft beneath its influence bowed,
A beam of hope will burst the cloud,
And heaven's celestial shore appears

Slow rising o'er the tide of years,
Guiding the spirit's darkling way
Through thorny paths to endless day.
Then the toils of life are done,
Youth and age are both as one;
Sorrow never more can sting,
Neglect or pain the bosom wring;
And the joys bless'd spirits prove,
Far exceeds all earthly love!"

EIGHT

Wearing Mourning for the Dead

"What is death? – my sister, say."
"Ask not, brother, breathing clay.
 Ask the earth on which we tread,
 That silent empire of the dead.
 Ask the sea – its myriad waves,
 Living, leap o'er countless graves!"
"Earth and ocean answer not,
 Life is in their depths forgot."
 Ask yon pale extended form,
 Unconscious of the coming storm,
 That breathed and spake an hour ago,
 Of heavenly bliss and penal woe; –
 Within yon shrouded figure lies
"The mystery of mysteries!"

S.M.

AMONG THE many absurd customs that the sanction of time and the arbitrary laws of society have rendered indispensable, there is not one that is so much abused, and to which mankind so fondly clings, as that of *wearing mourning for the dead!* – from the ostentatious public mourning appointed by governments for the loss of their rulers, down to the plain black badge, worn by the humblest peasant for the death of parent or child.

To attempt to raise one feeble voice against a practice

sanctioned by all nations, and hallowed by the most solemn religious rites, appears almost sacrilegious. There is something so beautiful, so poetical, so sacred, in this outward sign of a deep and heartfelt sorrow, that to deprive death of his sable habiliments – the melancholy hearse, funeral plumes, sombre pall, and a long array of drooping night-clad mourners, together with the awful clangour of the doleful bell – would rob the stern necessity of our nature of half its terrors, and tend greatly to destroy that religious dread which is so imposing, and which affords such a solemn lesson to the living.

Alas! Where is the need of all this black parade? Is it not a reproach to Him, who, in his wisdom, appointed death to pass upon all men? Were the sentence confined to the human species, we might have more reason for these extravagant demonstrations of grief: but in every object around us we see inscribed the mysterious law of change. The very mountains crumble and decay with years; the great sea shrinks and grows again; the lofty forest tree, that has drank the dews of heaven, laughed in the sunlight, and shook its branches at a thousand storms, yields to the same inscrutable destiny, and bows its tall forehead to the dust.

Life lives upon death, and death reproduces life, through endless circles of being, from the proud tyrant man down to the blind worm his iron heel tramples in the earth. Then wherefore should we hang out this black banner for those who are beyond the laws of change and chance?

> "Yea, they have finish'd:
> For them there is no longer any future.
> No evil hour knocks at their door
> With tidings of mishap – far off are they,
> Beyond desire or fear."

It is the dismal adjuncts of death which have invested it with those superstitious terrors that we would fain see removed. The gloom arising from these melancholy pageants forms a black cloud, whose dense shadow obscures the light of life to the living. And why, we ask, should death be invested with such horror? Death in itself is not dreadful; it is but the change of one mode of being for another – the breaking forth of the winged soul from its earthly chrysalis; or, as an old Latin poet has so happily described it –

> "Thus life for ever runs its endless race,
> Death as a line which but divides the space –
> A stop which can but for a moment last,
> A *point* between the *future* and the *past*."

Nature presents in all her laws such a beautiful and wonderful harmony, that it is as impossible for death to produce discord among them, as for night to destroy, by the intervention of its shadow, the splendour of the coming day. Were men taught from infancy to regard death as a natural consequence, a fixed law of their being, instead as an awful punishment for sin – as the friend and benefactor of mankind, not the remorseless tyrant and persecutor – to die would no longer be considered an evil. Let this hideous skeleton be banished into darkness, and replaced by a benignant angel, wiping away all tears, healing all pain, burying in oblivion all sorrow and care, calming every turbulent passion, and restoring man, reconciled to his Maker, to a state of purity and peace; young and old would then go forth to meet him with lighted torches, and hail his approach with songs of thanksgiving and welcome.

And this is really the case with all but the desperately wicked, who show that they despise the magnificent boon of life by the bad use they make of it, by their blasphemous defiance of God and good, and their unwillingness to be renewed in his image.

The death angel is generally met with more calmness by the dying than by surviving friends. By the former, the dreaded enemy is hailed as a messenger of peace, and they sink tranquilly into his arms, with a smile upon their lips.

The death of the Christian is a beautiful triumph over the fears of life. In Him who conquered death, and led captivity captive, he finds the fruition of his being, the eternal blessedness promised to him in the Gospel, which places him beyond the wants and woes of time. The death of such a man should be celebrated as a sacred festival, not lamented as a dreary execution, – as the era of a new birth, not the extinction of being.

It is true that death is a profound sleep, from which no one can awaken to tell his dreams. But why on that account should we doubt that it is less blessed than its twin brother, whose resemblance it bears, and whose presence we all sedulously court? Invest sleep, however, with the same dismal garb; let your bed be a coffin, your canopy a pall, your night-dress a shroud; let the sobs of mourners, and the tolling of bells lull you to repose, – and few persons would willingly, or tranquilly, close their eyes to sleep.

And then, this absurd fashion of wearing black for months and years for the dead; let us calmly consider the philosophy of the thing, its use and abuse. Does it confer any benefit on the dead? Does it afford any consolation to the living? Morally or physically, does it produce the least good? Does it soften one regretful pang, or dry one bitter tear, or make the wearers wiser or better? If it does not produce any ultimate benefit, it should be at once discarded as a superstitious relic of more barbarous times, when men could not gaze on the simple, unveiled face of truth, but obscured the clear daylight of her glance under a thousand fantastic masks.

The ancients were more consistent in their mourning than the civilized people of the present day. They sat upon the ground and fasted, with rent garments, and ashes strewn upon their heads. This mortification of the flesh was a sort of penance inflicted by the self-tortured mourner for his own sins, and those of the dead. If this grief were not of a deep or lasting nature, the mourner found relief for his mental agonies in humiliation and personal suffering. He did not array himself in silk, and wool, and fine linen, and garments cut in the most approved fashion of the day, like our modern beaux and belles, when they testify to the public their grief for the loss of relation or friend, in the most expensive and becoming manner.

Verily, if we must wear our sorrow upon our sleeve, why not return to the sackcloth and ashes, as the most consistent demonstration of that grief which, hidden in the heart, surpasseth show.

But, then, sackcloth is a most unmanageable material. A handsome figure would be lost, buried, annihilated, in a sackcloth gown; it would be so horribly rough; it would wound the delicate skin of a fine lady; it could not be confined in graceful folds by clasps of jet, and pearl, and ornaments in black and gold. "Sackcloth? Faugh! – away with it. It smells of the knotted scourge and the charnel-house." We, *too*, say, "Away with it!" True grief has no need of such miserable provocatives to woe.

The barbarians who cut and disfigured their faces for the dead, showed a noble contempt of the world, by destroying those personal attractions which the loss of the beloved had taught them to despise. But who now would have the fortitude and self-denial to imitate such an example? The mourners in crape, and silk, and French merino, would rather *die themselves* than sacrifice their beauty at the shrine of such a monstrous sorrow.

How often have I heard a knot of gossips exclaim, as some widow of a gentleman in fallen circumstances glided by in her rusty weeds, "What shabby black that woman wears for her husband! I should be ashamed to appear in public in such faded mourning."

And yet, the purchase of that *shabby black* may have cost the desolate mourner and her orphan children the price of many a necessary meal. Ah, this putting of a poor family into black, and all the funeral trappings for pall-bearers and mourners, what a terrible affair it is! what anxious thoughts! what bitter heartaches it costs!

But the usages of society demand the sacrifice, and it

must be made. The head of the family has suddenly been removed from his earthly toils, at a most complicated crisis of his affairs, which are so involved that scarcely enough can be collected to pay the expenses of the funeral, and put his family into decent mourning, but every exertion must be made to do this. The money that might, after the funeral was over, have paid the rent of a small house, and secured the widow and her young family from actual want, until she could look around and obtain some situation in which she could earn a living for herself and them, must all be sunk in conforming to a useless custom, upheld by pride and vanity in the name of grief.

"How will the funeral expenses ever be paid?" exclaims the anxious, weeping mother. "When it is all over, and the mourning bought, there will not remain a single copper to find us in bread." The sorrow of obtaining this useless outward show of grief engrosses all the available means of the family, and that is expended upon the dead which might, with careful management, have kept the living from starving. Oh, vanity of vanities! there is no folly on earth that exceeds the vanity of this!

There are many persons who put off their grief when they put on their mourning, and it is a miserable satire on mankind to see these somber-clad beings in festal halls mingling with the gay and happy, their melancholy garments affording a painful contrast to light laughter, and eyes sparkling with pleasure.

Their levity, however, must not be mistaken for hypocrisy. The world is in fault, not they. Their grief is already over, – gone like a cloud from before the sun; but they are forced to wear black for a *given time*. They are true to their nature, which teaches them that "no grief with man is permanent," that the storms of to-day will not darken the heavens tomorrow. It is complying with a *lying custom* makes them *hypocrites*; and, as the world always judges by appearances, it so happens that by adhering to one of its conventional rules, appearances in this instance are against them.

Nay, the very persons who, in the first genuine outburst of natural grief besought them to moderate their sorrow, to dry their tears, and be comforted for the loss they had sustained, are among the *first* to censure them for following advice so common and useless. Tears are as necessary to the afflicted as showers are to the parched earth, and are the best and sweetest remedy for excessive grief.

To the mourner we would say – Weep on; nature requires your tears. They are sent in mercy by Him who wept at the grave of his friend Lazarus. The man of sorrows himself taught us to weep.

We once heard a very beautiful volatile young lady exclaim, with something very like glee in her look and tone, after reading a letter she had received by the post, with its ominous black bordering and seal – "Grandmamma is dead! We shall have to go into deep mourning. I am so glad, for black is so becoming to me!"

An old aunt, who was present, expressed her surprise at this indecorous avowal; when the young lady replied, with great *naivete* – "I never saw grandmamma in my life. I cannot be expected to feel any grief for her death."

"Perhaps not," said the aunt. "But why, then, make a show of that which you do not feel?"

"Oh, it's the custom of the world. You know we must. It would be considered *shocking* not to go into very *deep* mourning for such a near relation."

The young lady inherited a very nice legacy, too, from her grandmamma; and, had she spoken the truth, she would have said, "*I cannot weep for joy.*"

Her mourning, in consequence, was of the deepest and most expensive kind; and she really did look charming in her "*love of a black crape bonnet!*" as she skipped before the glass, admiring herself and it, when it came home fresh from the milliner's.

In contrast to the pretty young heiress, we knew a sweet orphan girl whose grief for the death of her mother, to whom she was devotedly attached, lay deeper than this hollow tinsel show; and yet the painful thought that she was too poor to pay this mark of respect to the memory of her beloved parent, in a manner suited to her birth and station, added greatly to the poignancy of her sorrow.

A family who had long been burthened with a cross old aunt, who was a martyr to rheumatic gout, and whose violent temper kept the whole house in awe, and whom they dared not offend for fear of her leaving her wealth to strangers, were in the habit of devoutly wishing the old lady a *happy* release from her sufferings. When this long anticipated event at length took place, the very servants were put into the deepest mourning. What a solemn farce – we should say, lie – was this!

The daughters of a wealthy farmer had prepared everything to attend the great agricultural provincial show. Unfortunately, a grandfather to whom they all seemed greatly attached, died most inconveniently the day before, and as they seldom keep a body in Canada over the second day, he was buried early in the morning of the one appointed for their journey. They attended the remains to the grave, but after the funeral was over they put off their black garments and started for the show, and did not resume them again until after their return. People may think this very shocking, but it was not the laying aside the black that was so, but the fact of their being able to go from a grave to a scene of confusion and gaiety. The black clothes had nothing to do with this want of feeling, which would have remained the same under a black or a scarlet vestment.

A gentleman in this neighbourhood, since dead, who attended a public ball the same week that he had seen a lovely child consigned to the earth, would have remained the same heartless parent dressed in the deepest sables.

No instance that I have narrated of the business-like manner in which Canadians treat death, is more ridiculously striking than the following: –

The wife of a rich mechanic had a brother lying, it was supposed, at the point of death. His sister sent a note to me, requesting me to relinquish an engagement I had made with a sewing girl in her favour, as she wanted her immediately to make up her mourning, the doctor having told her that her brother could not live many days.

"Mrs. —— is going to be beforehand with death," I said, as I gave the girl the desired release. "I have known instances of persons being too late with their mourning to attend a funeral, but this is the first time I ever heard of it being made in anticipation."

After a week the girl returned to her former employment.

"Well, Anne, is Mr. —— dead?"

"No, ma'am, nor likely to die this time; and his sister is so vexed that she bought such expensive mourning, and all for no purpose!"

The brother of this provident lady is alive to this day, the husband of a very pretty wife, and the father of a family, while she, poor body, has been consigned to the grave for more than three years.

During her own dying illness, a little girl greatly disturbed her sick mother with the noise she made. Her husband, as an inducement to keep the child quiet, said, "Mary, if you do not quit that, I'll whip you; but if you keep still like a good girl, you shall go to ma's funeral."

An artist cousin of mine was invited, with many other members of the Royal Academy, to attend the funeral of the celebrated Nollekens the sculptor. The party filled twelve mourning coaches, and were furnished with silk gloves, scarfs, and hatbands, and a dinner was provided after the funeral was over at one of the large hotels. "A merrier set that we were on that day," said my cousin, "I never saw. We all got jovial, and it was midnight before any of us reached our respective homes. The whole affair vividly brought to my mind that description of the 'Gondola,' given so graphically by Byron, that it

'Contain'd much fun,
Like mourning coaches when the funeral's done.'"

Some years ago I witnessed the funeral of a young lady, the only child of very wealthy parents, who resided in

Bedford-square. The heiress of their enviable riches was a
very delicate, fragile-looking girl, and on the day that she
attained her majority her parents gave a large dinner
party, followed by a ball in the evening, to celebrate the
event. It was during the winter; the night was very cold,
the crowded rooms overheated, the young lady thinly but
magnificently clad. She took a chill in leaving the close
ballroom for the large, ill-warmed supper-room, and three
days after, the hope of these rich people lay insensible on
her bier.

I heard from every one that called upon Mrs. L——,
the relative and friend with whom I was staying, of the
magnificent funeral would be given to Miss C——. Ah,
little heeded that pale crushed flower of yesterday, the
pomp that was to convey her from the hot-bed of luxury
to the cold, damp vault of St. Giles's melancholy looking
church! I stood at Mrs. L——'s window, which com-
manded a view of the whole square, to watch the procession pass up Russell-street to the place of interment. The
morning was intensely cold, and large snow-flakes fell
lazily and heavily to the earth. The poor dingy sparrows,
with their feathers ruffled up, hopped mournfully along
the pavement in search of food; they,

> "In spite of all their feathers, were a-cold."

The mutes that attended the long line of mourning
coaches stood motionless, leaning on their long staffs
wreathed with white, like so many figures that the frost-
king had stiffened into stone. The hearse, with its snowy
plumes, drawn by six milk-white horses, might have
served for the regal car of his northern majesty, so ghost-
like and chilly were its sepulchral trappings. At length the
coffin, covered with black velvet, and a pall lined with
white silk and fringed with silver, was borne from the
house and deposited in the gloomy depths of the stately
hearse. The *hired* mourners, in their sable dresses and
long white hatbands and scarfs, rode slowly forward
mounted on white horses, to attend this bride of death to

her last resting place. The first three carriages that followed contained the family physician and surgeon, a clergyman, and the male servants of the house, in deep sables. The family carriage too was there, but *empty*, and of a procession in which 145 private carriages made a conspicuous show, all but those enumerated above were *empty*. Strangers drove strange horses to that vast funeral, and *hired servants* were the only members of the family that conducted the last scion of that family to the grave. Truly, it was the most dismal spectacle we ever witnessed, and we turned from it sick at heart, and with eyes moist with tears – not shed for the dead, for she had escaped from this vexatious vanity, but from the heartless mockery of all this fictitious woe.

The expense of such a funeral probably involved many hundred pounds, which had been better bestowed on charitable purposes.

Another evil arising out of this absurd custom, is the high price attached to black clothing, on account of the necessity that compels people to wear it for so long a period after the death of a near relation, making it a matter of still greater difficulty for the poorer class to comply with the usages of society.

"But who cares about the poor, whether they go into mourning for their friends or no? it is a matter of no consequence."

Ah, there it is. And this is not the least forcible argument we have to advance against this useless custom. If it becomes a moral duty for the rich to put on black for the death of a friend, it must be morally necessary for the poor to do the same. We see no difference in the degrees of moral feeling; the soul of man is of no rank, but of equal value in our eyes, whether belonging to rich or poor. But this usage is so general, and the neglect of it considered such a disgrace, that it leaves a very wide door open for the entrance of false pride.

Poverty is an evil which most persons, however humble their stations may be, most carefully endeavour to conceal. To avoid an exposure of their real circumstances, they will deprive themselves of the common necessaries of life, and incur debts which they have no prospect of paying, rather than allow their neighbours to suspect that they cannot afford a *handsome funeral* and good *mournings* for any deceased member of their family. If such persons would but follow the dictates of true wisdom, honesty, and truth, no dread of the opinion of others should tempt them to do what they cannot afford. Their grief for the dead would not be less sincere if they followed the body of the beloved in their ordinary costume to the grave; nor is the spectacle less imposing divested of all the solemn foppery which attends the funeral of persons who move in respectable society.

Some years ago, when it was the fashion in England (and may be it remains the fashion still) to give black silk scarfs and hatbands at funerals, mean and covetous persons threw themselves in the way of picking up these stray loaves and fishes. A lady, who lived in the same town with me after I was married, boasted to me that her husband (who always contrived to be a necessary attendant on such occasions) found her in all the black silk she required for articles of dress, and that he had not purchased a pair of gloves for many years.

About two years before old King George the Third died, a report got about that he could not survive many days. There was a general rush among all ranks to obtain mourning. Up went the price of black goods; Norwich crapes and bombazines rose ten per cent, and those who were able to secure a black garment at any price, to shew their loyalty, were deemed very fortunate. And after all this fuss, and hurry, and confusion, the poor mad old king disappointed the speculators in sables, and lived on in darkness and mental aberration for two whole years. The mourning of some on that occasion was *real*, not imaginary. The sorrow with them was not for the *king's death*, but that he had *not died*. On these public occasions of grief, great is the stir and bustle in economical families, who wish to show a decent concern for the death of the monarch, but who do not exactly like to go to the expense of buying new clothes for such a short period as a court mourning. All the old family stores are rummaged carefully over, and every stuff gown, worn ribbon, or shabby shawl, that can take a black dye, is handed over to the vat; and these second-hand black garments have a more *mournful appearance* than the glossy suits of the gay and wealthy, for it is actually humiliating to wear such, as they are both unbecoming to the young and old. Black, which is the most becoming and convenient colour for general wear, especially to the old and middle-aged, would no longer be regarded with religious horror as the type of mortality and decay, but would take its place on the same shelf with the gay tints that form the motley groups in our handsome stores. Could influential people be found to expose the folly and vanity of this practice, and refuse to comply with its demands, others would soon be glad to follow their example, and, before many years, it would sink into contempt and disuse.

If the Americans, the most practical people in the world, would but once take up the subject and publicly lecture on its absurdity, this dismal shadow of a darker age would no longer obscure our streets and scare our little ones. Men would wear their grief in their hearts and not around their hats; and widows would be better known by their serious deportment than by their weeds. I feel certain that every thinking person, who calmly investigates the subject, will be tempted to exclaim with me, "Oh, that the good sense of mankind would unite in banishing it for ever from the earth!"

THE SONG OF FAITH.

"House of clay! – frail house of clay!
  In the dust thou soon must lie;
 Spirit! spread thy wings – away,
  Strong in immortality;

To worlds more bright
 Oh wing thy flight,
To win the crown and robe of light.

"Hopes of dust! – false hopes of dust!
 Smiling as the morning fair;
Why do we confiding trust
 In trifles light as air?
  Like flowers that wave
  Above the grave,
Ye cheer, without the power to save.

"Joys of earth! – vain joys of earth!
 Sandy your foundations be;
Mortals overrate your worth,
 Sought through life so eagerly.
  Too soon we know
  That tears must flow, –
That bliss is still allied to woe!

"Human love! – fond human love!
 We have worshipp'd at thy shrine;
Envying not the saints above,
 While we deem'd thy power divine.
  But ah, thy light,
  So wildly bright,
Is born of earth to set in night.

"Love of heaven! – love of heaven!
 Let us pray for thine increase;
Happiness by thee is given,
 Hopes and joys that never cease.
  With thee we'll soar
  Death's dark tide o'er,
Where earth can stain the soul no more."

NINE

Odd Characters

"Dear merry reader, did you ever hear,
    Whilst travelling on the world's wide beaten road,
The curious reasoning, and opinions queer,
    Of men, who never in their lives bestow'd
One hour on study; whose existence seems
    A thing of course – a practical delusion –
A day of frowning clouds and sunny gleams –
    Of pain and pleasure, mix'd in strange confusion;
Who feel they move and breathe, they know not why –
Are born to eat and drink, and sleep and die."

S.M.

THE SHORES of the Prince Edward District become more bold and beautiful as the steamer pursues her course up the "Long Reach." Magnificent trees clothe these rugged banks to their very summits, and cast dense shadows upon the waters that slumber at their feet. The slanting rays of the evening sun stream through their thick foliage, and weave a network of gold around the corrugated trunks of the huge oak and maple trees that tower far above our heads. The glorious waters are dyed with a thousand changeful hues of crimson and saffron, and reflect from their unruffled surface the gorgeous tints of a Canadian sunset. The pines, with their hearse-like plumes, loom out darkly against the glowing evening sky, and frown austerely upon us, their gloomy aspect affording a striking contrast to the sun-lighted leaves of the feathery birch and the rock elm. It is a lonely hour, and one that nature seems to have set apart for prayer and praise; a devotional spirit seems to breathe over the earth, the woods, and waters, softening and harmonising the whole into one blessed picture of love and peace.

The boat has again crossed the bay, and stops to take in wood at "Roblin's wharf." We are now beneath the shadow of the "Indian woods," a reserve belonging to the Mohawks in the township of Tyendenaga, about twenty-four miles by water from Belleville. A broad belt of forest land forms the background to a cleared slope, rising gradually from the water until it reaches a considerable elevation above the shore. The frontage to the bay is filled up with neat farm houses, and patches of buck wheat and Indian corn, the only grain that remains unharvested at this season of the year. We have a fine view of the stone church built by the Indians, which stands on the top of the hill about a mile from the water. Queen Anne presented to this tribe three large marble tablets engraved with the Ten Commandments, which, after following them in all their ramblings for a century and a half, now grace the altar of this church, and are regarded with great veneration by the Indian settlers, who seem to look upon them with a superstitious awe. The church is built in the gothic style, and is one of the most picturesque village churches that I have seen in Canada. The Indians contributed a great part of the funds for erecting this building. I was never within the walls of the sacred edifice; but I have wandered round the quiet peaceful burial-ground, and admired the lovely prospect it commands of the bay and the opposite shores.

One side of the churchyard is skirted by a natural grove of forest trees, which separates it from the parsonage, a neat white building that fronts the water, and stands back from it at the head of a noble sweep of land covered with velvet turf, and resembling greatly a gentleman's park at home, by the fine groups of stately forest trees scattered over it, and a semicircular belt of the original forest, that, sloping from the house on either side, extends its wings until it meets the blue waters of the bay, leaving between its green arms a broad space of cleared land.

The first time my eyes ever rested on this beautiful spot it appeared to me a perfect paradise. It was a warm, balmy, moonlight evening in June. The rich resinous odour of the woods filled the air with delicious perfume; fire-flies were glancing like shooting stars among the dark foliage that hung over the water, and the spirit of love and peace sat brooding over the luxurious solitude, whose very silence was eloquent with praise of the great Maker. How I envied the residents of the parsonage their lovely home! How disappointed I felt, when Mrs. G—— told me that she felt it dull and lonely, that she was out of society, and that the Indians were very troublesome neighbours! Now, I have no doubt that this was all very true, and that I should have felt the same want that she did, after the bewitching novelty of the scene had become familiar; but it sadly destroyed the romance and poetry of it to me at the time.

This part of the township of Tyendenaga belongs almost exclusively to the Mohawk Indians, who have made a large settlement here, while the government has given them a good school for instructing their children in the Indian and English languages; and they have a resident clergyman of the Establishment always at hand, to minister to them the spiritual consolations of religion, and impart to them the blessed truths of the gospel. The Rev. S.G—— was for some years the occupant of the pretty parsonage-house, and was greatly beloved by his Indian congregation.

The native residents of these woods clear farms, and build and plant like their white neighbours. They rear horses, cattle, and sheep, and sow a sufficient quantity of grain to secure them from want. But there is a great lack of order and regularity in all their agricultural proceedings. They do not make half as much out of their lands –

which they suffer to be overgrown with thorns and thistles
– as their white neighbours; and their domestic arrangements within doors are never marked by that appearance
of comfort and cleanliness, which is to be seen in the
dwellings of the native Canadians and emigrants from
Europe.

The red man is out of his element when he settles
quietly down to a farm, and you perceive it at a glance. He
never appears to advantage as a resident among civilized
men; and he seems painfully conscious of his inferiority,
and ignorance of the arts of life. He has lost his identity, as
it were, and when he attempts to imitate the customs and
manners of the whites, he is too apt to adopt their vices
without acquiring their industry and perseverance, and
sinks into a sottish, degraded savage. The proud independence we admired so much in the man of the woods,
has disappeared with his truthfulness, honesty, and simple
manners. His pure blood is tainted with the dregs of a
lower humanity, degenerated by the want and misery of
over-populous European cities. His light eyes, crisp hair,
and whitey-brown complexion, too surely betray his
mixed origin; and we turn from the half educated, half-
caste Indian, with feelings of aversion and mistrust.

There is a Mohawk family who reside in this township
of the name of Loft, who have gained some celebrity in the
colony by their clever representations of the manners and
customs of their tribe. They sing Indian songs, dance the
war-dance, hold councils, and make grave speeches, in the
characters of Indian chiefs and hunters, in an artistic
manner that would gain the applause of a more fastidious
audience.

The two young squaws, who were the principal performers in this travelling Indian opera, were the most
beautiful Indian women I ever beheld. There was no base
alloy in their pure native blood. They had the large, dark,
humid eyes, the ebon locks tinged with purple, so peculiar
to their race, and which gives such a rich tint to the clear

olive skin and brilliant white teeth of the denizens of the Canadian wilderness.

Susannah Loft and her sister were the *beau ideal* of Indian women; and their graceful and symmetrical figures were set off to great advantage by their picturesque and becoming costume, which in their case was composed of the richest materials. Their acting and carriage were dignified and queen-like, and their appearance singularly pleasing and interesting.

Susannah, the eldest and certainly the most graceful of these truly fascinating girls, was unfortunately killed last summer by the collision of two steam-carriages, while travelling professionally with her sister through the States. Those who had listened with charmed ears to her sweet voice, and gazed with admiring eyes upon her personal charms, were greatly shocked at her untimely death.

A little boy and girl belonging to the same talented family have been brought before the public, in order to supply her place, but they have not been able to fill up the blank occasioned by her loss.

The steamboat again leaves the north shore, and stands across from the stone mills, which are in the Prince Edward district, and form one of the features of the remarkable scenery of what is called the "high shore." This mountainous ridge, which descends perpendicularly to the water's edge, is still in forest; and, without doubt, this is the most romantic portion of the bay, whose waters are suddenly contracted to half their former dimensions, and glide on darkly and silently between these steep wood-crowned heights.

There is a small lake upon the highest portion of this table-land, whose waters are led down the steep bank, and made to work a saw-mill, which is certainly giving a very unromantic turn to them. But here, as in the States, the beautiful and the ideal are instantly converted into the real and the practical.

This "lake of the mountains" is a favourite place for

picnics and pleasure trips from Northport and Belleville. Here the Sabbath-school children come, once during the summer, to enjoy a ramble in the woods, and spread their feast beneath the lordly oaks and maples that crown these heights. And the teetotallers marshall their bands of converts, and hold their cold water festival, beside the blue deep waters of this mysterious mountain-lake.

Strange stories are told of its unfathomable depth, of the quicksands that are found near it, and of its being supplied from the far-off inland ocean of Lake Huron. But like the cove in Tyendenaga, of which everybody in the neighbourhood has heard something, but which nobody has seen, these accounts of the lake of the mountain rest only upon hearsay.

The last rays of the sun still lingered on wood and stream when we arrived at Picton, which stands at the head of the "long reach." The bay here is not wider than a broad river. The banks are very lofty, and enclose the water in an oblong form, round which that part of the town which is near the shore is built.

Picton is a very beautiful place viewed from the deck of the steamer. Its situation is novel and imposing, and the number of pretty cottages that crown the steep ridge that rises almost perpendicularly from the water, peeping out from among fine orchards in full bearing, and trim gardens, give it quite a rural appearance. The steamboat enters this fairy bay by a very narrow passage; and, after delivering freight and passengers at the wharf, backs out by the way she came in. There is no turning a large vessel round this long half-circle of deep blue water. Few spots in Canada would afford a finer subject for the artist's pencil than this small inland town, which is so seldom visited by strangers and tourists.

The progress to wealth and importance made by this place is strikingly behind that of Belleville, which far exceeds it in size and population. Three years ago a very destructive fire consumed some of the principal buildings in the town, which has not yet recovered from its effects.

Trade is not so brisk here as in Belleville, and the streets are dull and monotonous, when compared with the stir and bustle of the latter, which, during the winter season, is crowded with sleighs from the country. The Bay of Quinte during the winter forms an excellent road to all the villages and towns on its shores. The people from the opposite side trade more with the Belleville merchants than with those in their own district; and during the winter season, when the bay is completely frozen from the mouth of the Trent to Kingston, loaded teams are passing to and fro continually. It is the favourite afternoon drive of young and old, and when the wind, sweeping over such a broad surface of ice, is not *too cold*, and you are well wrapped up in furs and buffalo robes, a sleigh ride on the ice is very delightful. Not that I can ever wholly divest myself of a vague, indistinct sense of danger, whilst rapidly gliding over this frozen mirror. I would rather be out on the bay, in a gale of wind in a small boat, than overtaken by a snow storm on its frozen highways. Still it is a pleasant sight of a bright, glowing, winter day, when the landscape glitters like a world composed of crystals, to watch the handsome sleighs, filled with well-dressed men and women, and drawn by spirited horses, dashing in all directions over this brilliant field of dazzling white.

Night has fallen rapidly upon us since we left Picton in the distance. A darker shade is upon the woods, the hills, the waters, and by the time we approach Fredericksburg it will be dark. This too is a very pretty place on the north side of the bay; beautiful orchards and meadows skirt the water, and fine bass-wood and willow-trees grow beside, or bend over the waves. The green smooth meadows, out of which the black stumps rotted long ago, show noble groups of hiccory and butter-nut, and sleek fat cows are reposing beneath them, or standing mid-leg in the small creek that wanders through them to pour its fairy tribute into the broad bay.

We must leave the deck and retreat into the ladies' cabin, for the air from the water grows chilly, and the sense of seeing can no longer be gratified by remaining where we are. But if you open your eyes to see, and your ears to hear, all the strange sayings and doings of the odd people you meet in a steamboat, you will never lack amusement.

The last time I went down to Kingston, there was a little girl in the cabin who rejoiced in the possession of a very large American doll, made so nearly to resemble an infant, that at a distance it was easy to mistake it for one. To render the deception more striking, you could make it cry like a child by pressing your hand upon its body. A thin, long-faced farmer's wife came on board, at the wharf we have just quitted, and it was amusing to watch her alternately gazing at the little girl and her doll.

"Is that your baby, Cisy?"

"No; it's my doll."

"Mi! what a strange doll! Isn't that something *oncommon?* I took it for a real child. Look at its bare feet and hands, and bald head. Well, I don't think it's 'zactly right to make a piece of wood look so like a human critter."

The child good-naturedly put the doll into the woman's hands, who, happening to take it rather roughly, the wooden baby gave a loud squall; the woman's face expressed the utmost horror, and she dropped it on the floor as if it had been a hot coal.

"Gracious, goodness me, the thing's alive!"

The little girl laughed heartily, and, taking up the discarded doll, explained to the woman the simple method employed to produce the sound.

"Well, it do sound quite *nataral*," said her astonished companion. "What will they find out next? It beats the railroad and the telegraph holler."

"Ah, but I saw a big doll that could speak when I was with mamma in New York," said the child, with glistening eyes.

"A doll that could speak? You don't say. Oh, do tell!"

While the young lady described the automaton doll, it was amusing to watch the expressions of surprise, wonder, and curiosity, that flitted over the woman's long cadaverous face. She would have made a good study for a painter.

A young relative of mine went down in the steamboat, to be present at the Provincial Agricultural Show that was held that year in the town of Buckville, on the St. Lawrence. It was the latter end of September; the weather was wet and stormy, and the boat loaded to the water's edge with cattle and passengers. The promenade decks were filled up with pigs, sheep and oxen. Cows were looking sleepily in at the open doors of the ladies' cabin, and bulls were fastened on the upper deck. Such a motley group of bipeds and quadrupeds were never before huddled into such a narrow space; and, amidst all this din and confusion, a Scotch piper was playing lustily on the bagpipes, greatly to the edification, I've no doubt, of himself and the crowd of animal life around him.

The night came on very dark and stormy, and many of the women suffered as much from the pitching of the boat as if they had been at sea. The ladies' cabin was crowded to overflowing; every sofa, bed, and chair was occupied; and my young friend, who did not feel any inconvenience from the storm, was greatly entertained by the dialogues carried on across the cabin by the women, who were reposing in their berths, and lamenting over the rough weather and their own sufferings in consequence. They were mostly the wives of farmers and respectable mechanics, and the language they used was neither very choice nor grammatical.

"I say, Mrs. C——, how be you?"

"I feel bad, any how," with a smothered groan.

"Have you been sick?"

"Not yet; but feel as if I was going to."

"How's your head coming on, Mrs. N——?"

"It's just splitting, I thank you."

"Oh, how awful the boat do pitch!" cries a third.

"If she should sink, I'm afeard we shall all go to the bottom."

"And think of all the poor sheep and cattle!"

"Well, of course, they'd have to go too."

"Oh, mi! I'll get up, and be ready for a start, in case of the worst," cried a young girl.

"Mrs. C——, do give me something good out of your basket, to keep up my spirits."

"Well, I will. Come over here, and you and I will have some talk. My basket's at the foot of my berth. You'll find in it a small bottle of brandy and some curls."

So up got several of the sick ladies, and kept up their spirits by eating cakes, chewing gum, and drinking cold brandy punch.

"Did Mrs. H—— lose much in the fire last night?" said one.

"Oh, dear, yes; she lost all her clothes, and three large jars of preserves she made about a week ago, and *sarce in accordance!*"*

There was an honest Yorkshire farmer and his wife on board, and when the morning at length broke through pouring rain and driving mist, and the port to which they were bound loomed through the haze, the women were very anxious to know if their husbands, who slept in the gentlemen's cabin, were awake."

"They arn't stirring yet," said Mrs. G——," for I hear Isaac (meaning her husband) *breezing* below" – a most expressive term for very hard snoring.

The same Isaac, when he came up to the ladies' cabin to take his wife on shore, complained, in his broad Yorkshire dialect, that he had been kept awake all night by a jovial gentleman who had been his fellow-traveller in the cabin.

"We had terrible noisy chap in t'cabin. They called him Mr. D——, and said he 'twas t'mayor of Belleville; but I thought they were a-fooning. He wouldn't sleep himself, nor let t'others sleep. He gat piper, an' put him top o' table, and kept him playing all t'night."

One would think that friend Isaac had been haunted by

*A common Yankee phrase, often used instead of the word proportion.

the vision of the piper in his dreams; for, certes, the jovial buzzing of the pipes had not been able to drown the deep drone of his own nasal organ.

A gentleman who was travelling in company with Sir A—— told me an anecdote of him, and how he treated an impertinent fellow on board one of the lake boats, that greatly amused me.

The state cabins in these large steamers open into the great saloon; and as they are often occupied by married people, each berth contains two beds, one placed above the other. Now it often happens, when the boat is greatly crowded, that two passengers of the same sex are forced to occupy the same sleeping room. This was Sir A——'s case, and he was obliged, though very reluctantly, to share his sleeping apartment with a well-dressed American, but evidently a man of low standing, from the familiarity of his manners and the bad grammar he used.

In the morning, it was necessary for one gentleman to rise before the other, as the space in front of their berths was too narrow to allow of more than one performing his ablutions at a time.

Our Yankee made a fair start, and had nearly completed his toilet, when he suddenly spied a tooth-brush and a box of tooth-powder in the dressing-case his companion had left open on the washstand. Upon these he pounced, and having made a liberal use of them, flung them back into the case, and sat down upon the only chair the room contained, in order to gratify his curiosity by watching how his sleeping partner went through the same process.

Sir A——, greatly annoyed by the fellow's assurance, got out of bed; and placing the washhand basin on the floor, put his feet into the water, and commenced scrubbing his toe-nails with the desecrated tooth-brush. Jonathan watched his movements for a few seconds in silent horror; at length, unable to contain himself, he exclaimed.

"Well, stranger! that's the dirtiest use I ever see a tooth-brush put to, any how."

"I saw it put to a dirtier, just now," said Sir A——, very coolly. "I always use that brush for cleaning my toes."

The Yankee turned very green, and fled to the deck, but his nausea was not sea-sickness.

The village of Nappanee, on the north side of the Bay, is situated on a very pretty river that bears the same name, – Nappanee, in the Mohawk language, signifying flour. The village is a mile back from the Bay, and is not much seen from the water. There are a great many mills here, both grist and saw mills, from which circumstance it most likely derives its name.

Amherst Island, which is some miles in extent, stands between Ontario and the Bay of Quinte, its upper and lower extremity forming the two straits that are called the Upper and Lower Gap, – and the least breeze, which is not perceptible in the other portions of the bay, is felt here. Passing through these gaps on a stormy day creates as great a nausea as a short chopping sea on the Atlantic, and I have seen both men and women retreat to their berths to avoid disagreeable consequences. Amherst Island is several miles in extent, and there are many good farms in high cultivation upon it, while its proximity on all sides to the water affords excellent sport to the angler and gunner, as wild ducks abound in this vicinity.

Just after you pass the island and enter the lower gap, there are three very small islands in a direct line with each other, that are known as the three brothers. A hermit has taken up his abode on the centre one, and built a very Robinson Crusoe looking hut near the water, composed of round logs and large stones cemented together with clay. He gets his living by fishing and fowling, and you see his well-worn, weather-beaten boat, drawn up in a little cove near his odd dwelling. I was very curious to obtain some particulars of the private history of this eccentric individual, but beyond what I have just related, my informants could tell me nothing, or why he had chosen this solitary abode in such an exposed situation, and so far apart from all the comforts of social life.

The town of Bath is the last place of any note on this portion of the Bay, until you arrive at Kingston.

A MORNING SONG.

"The young wheat is springing
    All tender and green,
And the blackbird is singing
    The branches between;
The leaves of the hawthorn
    Have burst from their prison,
And the bright eyes of morn
    On the earth have arisen.

"While sluggards are sleeping,
    Oh hasten with me;
While the night mists are weeping
    Soft showers on each tree,
And nature is glowing
    Beneath the warm beam,
The young day is throwing
    O'er mountain and stream.

"And the shy colt is bounding
    Across the wide mead,
And his wild hoofs resounding,
    Increases his speed;
Now starting and crossing
    At each shadow he sees,
Now wantonly tossing
    His mane in the breeze.

"The sky-lark is shaking
    The dew from her wing,
And the clover forsaking,

Soars upwards to sing,
In rapture outpouring
Her anthem of love,
Where angels adoring
Waft praises above.

"Shake dull sleep from your pillow,
Young dreamer arise,
On the leaves of the willow
The dew-drop still lies,
And the mavis is trilling
His song from the brake,
And with melody filling
The wild woods – awake!"

TEN

Grace Marks

"I dare not think – I cannot pray;
   To name the name of God were sin:
No grief of mine can wash away
   The consciousness of guilt within.
The stain of blood is on my hand,
   The curse of Cain is on my brow; –
I see that ghastly phantom stand
   Between me and the sunshine now!
That mocking face still haunts my dreams,
   That blood-shot eye that never sleeps,
In night and darkness – oh, it gleams,
   Like red-hot steel – but never weeps!
And still it bends its burning gaze
   On mine, till drops of terror start
From my hot brow, and hell's fierce blaze
   Is kindled in my brain and heart.
I long for death, yet dare not die,
   Though life is now a weary curse;
But oh, that dread eternity
   May bring a punishment far worse!"

So MUCH has been written about the city of Kingston, so lately the seat of government, and so remarkable for its fortifications, and the importance it ever must be to the colony as a military depôt and place of defence, that it

is not my intention to enter into a minute description of it
here. I was greatly pleased, as I think every stranger must
be, with its general aspect, particularly as seen from the
water, in which respect it has a great advantage over
Toronto. The number of vessels lying at the different
wharfs, and the constant arrival of noble steamers both
from the United States and the Upper and Lower Province, give it a very business-like appearance. Yet, upon
landing, you are struck with the want of stir and bustle in
the principal thoroughfares, when contrasted with the size
and magnitude of the streets.

The removal of the seat of government has checked the
growth of Kingston for a while; but you feel, while examining its commanding position, that it must always be the
key of the Upper Province, the great rallying point in case
of war or danger. The market house is a very fine building,
and the wants of the city could be supplied within its area,
were it three times the size that it is at present. The market
is decidedly one of the chief attractions of the place.

The streets are wide and well paved, and there are a
great many fine trees in and about Kingston, which give to
it the appearance of a European town. The houses are
chiefly of brick and stone along the public thoroughfares,
and there are many neat private dwellings inclosed in trim
well-kept gardens. The road leading to the Provincial Penitentiary runs parallel with the water, and forms a delightful drive.

It is about three years ago that I paid a visit with my
husband to the Penitentiary, and went over every part of
it. I must own that I felt a greater curiosity to see the
convicts than the prison which contained them, and my
wishes were completely gratified, as my husband was
detained for several hours on business, and I had a long
interval of leisure to examine the workshops, where the
convicts were employed at their different trades, their
sleeping cells, chapel, and places of punishment. The
silence system is maintained here, no conversation being
allowed between the prisoners. I was surprised at the neat-

ness, cleanliness, order, and regularity of all the arrangements in the vast building, and still more astonished that forty or fifty strong active looking men, unfettered, with the free use of their limbs, could be controlled by one person, who sat on a tall chair as overseer of each ward. In several instances, particularly in the tailoring and shoe-making department, the overseers were small delicate-looking men; but such is the force of habit, and the want of moral courage which generally accompanies guilt, that a word or a look from these men was sufficient to keep them at work.

The dress of the male convicts was warm and comfortable, though certainly not very elegant, consisting (for it was late in the fall) of a thick woollen jacket, one side of it being brown, the other yellow, with trowsers to correspond, a shirt of coarse factory cotton, but very clean, and good stout shoes, and warm knitted woollen socks. The letters P.P. for "Provincial Penitentiary," are sewed in coloured cloth upon the dark side of the jacket. Their hair is cut very short to the head, and they wear a cloth cap of the same colours that compose their dress.

The cells are narrow, just wide enough to contain a small bed, a stool, and a wash-bowl, and the prisoners are divided from each other by thick stone walls. They are locked in every night at six o'clock, and their cell is so constructed, that one of the keepers can always look in upon the convict without his being aware of the scrutiny. The bedding was scrupulously clean, and I saw a plain Bible in each cell.

There is a sort of machine resembling a stone coffin, in which mutinous convicts are confined for a given time. They stand in an upright position; and as there are air-holes for breathing, the look and name of the thing is more dreadful than the punishment, which cannot be the least painful. I asked the gentleman who showed us over the building, what country sent the most prisoners to the "Penitentiary?" He smiled, and told me "guess." I did so, but was wrong.

"No," said he; "we have more French Canadians and men of colour. Then Irish, English, and run-a-way loafers from the States. Of the Scotch we have very few; but they are very bad – the most ungovernable, sullen, and disobedient. When a Scotchman is bad enough to be brought here, he is like Jeremiah's bad figs – only fit for the gallows."

Mr. Moodie's bailiffs had taken down a young fellow, about twenty years of age, who had been convicted at the assizes for stealing curious coins from a person who had brought them out to this country as old family relics. The evidence was more circumstantial than positive, and many persons believed the lad innocent.

He had kept up his spirits bravely on the voyage, and was treated with great kindness by the men who had him in custody; but when once within the massy walls of the huge building, his courage seemed to forsake him all at once. We passed him as he sat on the bench, while the barber was cutting his hair and shaving off his whiskers. His handsome suit had been removed – he was in the party-coloured dress before described. There was in his face an expression of great anguish, and tears were rolling in quick succession down his cheeks. Poor fellow! I should hardly have known him again, so completely was he humbled by his present position.

Mr. M——y told me that they had some men in the "Penitentiary" who had returned three different times to it, and had grown so attached to their prison that they preferred being there, well clothed and well fed, to gaining a precarious living elsewhere.

Executions in Canada are so rare, even for murder, that many atrocious criminals are found within these walls – men and women – who could not possibly have escaped the gallows in England.

At twelve o'clock I followed Mr. M—— to the great hall, to see the prisoners dine. The meal consisted of excellent soups, with a portion of the meat which had been boiled in it, potatoes, and brown bread, all very clean and good of their kind. I took a plate of the soup and a piece of the bread, and enjoyed both greatly.

I could not help thinking, while watching these men in their comfortable dresses, taking their wholesome, well-cooked meal, how much better they were fed and lodged than thousands of honest industrious men, who had to maintain large families upon a crust of bread, in the great manufacturing cities at home.

Most of these men had very bad countenances, and I never felt so much convinced of the truth of phrenology as while looking at their heads. The extraordinary formation, or rather *mal*-formation, of some of them, led me to think that their possessors were hardly accountable for their actions. One man in particular, who had committed a very atrocious murder, and was confined for life, had a most singular head, such as one, indeed, as I never before saw on a human body. It was immensely large at the base, and appeared perfectly round, while at the crown it rose to a point like a sugar-loaf. He was of a dull, drab-coloured complexion, with large prominent eyes of a pale green colour; his expression, the most repulsively cruel and sinister. The eye involuntarily singled him out among all his comrades, as something too terrible to escape observation.

Among such a number of men, 448, who were there present, I was surprised at seeing so few with red or fair hair. I noticed this to my companion. He had never observed it before, but said it was strange. The convicts were mostly of a dull grey complexion, large eyed, stolid looking men, or with very black hair, and heavy black brows.

I could only account for this circumstance from the fact, that though fair-haired people are often violently passionate and easily excited, their anger is sudden and quick, never premeditated, but generally the work of the moment. Like straw on a fire, it kindles into a fierce blaze, but it is over in an instant. They seldom retain it, or bear malice. Not so the dull, putty-coloured, sluggish man. He is slow to act, but he broods over a supposed affront or injury, and never forgets it. He plans the moment of retaliation, and stabs his enemy when least prepared. There were many stolid, heavy-looking men in that prison – many with black, jealous, fiery-looking eyes, in whose gloomy depths suspicion and revenge seemed to lurk. Even to look at these men as they passed on, seemed to arouse their vindictive feelings, and they scowled disdainfully upon us as they walked on to their respective places.

There was one man among these dark, fierce-looking criminals, who, from his proud carriage and bearing, particularly arrested my attention. I pointed him out to Mr.——. "That man has the appearance of an educated person. He looks as if he had been a gentleman."

"You are right," was his reply. "He *was* a gentleman, the son of a district judge, and brought up to the law. A clever man too; but these walls do not contain a worse in every respect. He was put in here for arson, and an attempt to murder. Many a poor man has been hung with half his guilt."

"There are two men near him," I said, "who have not the appearance of criminals at all. What have they done?"

"They are not felons, but two soldiers put in here for a week for disorderly conduct."

"What a shame," I cried, "to degrade them in this manner! What good can it do?"

"Oh," said he, laughing; "it will make them desert to the States the moment they get out."

"And those two little boys; what are they here for?"

"For murder!" whispered he.

I almost sprang from my seat; it appeared too dreadful to be true.

"Yes," he continued. "That child to the right is in for shooting his sister. The other, to the left, for killing a boy of his own age with a hoe, and burying him under the roots of a fallen tree. Both of these boys come from the neighbourhood of Peterboro'. Your district, by the bye, sends fewer convicts to the 'Penitentiary' than any part of the Upper Province."

It was with great pleasure I heard him say this. During a residence of thirteen years at Belleville, there has not been one execution. The county of Hastings is still unstained with the blood of a criminal. There is so little robbery committed in this part of the country, that the thought of thieves or housebreakers never for a moment disturbs our rest. This is not the case in Hamilton and Toronto, where daring acts of housebreaking are of frequent occurrence.

The constant influx of runaway slaves from the States has added greatly to the criminal lists on the frontier. The addition of these people to our population is not much to be coveted. The slave, from his previous habits and education, does not always make a good citizen. During the last assizes at Cobourg, a black man and his wife were condemned to be hung for a most horrible murder, and their son, a young man of twenty years of age, offered the sheriff to hang his own father and mother for a new suit of clothes. Those who laud the black man, and place him above the white, let them produce in the whole annals of human crime a more atrocious one than this! Yet *it was not a hanging matter*.

I heard a gentleman exclaim with honest indignation, when this anecdote was told in his hearing – "If a man were wanting to hang that monster, I would do it myself."

But leaving the male convicts, I must now introduce my reader to the female inmates of this house of woe and crime. At the time of my visit, there were only forty women in the "Penitentiary." This speaks much for the superior moral training of the feebler sex. My chief object in visiting their department was to look at the celebrated murderess, Grace Marks, of whom I had heard a great deal, not only from the public papers, but from the gentleman who defended her upon her trial, and whose able pleading saved her from the gallows, on which her wretched accomplice closed his guilty career.

As many of my English readers may never have heard even the name of this remarkable criminal, it may not be uninteresting to them to give a brief sketch of the events which placed her here.

About eight or nine years ago – I write from memory, and am not very certain as to dates – a young Irish emigrant girl was hired into the service of Captain Kinnaird, an officer on half-pay, who had purchased a farm about thirty miles in the rear of Toronto; but the name of the township, and the county in which it was situated, I have forgotten; but this is of little consequence to my narrative. Both circumstances could be easily ascertained by the curious. The captain had been living for some time on very intimate terms with his housekeeper, a handsome young woman of the name of Hannah Montgomery, who had been his servant of all work. Her familiarity with her master, who, it appears, was a very fine-looking, gentlemanly person, had rendered her very impatient of her former menial employments, and she soon became virtually the mistress of the house. Grace Marks was hired to wait upon her, and perform all the coarse drudgery that Hannah considered herself too fine a lady to do.

While Hannah occupied the parlour with her master, and sat at his table, her insolent airs of superiority aroused the jealousy and envy of Grace Marks, and the man-servant, Macdermot, who considered themselves quite superior to their self-elected mistress. Macdermot was the son of respectable parents; but from being a wild, ungovernable boy, he became a bad, vicious man, and early abandoned the parental roof to enlist for a soldier. He was soon tired of his new profession, and, deserting from his regiment, escaped detection, and emigrated to Canada. Having no means of his own, he was glad to engage with Captain Kinnaird as his servant, to whom his character and previous habits were unknown.

These circumstances, together with what follows, were

drawn from his confession, made to Mr. Mac——ie, who had conducted his defence, the night previous to his execution. Perhaps it will be better to make him the narrator of his own story.

"Grace Marks was hired by Captain Kinnaird to wait upon his housekeeper, a few days after I entered his service. She was a pretty girl, and very smart about her work, but of a silent, sullen temper. It was very difficult to know when she was pleased. Her age did not exceed seventeen years. After the work of the day was over, she and I generally were left to ourselves in the kitchen, Hannah being entirely taken up with her master. Grace was very jealous of the difference made between her and the housekeeper, whom she hated, and to whom she was often very insolent and saucy. Her whole conversation to me was on this subject. 'What is she better than us?' she would say, 'that she is to be treated like a lady, and eat and drink of the best. She is not better born than we are, or better educated. I will not stay here to be domineered over by her. Either she or I must soon leave this.' Every little complaint Hannah made of me, was repeated to me with cruel exaggerations, till my dander was up, and I began to regard the unfortunate woman as our common enemy. The good looks of Grace had interested me in her cause; and though there was something about the girl that I could not exactly like, I had been a very lawless, dissipated fellow, and if a woman was young and pretty, I cared very little about her character. Grace was sullen and proud, and not very easily won over to my purpose; but in order to win her liking, if possible, I gave a ready ear to all her discontented repinings.

"One day Captain Kinnaird went to Toronto, to draw his half-year's pay, and left word with Hannah that he would be back by noon the next day. She had made some complaint against us to him, and he had promised to pay us off on his return. This had come to the ears of Grace, and her hatred to the housekeeper was increased to a tenfold degree. I take heaven to witness, that I had no designs against the life of the unfortunate woman when my master left the house.

"Hannah went out in the afternoon, to visit some friends she had in the neighbourhood, and left Grace and I alone together. This was an opportunity too good to be lost, and, instead of minding our work, we got recapitulating our fancied wrongs over some of the captain's whisky. I urged my suit to Grace; but she would not think of anything, or listen to anything, but the insults and injuries she had received from Hannah, and her burning thirst for revenge. 'Dear me,' said I, half in jest, 'if you hate her so much as all that, say but the word, and I will soon rid you of her for ever.'

"I had not the least idea that she would take me at my word. Her eyes flashed with a horrible light. 'You dare not do it!' she replied, with a scornful toss of her head.

" 'Dare not do what?'

" 'Kill that woman for me!' she whispered.

" 'You don't know what I dare, or what I dar'n't do!' said I, drawing a little back from her. 'If you will promise to run off with me afterwards, I will see what I can do with her.'

" 'I'll do anything you like; but you must first kill her.'

" 'You are not in earnest, Grace?'

" 'I mean what I say!'

" 'How shall we be able to accomplish it? She is away now, and she may not return before her master comes back.'

" 'Never doubt her. She will be back to see after the house, and that we are in no mischief.'

" 'She sleeps with you?'

" 'Not always. She will to-night.'

" 'I will wait till you are asleep, and then I will kill her with a blow of the axe on the head. It will be over in a minute. Which side of the bed does she lie on?'

" 'She always sleeps on the side nearest the wall, and she bolts the door the last thing before she puts out the light. But I will manage both these difficulties for you. I will pretend to have the toothache very bad, and will ask to sleep next the wall to-night. She is kind to the sick, and will not refuse me; and after she is asleep, I will steal out at the foot of the bed, and unbolt the door. If you are true to your promise, you need not fear that I shall neglect mine.'

"I looked at her with astonishment. 'Good God!' thought I, 'can this be a woman? A pretty, soft-looking woman too – and a mere girl! What a heart she must have!' I felt equally tempted to tell her she was a devil, and that I would have nothing to do with such a horrible piece of business; but she looked so handsome, that somehow or another I yielded to the temptation, though it was not without a struggle; for conscience loudly warned me not to injure one who had never injured me.

"Hannah came home to supper, and she was unusually agreeable, and took her tea with us in the kitchen, and laughed and chatted as merrily as possible. And Grace, in order to hide the wicked thoughts working in her mind, was very pleasant too, and they went laughing to bed, as if they were the best friends in the world.

"I sat by the kitchen fire after they were gone, with the axe between my knees, trying to harden my heart to commit the murder; but for a long time I could not bring myself to do it. I thought over all my past life. I had been a bad, disobedient son – a dishonest, wicked man; but I had never shed blood. I had often felt sorry for the error of my ways, and had even vowed amendment, and prayed God to forgive me, and make a better man of me for the time to come. And now, here I was, at the instigation of a young girl, contemplating the death of a fellow-creature, with whom I had been laughing and talking on apparently friendly terms a few minutes ago. Oh, it was dreadful, too dreadful to be true! and then I prayed God to remove the temptation from me, and to convince me of my sin. 'Ah, but,' whispered the devil, 'Grace Marks will laugh at you. She will twit you with your want of resolution, and say that she is the better man of the two.'

"I sprang up, and listened at their door, which opened

into the kitchen. All was still. I tried the door; – for the damnation of my soul, it was open. I had no need of a candle, the moon was at full; there was no curtain to their window, and it shone directly upon the bed, and I could see their features as plainly as by the light of day. Grace was either sleeping, or pretending to sleep – I think the latter, for there was a sort of fiendish smile upon her lips. The housekeeper had yielded to her request, and was lying with her head out over the bed-clothes, in the best possible manner for receiving a death-blow upon her temples. She had a sad, troubled look upon her handsome face; and once she moved her hand, and said 'Oh dear!' I wondered whether she was dreaming of any danger to herself and the man she loved. I raised the axe to give the death-blow, but my arm seemed held back by an invisible hand. It was the hand of God. I turned away from the bed, and left the room; I could not do it. I sat down by the embers of the fire, and cursed my own folly. I made a second attempt – a third – and fourth; yes, even to a ninth – and my purpose was each time defeated. God seemed to fight for the poor creature; and the last time I left the room I swore, with a great oath, that if she did not die till I killed her, she might live on till the day of judgment. I threw the axe on to the wood heap in the shed, and went to bed, and soon fell fast asleep.

"In the morning, I was coming into the kitchen to light the fire, and met Grace Marks with the pails in her hand, going out to milk the cows. As she passed me, she gave me a poke with the pail in the ribs, and whispered with a sneer, 'Arn't you a coward!'

"As she uttered those words, the devil, against whom I had fought all night, entered into my heart, and transformed me into a demon. All feelings of remorse and mercy forsook me from that instant, and darker and deeper plans of murder and theft flashed through my brain. 'Go and milk the cows,' said I with a bitter laugh, 'and you shall soon see whether I am the coward you take me for.' She went out to milk, and I went in to murder the unsuspicious housekeeper.

"I found her at the sink in the kitchen, washing her face in a tin basin. I had the fatal axe in my hand, and without pausing for an instant to change my mind – for had I stopped to think, she would have been living to this day – I struck her a heavy blow on the back of the head with my axe. She fell to the ground at my feet without uttering a word; and, opening the trap-door that led from the kitchen into a cellar where we kept potatoes and other stores, I hurled her down, closed the door, and wiped away the perspiration that was streaming down my face. I then looked at the axe and laughed. 'Yes; I have tasted blood now, and this murder will not be the last. Grace Marks, you have raised the devil – take care of yourself now!'

"She came in with her pails, looking as innocent and demure as the milk they contained. She turned pale when her eye met mine. I have no doubt but that I looked the fiend her taunt had made me.

" 'Where's Hannah?' she asked, in a faint voice.

" 'Dead,' said I. 'What! are you turned coward now?'

" 'Macdermot, you look dreadful. I am afraid of *you*, not of her.'

" 'Aha, my girl! you should have thought of that before. The hound that laps blood once will lap again. You have taught me how to kill, and I don't care who, or how many I kill now. When Kinnaird comes home I will put a ball through his brain, and send him to keep company below with the housekeeper.'

"She put down the pails, – she sprang towards me, and, clinging to my arm, exclaimed in frantic tones –

" 'You won't kill him?'

" 'By –, I will! why should he escape more than Hannah? And hark you, girl, if you dare to breathe a word to any one of my intention, or tell to any one, by word or sign, what I have done, I'll kill you!'

"She trembled like a leaf. Yes, that young demon trembled. 'Don't kill me,' she whined, 'don't kill me, Macdermot! I swear that I will not betray you; and oh, don't kill him!'

" 'And why the devil do you want me to spare him?'

" 'He is so handsome!'

" 'Pshaw!'

" 'So good-natured!'

" 'Especially to you. Come, Grace; no nonsense. If I had thought that you were jealous of your master and Hannah, I would have been the last man on earth to have killed her. You belong to me now; and though I believe that the devil has given me a bad bargain in you, yet, such as you are, I will stand by you. And now, strike a light and follow me into the cellar. You must help me to put Hannah out of sight.'

"She never shed a tear, but she looked dogged and sullen, and did as I bid her.

"That cellar presented a dreadful spectacle. I can hardly bear to recall it now; but then, when my hands were still red with her blood, it was doubly terrible. Hannah Montgomery was not dead, as I had thought; the blow had only stunned her. She had partially recovered her senses, and was kneeling on one knee as we descended the ladder with the light. I don't know if she heard us, for she must have been blinded with the blood that was flowing down her face; but she certainly heard us, and raised her clasped hands, as if to implore mercy.

"I turned to Grace. The expression of her livid face was even more dreadful than that of the unfortunate woman. She uttered no cry, but she put her hand to her head, and said, –

" 'God has damned me for this.'

" 'Then you have nothing more to fear,' says I. 'Give me that handkerchief off your neck.' She gave it without a word. I threw myself upon the body of the housekeeper, and planting my knee on her breast, I tied the handkerchief round her throat in a single tie, giving Grace one end to hold, while I drew the other tight enough to finish my terrible work. Her eyes literally started from her head, she gave one groan, and all was over. I then cut the body in four pieces, and turned a large washtub over them.

" 'Now, Grace, you may come up and get my breakfast.'

" 'Yes, Mr. M——.' You will not perhaps believe me, yet I assure you that we went up-stairs and ate a good breakfast; and I laughed with Grace at the consternation the captain would be in when he found that Hannah was absent.

"During the morning a pedlar called, who travelled the country with second-hand articles of clothing, taking farm produce in exchange for his wares. I bought of him two good linen-breasted shirts, which had been stolen from some gentleman by his housekeeper. While I was chatting with the pedlar, I remarked that Grace had left the house, and I saw her through the kitchen-window talking to a young lad by the well, who often came across to borrow an old gun from my master to shoot ducks. I called to her to come in, which she appeared to me to do very reluctantly. I felt that I was in her power, and I was horribly afraid of her betraying me in order to save her own and the captain's life. I now hated her from my very soul, and could have killed her without the least pity or remorse.

" 'What do you want, Macdermot!' she said sullenly.

" 'I want you. I dare not trust you out of my sight. I know what you are, – you are plotting mischief against me; but if you betray me I will be revenged, if I have to follow you to – for that purpose.'

" 'Why do you doubt my word, Macdermot? Do you think I want to hang myself?'

" 'No, not yourself, but me. You are too bad to be trusted. What were you saying just now to that boy?'

" 'I told him that the captain was not at home, and I dared not lend him the gun.'

" 'You were right. The gun will be wanted at home.'

"She shuddered and turned away. It seems that she had had enough of blood, and shewed some feeling at last. I kept my eye upon her, and would not suffer her for a moment out of my sight.

"At noon the captain drove into the yard, and I went out to take the horse. Before he had time to alight, he asked for Hannah. I told him that she was out, – that she went off the day before, and had not returned, but that we expected her in every minute.

"He was very much annoyed, and said that she had no business to leave the house during his absence, – that he would give her a good rating when she came home.

"Grace asked if she should get his breakfast?

"He said, 'He wanted none. He would wait till Hannah came back, and then he would take a cup of coffee.'

"He then went into the parlour; and throwing himself down upon the sofa, commenced reading a magazine he had brought with him from Toronto.

"'I thought he would miss the young lady,' said Grace. 'He has no idea how close she is to him at this moment. I wonder why I could not make him as good a cup of coffee as Hannah. I have often made it for him when he did not know it. But what is sweet from her hand, would be poison from mine. But I have had my revenge!'

"Dinner time came, and out came the captain to the kitchen, book in hand.

"'Isn't Hannah back yet?'

"'No, Sir.'

"'It's strange. Which way did she go?'

"'She did not tell us where she was going; but said that, as you were out, it would be a good opportunity of visiting an old friend.'

"'When did she say she would be back?"

"'We expected her last night,' said Grace.

"'Something must have happened to the girl, Macdermot,' turning to me. 'Put the saddle on my riding horse. I will go among the neighbours, and inquire if they have seen her.'

"Grace exchanged glances with me.

" 'Will you not stay till after dinner, Sir?'

" 'I don't care,' he cried impatiently, 'a – for dinner. I feel too uneasy about the girl to eat. Macdermot, be quick and saddle Charley; and you, Grace, come and tell me when he is at the door.'

"He went back into the parlour, and put on his riding-coat; and I went into the harness-house, not to obey his orders, but to plan his destruction.

"I perceived that it was more difficult to conceal a murder than I had imagined; that the inquiries he was about to make would arouse suspicion among the neigh-bours, and finally lead to a discovery. The only way to prevent this was to murder him, take what money he had brought with him from Toronto, and be off with Grace to the States. Whatever repugnance I might have felt at the commission of this fresh crime, was drowned in the selfish necessity of self-preservation. My plans were soon matured, and I hastened to put them in a proper train.

"I first loaded the old duck gun with ball, and putting it behind the door of the harness-house, I went into the parlour. I found the captain lying on the sofa reading, his hat and gloves beside him on the table. He started up as I entered.

" 'Is the horse ready?'

" 'Not yet, Sir. Some person has been in during the night, and cut your new English saddle almost to pieces. I wish you would step out and look at it. I cannot put it on Charley in its present state.'

" 'Don't bother me,' he cried angrily; 'it is in your charge, – you are answerable for that. Who the devil would think it worth their while to break into the harness-house to cut a saddle, when they could have carried it off entirely? Let me have none of your tricks, Sir! You must have done it yourself!'

" 'That is not very likely, Captain Kinnaird. At any rate, it would be a satisfaction to me if you would come and look at it.'

" 'I'm in too great a hurry. Put on the old one.'

"I still held the door in my hand. 'It's only a step from here to the harness-house.'

"He rose reluctantly, and followed me into the kitchen. The harness-house formed part of a lean-to off the kitchen, and you went down two steps into it. He went on before me, and as he descended the steps, I clutched the gun I had left behind the door, took my aim between his shoulders, and shot him through the heart. He staggered forward and fell, exclaiming as he did so, 'O God, I am shot!'

"In a few minutes he was lying in the cellar, beside our other victim. Very little blood flowed from the wound; he bled internally. He had on a very fine shirt; and after rifling his person, and possessing myself of his pocket-book, I took off his shirt, and put on the one I had bought of the pedlar."

"Then," cried Mr. Mac——ie, to whom this confession was made, "that was how the pedlar was supposed to have had a hand in the murder. That circumstance confused the evidence, and nearly saved your life."

"It was just as I have told you," said Macdermot.

"And tell me, Macdermot, the reason of another circumstance that puzzled the whole court. How came that magazine, which was found in the housekeeper's bed saturated with blood, in that place, and so far from the spot where the murder was committed?"

"That, too, is easily explained, though it was such a riddle to you gentlemen of the law. When the captain came out to look at the saddle, he had the book open in his hand. When he was shot, he clapped the book to his breast with both his hands. Almost all the blood that flowed from it was caught in that book. It required some force on my part to take it from his grasp after he was dead. Not knowing what to do with it, I flung it into the housekeeper's bed. While I harnessed the riding-horse into his new buggy, Grace collected all the valuables in the house. You know, Sir, that we got safe on board the steamer at Toronto; but, owing to an unfortunate delay, we were apprehended, sent to jail, and condemned to die.

"Grace, you tell me, has been reprieved, and her sentence commuted into confinement in the Penitentiary for life. This seems very unjust to me, for she is certainly more criminal than I am. If she had not instigated me to commit the murder, it never would have been done. But the priest tells me that I shall not be hung, and not to make myself uneasy on that score."

"Macdermot," said Mr. Mac——ie, "it is useless to flatter you with false hopes. You will suffer the execution of your sentence to-morrow, at eight o'clock, in front of the jail. I have seen the order sent by the governor to the sheriff, and that was my reason for visiting you to-night. I was not satisfied in my own mind of your guilt. What you have told me has greatly relieved my mind; and I must add, if ever man deserved his sentence, you do yours."

"When this unhappy man was really convinced that I was in earnest – that he must pay with his life the penalty of his crime," continued Mr. Mac——ie, "his abject cowardice and the mental agonies he endured were too terrible to witness. He dashed himself on the floor of his cell, and shrieked and raved like a maniac, declaring that he could not, and would not die; that the law had no right to murder a man's soul as well as his body, by giving him no time for repentance; that if he was hung like a dog, Grace Marks, in justice, ought to share his fate. Finding that all I could say to him had no effect in producing a better frame of mind, I called in the chaplain, and left the sinner to his fate.

"A few months ago I visited the Penitentiary; and as my pleading had been the means of saving Grace from the same doom, I naturally felt interested in her present state. I was permitted to see and speak to her and Mrs. M——. I never shall forget the painful feelings I experienced during this interview. She had been five years in the Penitentiary, but still retained a remarkably youthful appearance. The sullen assurance that had formerly marked her coun-

tenance, had given place to a sad and humbled expression.
She had lost much of her former good looks, and seldom
raised her eyes from the ground.

"'Well, Grace,' I said, 'how is it with you now?'

"'Bad enough, Sir,' she answered, with a sigh; 'I ought
to feel grateful to you for all the trouble you took on my
account. I thought you my friend then, but you were the
worst enemy I ever had in my life.'

"'How is that, Grace?'

"'Oh, Sir, it would have been better for me to have died
with Macdermot than to have suffered for years, as I have
done, the torments of the damned. Oh, Sir, my misery is
too great for words to describe! I would gladly submit to
the most painful death, if I thought that it would put an
end to the pangs I daily endure. But though I have
repented of my wickedness with bitter tears, it has pleased
God that I should never again know a moment's peace.
Since I helped Macdermot to strangle Hannah Montgomery, her terrible face and those horrible bloodshot eyes
have never left me for a moment. They glare upon me by
night and day, and when I close my eyes in despair, I see
them looking into my soul – it is impossible to shut them
out. If I am at work, in a few minutes that dreadful head is
in my lap. If I look up to get rid of it, I see it in the far
corner of the room. At dinner, it is in my plate, or grin-
ning between the persons who sit opposite to me at table.
Every object that meets my sight takes the same dreadful
form; and at night – at night – in the silence and loneliness
of my cell, those blazing eyes make my prison as light as
day. No, not as day – they have a terribly hot glare, that
has not the appearance of anything in this world. And
when I sleep, that face just hovers above my own, its eyes
just opposite to mine; so that when I awake with a shriek
of agony, I find them there. Oh! this is hell, Sir – these are
the torments of the damned! Were I in that fiery place, my
punishment could not be greater than this.'

"The poor creature turned away, and I left her, for who
could say a word of comfort to such grief? it was a matter

solely between her own conscience and God."

Having heard this terrible narrative, I was very anxious to behold this unhappy victim of remorse. She passed me on the stairs as I proceeded to the part of the building where the women were kept; but on perceiving a stranger, she turned her head away, so that I could not get a glimpse of her face.

Having made known my wishes to the matron, she very kindly called her in to perform some trifling duty in the ward, so that I might have an opportunity of seeing her. She is a middle-sized woman, with a slight graceful figure. There is an air of hopeless melancholy in her face which is very painful to contemplate. Her complexion is fair, and must, before the touch of hopeless sorrow paled it, have been very brilliant. Her eyes are a bright blue, her hair auburn, and her face would be rather handsome were it not for the long curved chin, which gives, as it always does to most persons who have this facial defect, a cunning, cruel expression.

Grace Marks glances at you with a sidelong stealthy look; her eye never meets yours, and after a furtive regard, it invariably bends its gaze upon the ground. She looks like a person rather above her humble station, and her conduct during her stay in the Penitentiary was so unexceptionable, that a petition was signed by all the influential gentlemen in Kingston, which released her from her long imprisonment. She entered the service of the governor of the Penitentiary, but the fearful hauntings of her brain have terminated in madness. She is now in the asylum at Toronto; and as I mean to visit it when there, I may chance to see this remarkable criminal again. Let us hope that all her previous guilt may be attributed to the incipient workings of this frightful malady.

TO THE WIND.

"Stern spirit of air, wild voice of the sky!
    Thy shout rends the heavens, and earth trembles with dread;

In hoarse hollow murmurs the billows reply,
   And ocean is roused in his cavernous bed.

"On thy broad rushing pinions destruction rides free,
   Unfettered they sweep the wide deserts of air;
The hurricane bursts over mountain and sea,
   And havoc and death mark thy track with despair.

"When the thunder lies cradled within its dark cloud,
   And earth and her tribes crouch in silence and dread,
Thy voice shakes the forest, the tall oak is bowed,
   That for ages had shook at the tempest its head.

"When the Lord bowed the heavens, and came down in his
     might,
   Sublimely around were the elements cast;
At his feet lay the dense rolling shadows of night,
   But the power of Omnipotence rode on the blast.

"From the whirlwind he spake, when man wrung with pain,
   In the strength of his anguish dare challenge his God;
'Mid its thunders he told him his reasoning was vain,
   Till he bowed to correction, and kiss'd the just rod.

"When call'd by the voice of the prophet of old,
   In the 'valley of bones,' to breathe over the dead;
Like the sands of the sea, could their number be told,
   They started to life when the mandate had sped.

"Those chill mouldering ashes thy summons could bind,
   And the dark icy slumbers of ages gave way;
The spirit of life took the wings of the wind,
   Rekindling the souls of the children of clay.

"Shrill trumpet of God! I shrink at thy blast,
   That shakes the firm hills to their centre with dread,
And have thought in that conflict – earth's saddest and last –
   That thy deep chilling sigh will awaken the dead!"

ELEVEN

Michael Macbride

"His day of life is closing – the long night
Of dreamless rest a dusky shadow throws,
Between the dying and the things of earth,
Enfolding in a chill oblivious pall
The last sad struggles of a broken heart.
Yes! ere the rising of to-morrow's sun,
The bitter grief that brought him to this pass
Will be forgotten in the sleep of death."

S.M.

W E LEFT Kingston at three o'clock, P.M., in the "Pass-port," for Toronto. From her commander, Captain Towhy, a fine British heart of oak, we received the kindest attention; his intelligent conversation, and interesting descriptions of the many lands he had visited during a long acquaintance with the sea, greatly lightening the tedium of the voyage.

When once fairly afloat on the broad blue inland sea of Ontario, you soon lose sight of the shores, and could imagine yourself sailing on a calm day on the wide ocean. There is something, however, wanting to complete the deception, – the invigorating freshness – the peculiar smell of the salt water, that is so exhilarating, and which produces a sensation of freedom and power that is never experienced on these fresh-water lakes. They want the depth, the

fulness, the grandeur of the ocean, though the wide
expanse of water and sky are, in all other respects, the
same.

The boat seldom touches at any place before she
reaches Cobourg, which is generally at night. We stopped
a short time at the wharf to put passengers and freight on
shore, and to receive fresh passengers and freight in
return. The sight of this town, which I had not seen for
many years, recalled forcibly to my mind a melancholy
scene in which I chanced to be an actor. I will relate it
here.

When we first arrived in Canada, in 1832, we remained
for three weeks at an hotel in this town, though, at that
period, it was a place of much less importance than it is at
present, deserving little more than the name of a pretty
rising village, pleasantly situated on the shores of Lake
Ontario. The rapid improvement of the country has converted Cobourg into a thriving, populous town, and it has
trebled its population during the lapse of twenty years. A
residence in a house of public entertainment, to those who
have been accustomed to the quiet and retirement of a
country life, is always unpleasant, and to strangers as we
were, in a foreign land, it was doubly repugnant to our
feelings. In spite of all my wise resolutions not to give way
to despondency, but to battle bravely against the change
in my circumstances, I found myself daily yielding up my
whole heart and soul to that worst of all maladies, home
sickness.

It was during these hours of loneliness and dejection,
while my husband was absent examining farms in the
neighbourhood, that I had the good fortune to form an
acquaintance with Mrs. C——, a Canadian lady, who
boarded with her husband in the same hotel. My new
friend was a young woman agreeable in person, and perfectly unaffected in her manners, which were remarkably
frank and kind. Hers was the first friendly face I had seen
in the colony, and it will ever be remembered by me with
affection and respect.

One afternoon while alone in my chamber, getting my baby, a little girl of six months old, to sleep, and thinking many sad thoughts, and shedding some bitter tears for the loss of the dear country and friends I had left for ever, a slight tap at the door roused me from my painful reveries, and Mrs. C—— entered the room. Like most of the Canadian women, my friend was small of stature, slight and delicately formed, and dressed with the smartness and neatness so characteristic of the females of this continent, who, if they lack some of the accomplishments of English women, far surpass them in their taste in dress, their choice of colours, and the graceful and becoming manner in which they wear their clothes. If my young friend had a weakness, it was on this point; but as her husband was engaged in a lucrative mercantile business, and they had no family, it was certainly excusable. At this moment her pretty neat little figure was a welcome and interesting object to the home-sick emigrant.

"What! always in tears," said she, carefully closing the door. "What pleasure it would give me to see you more cheerful! This constant repining will never do."

"The sight of you has made me feel better already," said I, wiping my eyes, and trying to force a smile. "M—— is away on a farm-hunting expedition, and I have been alone all day. Can you wonder, then, that I am so depressed? Memory is my worst companion; for by constantly recalling scenes of past happiness, she renders me discontented with the present, and hopeless of the future, and it will require all your kind sympathy to reconcile me to Canada."

"You will like it better by and by; a new country always improves upon acquaintance."

"Ah, never! Did I only consult my own feelings, I would be off by the next steam-boat for England; but then – my husband, my child, our scanty means. Yes! yes! I must submit, but I find it a hard task."

"We have all our trials, Mrs. M——; and, to tell you the truth, I do not feel in the best spirits myself this afternoon. I came to ask you what I am certain you will consider a strange question."

This was said in a tone so unusually serious, that I looked up from the cradle in surprise, which her solemn aspect, and pale, tearful face, did not tend to diminish. Before I could ask the cause of her dejection, she added quickly –

"Dare you read a chapter from the Bible to a dying man?"

"Dare I? Yes, certainly! Who is ill? Who is dying?"

"It's a sad story," she continued, wiping the tears from her kind eyes. "I will tell you, however, what I know of it, just to satisfy you as to the propriety of my request. There is a poor young man in this house who is very sick – dying, I believe, of consumption. He came here about three weeks ago, without food, without money, and in a dreadfully emaciated state. He took our good landlord, Mr. S——, on one side, and told him how he was situated, and begged that he would give him something to eat and a night's lodging, promising that if ever he was restored to health, he would repay the debt in work. You know what a kind, humane man, Mr. S—— is, although," she added, with a sly smile, "*he is a Yankee*, and so am I by right of parentage, though not of birth. Mr. S—— saw at a glance that the suppliant was an object of real charity, and instantly complied with his request. Without asking further particulars, he gave him a good bed, sent him up a bowl of hot soup, and bade him not distress himself about the future, but try and get a good night's rest. The next day, the young man was too ill to leave his chamber. Mr. S—— sent for old Dr. Morton, who, after examining the lad, informed his employer that he was in the last stage of consumption, and had not many days to live, and it would be advisable for Mr. S—— to have him removed to the hospital – (a pitiful shed erected for emigrants who may chance to arrive ill with the cholera). Mr. S—— not only refused to send the young man away, but has nursed him with the greatest care, his wife and daughters taking it by turns to sit up nightly with the poor patient."

My friend said nothing about her own attendance on the invalid, which, I afterwards learned from Mrs. S——, had been unremitting.

"And what account does the lad give of himself?" said I.

"All that we know about him is, that his name is Macbride,* and that he is nephew to Mr. C——, of Peterboro', an Irishman by birth, and a Catholic by religion. Some violent altercation took place between him and his uncle a short time ago, which induced Michael to leave his house, and look out for a situation for himself. Hearing that his parents had arrived in this country, and were on their way to Peterboro', he came down as far as Cobourg in the hope of meeting them, when his steps were arrested by poverty and sickness on this threshold.

"By a singular coincidence, his mother came to the hotel yesterday evening to inquire the way to Peterboro', and Mr. S—— found out, from her conversation, that she was the mother of the poor lad, and he instantly conducted her to the bed-side of her son. I was sitting with him when the interview between him and his mother took place, and I assure you that it was almost too much for my nerves – his joy and gratitude were so great at once more beholding his parent, while the grief and distraction of the poor woman, on seeing him in a dying state, was agonising; and she gave vent to her feelings in uttering the most hearty curses against the country, and the persons who by their unkindness had been the cause of his sickness. The young man seemed shocked at the unfeminine conduct of his mother, and begged me to excuse the rude manner in which she answered me; 'for,' says he, 'she is ignorant and beside herself, and does not know what she is saying or doing.'

*Michael Macbride was not the real name of this poor young man, but is one substituted by the author.

"Instead of expressing the least gratitude to Mr. S——
for the attention bestowed on her son, by some strange
perversion of intellect she seems to regard him and us as
his especial enemies. Last night she ordered us from his
room, and declared that her 'precious *bhoy* was not going
to die like a *hathen*, surrounded by a parcel of heretics;'
and she sent off a man on horseback for the priest and for
his uncle – the very man from whose house he fled, and
whom she accuses of being the cause of her son's death.
Michael anticipates the arrival of Mr. C—— with feelings
bordering on despair, and prays that God may end his
sufferings before he reaches Cobourg.

"Last night Mrs. Macbride sat up with Michael herself,
and would not allow us to do the least thing for him. This
morning her fierce temper seems to have subsided, until
her son awoke from a broken and feverish sleep, and
declared that he would not die a Roman Catholic, and
earnestly requested Mr. S—— to send for a Protestant
clergyman. This gave rise to a violent scene between Mrs.
Macbride and her son, which ended in Mr. S—— sending
for Mr. B——, the clergyman of our village, who, unfortunately, had left this morning for Toronto, and is not
expected home for several days. Michael eagerly asked if
there was any person present who would read to him from
the Protestant Bible. This excited in the mother such a fit
of passion, that none of us dared attempt the task. I then
thought of you, that, as a perfect stranger, she might
receive you in a less hostile manner. If you are not afraid
to encounter the fierce old woman, do make the attempt
for the sake of the dying creature, who languishes to hear
the words of life. I will watch the baby while you are
gone."

"She is asleep, and needs no watching. I will go as you
seem so anxious about it," and I took my pocket Bible
from the table. "But you must go with me, for I do not
know my way in this strange house."

"Carefully closing the door upon the sleeping child, I
followed the light steps of Mrs. C—— along the passage,

until we reached the head of the main staircase, then, turning to the right, we entered the large public ball-room. In the first chamber of many that opened into this spacious apartment we found the object that we sought.

Stretched upon a low bed, with a feather fan in his hand, to keep off the flies that hovered in tormenting clusters round his head, lay the dying Michael Macbride.

The face of the young man was wasted by disease and mental anxiety; and if the features were not positively handsome, they were well and harmoniously defined, and a look of intelligence and sensibility pervaded his counte-nance, which greatly interested me in his behalf. His face was deathly pale, as pale as marble, and his large sunken eyes shone with unnatural brilliancy, their long dark lashes adding an expression of intense melancholy to the patient endurance of suffering that marked his fine coun-tenance. His nose was shrunk and drawn in about the nostrils, his feverish lips apart, in order to admit a free passage for the labouring breath, their bright red glow affording a painful contrast to the ghastly glitter of the brilliant white teeth within. The thick black curls that clustered round his high forehead were moist with perspi-ration, and the same cold unwholesome dew trickled in large drops down his hollow temples. It was impossible to mistake these signs of approaching dissolution – it was evident to all present that death was not far distant.

An indescribable awe crept over me. He looked so tran-quil, so sublimed by suffering, that I felt my self unworthy to be his teacher.

"Michael," I said, taking the long thin white hand that lay so listlessly on the coverlid, "I am sorry to see you so ill."

He looked at me attentively for a few minutes. – "Do not say sorry, Ma'am; rather say glad. I am glad to get away from this bad world – young as I am – I am so weary of it."

He sighed deeply, and tears filled his eyes.

"I heard that you wished some one to read to you."

"Yes, the Bible!" he cried, trying to raise himself in the bed, while his eager eyes were turned to me with an earnest, imploring expression.

"I have it here. Are you able to read it for yourself?"

"I can read – but my eyes are so dim. The shadows of death float between me and the world; I can no longer see objects distinctly. But oh, Madam, if my soul were light, I should not heed this blindness. But all is dark here," laying his hand on his breast, – "dark as the grave."

I opened the sacred book, but my own tears for a moment obscured the page. While I was revolving in my own mind what would be the best to read to him, the book was rudely wrenched from my hand by a tall, gaunt woman, who just then entered the room.

"Och! what do you mane by disturbing him in his dying moments wid yer thrash? It is not the likes o' you that shall throuble his sowl! The praste will come and administher consolation to him in his last exthremity."

Michael shook his head, and turned his face sorrowfully to the wall.

"Oh, mother," he murmured, "is that the way you treat the lady?"

"Lady, or no lady, and I mane no disrispict; it is not for the like o' her to take this on hersel'. If she will be rading, let her rade this," and she tried to force a book of devotional prayers into my hand. Michael raised himself, and with an impatient gesture exclaimed –

"Not that – not that! It speaks no comfort to me. I will not listen to it. Mother, mother! do not stand between me and my God. I know that you love me – that what you do is done for the best; but the voice of conscience will be heard above your voice. I hunger and thirst to hear the word as it stands in the Bible, and I cannot die in peace unsatisfied. For the love of Christ, Ma'am, read a few words of comfort to a dying sinner!"

Here the mother again interposed.

"My good woman," I said gently putting her back, "you hear your son's earnest request. If you really love him, you will offer no opposition to his wishes. It is not a question of creeds that is here to be determined, as to which is the best – yours or mine. I trust that all the faithful followers of Christ, however named, hold the same faith, and will be saved by the same means. I shall make no comment on what I read to your son. The Bible is its own interpreter. The Spirit of God, by whom it was dictated, will make it clear to his comprehension. Michael, shall I commence now?"

"Yes," he replied, "with the blessing of God!"

After putting up a short prayer I commenced reading, and continued to do so until night, taking care to select those portions of Scripture most applicable to his case. Never did human creature listen with more earnestness to the words of truth. Often he repeated whole texts after me, clasping his hands together in a sort of ecstasy, while tears streamed from his eyes. The old woman glared upon me from a far corner, and muttered over her beads, as if they were a spell to secure her against some diabolical art. When I could no longer see to read, Michael took my hand, and said with great earnestness –

"May God bless you, Madam! You have made me very happy. It is all clear to me now. In Christ alone I shall obtain mercy and forgiveness for my sins. It is his righteousness, and not any good works of my own, that will save me. Death no longer appears so dreadful to me. I can now die in peace."

"You believe that God will pardon you, Michael, for Christ's sake; but have you forgiven all your enemies?"

I said this in order to try his sincerity, for I had heard that he entertained hard thoughts against his uncle.

He covered his face with his thin, wasted hands, and did not answer for some minutes; at length he looked up with a calm smile upon his lips, and said –

"Yes, I have forgiven all – even *him!* –"

Oh, how much was contained in the stress laid so strongly and sadly upon that little word *Him!* How I longed to hear the story of his wrongs from his own lips!

but he was too weak and exhausted for me to urge such a request. Just then Dr. Morton came in, and after standing for some minutes at the bed-side, regarding his patient with fixed attention, he felt his pulse, spoke a few kind words, gave some trifling order to his mother and Mrs. C——, and left the room. Struck by the solemnity of his manner, I followed him into the outer apartment.

"Excuse the liberty I am taking Dr. Morton; but I feel deeply interested in your patient. Is he better or worse?"

"He is dying. I did not wish to disturb him in his last moments. I can be of no further use to him. Poor lad, it's a pity! he is really a fine young fellow."

I had judged from Michael's appearance that he had not long to live, but I felt inexpressibly shocked to find his end so near. On returning to the sick room, Michael eagerly asked what the doctor thought of him?

I did not answer – I could not.

"I see," he said, "that I must die. I will prepare myself for it. If I live until the morning, will you, Madam, come and read to me again?"

I promised him that I would – or during the night, if he wished it.

"I feel very sleepy," he said. "I have not slept for many nights, but for a few minutes at a time. Thank God, I am entirely free from pain: it is very good of Him to grant me this respite."

His mother and I adjusted his pillows, and in a few seconds he was slumbering as peacefully as a little child.

The feelings of the poor woman seemed softened towards me, and for the first time since I entered the room she shed tears. I asked the age of her son? She told me that he was two-and-twenty. She wrung my hand hard as I left the room, and thanked me for my kindness to her poor *bhoy*.

It was late that night when my husband returned from the country, and we sat for several hours talking over our affairs, and discussing the soil and situation of the various farms he had visited during the day. It was past twelve when we retired to rest, but my sleep was soon disturbed by some one coughing violently, and my thoughts instantly reverted to Michael Macbride, as the hoarse sepulchral sounds echoed through the large empty room beyond which he slept. The coughing continued for some minutes, and I was so much overcome by fatigue and the excitement of the evening that I fell asleep, and did not awake until six o'clock the following morning.

Anxious to hear how the poor invalid had passed the night, I dressed myself and hurried to his chamber.

On entering the ball-room I found the doors and windows all open, as well as the one that led to the sick man's chamber. My foot was arrested on the threshold – for death was there. Yes! that fit of coughing had terminated his life – Michael had expired without a struggle in the arms of his mother.

The gay broad beams of the sun were not admitted into that silent room. The window was open, but the green blinds were carefully closed, admitting a free circulation of air, and just light enough to render the objects within distinctly visible. The body was laid out upon the bed enveloped in a white sheet; the head and hands alone were bare. All traces of sorrow and disease had passed away from the majestic face, that, interesting in life, now looked beautiful and holy in death – and happy, for the seal of heaven seemed visibly impressed upon the pure pale brow. He was at peace, and though tears of human sympathy for a moment dimmed my sight, I could not regret that it was so.

While I still stood in the door-way, Mrs. Macbride, whom I had not observed until then, rose from her knees beside the bed. She seemed hardly in her right mind, and began talking and muttering to herself.

"Och hone! he is dead – my fine bhoy is dead – widout a praste to pray wid him, or bless him in the last hour – wid none of his frinds and relations to lamint iver him, or wake him, but his poor heartbroken mother – Och hone! och hone! that I should ever live to see this day. Get up, my fine bhoy – get up wid ye! Why do you lie there? – owlder folk nor you are abroad in the sunshine. – Get up, and show them how supple you are!"

Then laying her cheek down to the cold cheek of the dead, she exclaimed, amid broken sobs and groans –

"Oh, spake to me – spake to me, Mike – my own Mike – 'tis the mother that axes ye."

There was a deep pause, when the bereaved parent again broke forth –

"Mike, Mike – why did your uncle rare you like a jintleman to bring you to this. Och hone! och hone! – oh, never did I think to see your head lie so low. – My bhoy! my bhoy! – why did you die? – Why did you lave your frinds, and your money, and your good clothes, and your poor owld mother?"

Convulsive sobs again choked her utterance. She flung herself upon the neck of the corpse, and bathed the face and hands of him, who had once been her own, with burning tears.

I now came forward, and offered a few words of consolation. Vain – all in vain. The ear of sorrow is deaf to all save its own agonised moans. Grief is as natural to the human mind as joy, and in their own appointed hour both will have their way.

The grief of this unhappy Irish mother, like the downpouring of a thunder shower, could not be restrained. But her tears soon flowed in less violent gushes – exhaustion rendered her more calm. She sat upon the bed, and looked cautiously round – "Hist! – did not you hear a voice? It was him who spake – yes – it was his own swate voice. I knew he was not dead. See, he moves!" This was the fond vain delusion of maternal love. She took his cold hand, and clasped it to her heart.

"Och hone! – he is gone, and left me for ever and ever. Oh, that my cruel brother was here – that I might point to my murthered child, and curse him to his face!"

"Is Mr. C—— your brother?" said I, taking this opportunity to divert her grief into another channel.

"Yes – yes – he is my brother, bad cess to him! and uncle to the bhoy. Listen to me, and I will tell you some of my mind. It will ease my sorrow, for my poor heart is breaking entirely, and he is there," pointing to the corpse, "and he knows that what I am afther telling you is thrue.

"I came of poor but dacent parints. There was but the two of us, Pat C—— and I. My father rinted a good farm, and he sint Pat to school, and gave him the eddication of a jintleman. Our landlord took a liking for the bhoy, and gave him the manes to emigrate to Canady. This vexed my father intirely, for he had no one barring myself to help him on the farm. Well, by and by, I joined myself to one whom my father did not approve – a bhoy he had hired to work wid him in the fields – an' he wrote to my brother (for my mother had been dead ever since I was a wee thing) to ax him in what manner he had best punish my disobedience; and he jist advises him to turn us off the place. I suffered, wid my husband, the extremes of poverty: we had seven childer, but they all died of the faver, and hard times, save Mike and the two weeny ones. In the midst of our disthress, it plased the Lord to remove my father, widout softenin' his heart towards me. But he left my Mike three hunder pounds, to be his whin he came to a right age; and he appointed my brother Pat guardian to the bhoy.

"My brother returned to Ireland when he got the news of my father's death, in order to get his share of the property, for my father left him the same as he did my son. He took away my bhoy wid him to Canady, in order to make a landed jintleman of him. Och hone! I thought my heart would broken thin, whin he took away my swate bhoy; but I was to live to see a darker day yet."

Here a long burst of passionate weeping interrupted her story.

"Many long years came an' wint, and we niver got the scrape of a pen from my brother to tell us of the bhoy at all at all. He might jist as well have been dead, for aught we knew to the conthrary; but we consowled oursilves wid the thought, that he would niver go about to harm his own flesh and blood.

"At last a letther came, written in Mike's own hand; and a beautiful hand it was that same, – the good God bless him for the throuble he took in makin' it so nate an' aisy for us poor folk to rade. It was full of love and respict to his poor parents, an' he longin' to see them in 'Meriky; but he said he had written by stealth, for he was very unhappy intirely, – that his uncle thrated him hardly, becaze he would not be a praste, – an' wanted to lave him, to work for himsel'; an' he refused to buy him a farm wid the money his grandfather left him, which he was bound by the will to do, as Mike was now of age, an' his own masther.

"Whin we got the word from the lad, we gathered our little all together, an' took passage for Canady, first writin' to Mike whin we should start, an' the name of the vessel; an' that we should wait at Cobourg until sich time as he came to fetch us himsel' to his uncle's place.

"But oh, Ma'am, our throubles had only begun. My poor husband and my youngest bhoy died of the cholera comin' out; an' I saw their prechious bodies cast into the salt, salt saa. Still the hope of seeing Mike consowled me for all my disthress. Poor Pat an' I were worn out entirely whin we got to Kingston, an' I left the child wid a frind, an' came on alone, – I was so eager to see Mike, an' tell him all my throubles; an' there he lies, och hone! my heart, my poor heart, it will break entirely."

"And what caused your son's separation from his uncle?" said I.

The woman shook her head. "The thratement he got from him was too bad. But shure he would not disthress me by saying aught agin my mother's son. Did he not break his heart, and turn him dying an' pinniless on the wide world? An' could he have done worse had he stuck a knife into his heart?"

"Ah!" she continued, with bitterness, "it was the gowld, the dhirty gowld, that kilt my poor bhoy. His uncle knew that if Mike were dead, it would come to Pat as the ne'est in degree, an' he could keep it all to himsel' for the ne'est ten years."

This statement appeared only too probable. Still there was a mystery about the whole affair that required a solution, and it was several years before I accidentally learned the sequel of this sad history.

In the meanwhile the messenger, despatched by the kind Mr. S—— to Peterboro' to inform Michael's uncle of the dying state of his nephew, returned without that worthy, and with this unfeeling message – that Michael Macbride had left him without any just cause, and should receive no consolation from him in his last moments.

Mr. S—— did not inform the poor bereaved widow of her brother's cruel message; but finding that she was unable to defray the expenses attendant on her son's funeral, like a true Samaritan, he supplied them out of his own pocket, and followed the remains of the unhappy stranger that Providence had cast upon his charity to the grave. In accordance with Michael's last request, he was buried in the cemetry of the English church.

Six years after these events took place, Mr. W—— called upon me at our place in Douro, and among other things told me of the death of Michael's uncle, Mr. C——. Many things were mentioned by Mr. W——, who happened to know him, to his disadvantage. "But of all his evil acts," he said, "the worst thing I knew of him was his conduct to his nephew."

"How was that?" said I, as the death-bed of Michael Macbride rose distinctly before me.

"It was a bad business. My housekeeper lived with the old man at the time, and from her I heard all about it. It seems that he had been left guardian to this boy, whom he brought out with him some years ago to this country, together with a little girl about two years younger, who was the child of a daughter of his mother by a former marriage, so that the children were half-cousins to each other. Elizabeth was a modest, clever little creature, and grew up a very pretty girl. Michael was strikingly handsome, had a fine talent for music, and in person and manners was far above his condition. There was some property, to the amount of several hundred pounds, coming to the lad when he reached the age of twenty-one. This legacy had been left him by his grandfather, and Mr. C—— was to invest it in land for the boy's use. This, for reasons best known to himself, he neglected to do, and brought the lad up to the service of the altar, and continually urged him to become a priest. This did not at all accord with Michael's views and wishes, and he obstinately refused to study for the holy office, and told his uncle that he meant to become a farmer as soon as he obtained his majority.

"Living constantly in the same house, and possessing a congeniality of tastes and pursuits, a strong affection had grown up between Michael and his cousin, which circumstance proved the ostensible reason given by Mr. C—— for his ill conduct to the young people, as by the laws of his church they were too near of kin to marry. Finding that their attachment was too strong to be wrenched asunder by threats, and that they had actually formed a design to leave him, and embrace the Protestant faith, he confined the girl to her chamber, without allowing her a fire during a very severe winter. Her constitution, naturally weak, sunk under these trials, and she died early in the spring of 1832, without being allowed the melancholy satisfaction of seeing her lover before she closed her brief life.

"Her death decided Michael's fate. Rendered desperate by grief, he reproached his bigoted uncle as the author of his misery, and demanded of him a settlement of his property, as it was his intention to quit his roof for ever. Mr. C—— laughed at his reproaches, and treated his threats with scorn, and finally cast him friendless upon the world.

"The poor fellow played very well upon the flute, and possessed an excellent tenor voice; and, by the means of these accomplishments, he contrived for a few weeks to obtain a precarious living.

"Broken-hearted and alone in the world, he soon fell a victim to hereditary disease of the lungs, and died, I have been told, at an hotel in Cobourg; and was buried at the expense of Mr. S——, the tavern-keeper, out of charity."

"The latter part of your statement I know to be correct; and the whole of it forcibly corroborates the account given to me by the poor lad's mother. I was at Michael's death-bed; and if his life was replete with sorrow and injustice, his last hours were peaceful and happy."

I could now fully comprehend the meaning of the sad stress laid upon the one word, which had struck me so forcibly at the time, when I asked him if he had forgiven *all* his enemies, and he replied, after that lengthened pause, "Yes; I have forgiven them all – even *him!*"

It did, indeed, require some exertion of Christian forbearance to forgive such injuries.

SONG.

"There's hope for those who sleep
    In the cold and silent grave,
For those who smile, for those who weep,
    For the freeman and the slave!

"There's hope on the battle plain,
    'Mid the shock of charging foes;
On the dark and troubled main,
    When the gale in thunder blows.

"He who dispenses hope to all,
    Withholds it not from thee;
He breaks the woe-worn captive's thrall,
    And sets the prisoner free!"

TWELVE

Jeanie Burns

"Ah, human hearts are strangely cast,
   Time softens grief and pain;
Like reeds that shiver in the blast,
   They bend to rise again.
But she in silence bowed her head,
   To none her sorrow would impart:
Earth's faithful arms enclose the dead,
   And hide for aye her broken heart."

S.M.

WHILE THE steamboat is leaving Cobourg in the distance, and, through the hours of night and darkness, holds on her course to Toronto, I will relate another true but mournful history from the romance of real life, that was told to me during my residence in this part of the country.

One morning our man-servant, James N——, came to me to request the loan of one of the horses to attend a funeral. M—— was absent on business at Toronto, and the horses and the man's time were both greatly needed to prepare the land for the full crop of wheat. I demurred; James looked anxious and disappointed; and the loan of the horse was at length granted, but not without a strict injunction that he should return to his work directly the funeral was over. He did not come back until late that evening.

I had just finished my tea, and was nursing my wrath at his staying out the whole day, when the door of the room (we had but one, and that was shared in common with the servants) opened, and the delinquent at last appeared. He hung up the new English saddle, and sat down before the blazing hearth without speaking a word.

"What detained you so long, James? You ought to have had half an acre of land, at least, ploughed to-day."

"Verra true, mistress; it was nae fau't o' mine. I had mista'en the hour; the funeral did na come in afore sundoon, an' I cam' awa' as sune as it was owre."

"Was it any relation of yours?"

"Na'na', jest a freend, an auld acquaintance, but nane o' mine ain kin. I never felt sae sad in a' my life as I ha'e dune this day. I ha'e seen the clods piled on mony a heid, an' never felt the saut tear in my een. But puir Jeanie! puir lass! it was a sair sight to see them thrown down upon her."

My curiosity was excited; I pushed the tea-things from me, and told Bell, my maid, to give James his supper.

"Naething for me the night, Bell. I canna' eat; my thoughts will a'run on that puir láss. Sae young, sae bonnie, an'a few months ago as blythe as a lark, an' noo a clod o' the airth. Hout! we maun a' dee when our ain time comes; but, somehow, I canna think that Jeanie ought to ha'e gane sae sune."

"Who is Jeanie Burns? Tell me, James, something about her?"

In compliance with my request, the man gave me the following story. I wish I could convey it in his own words; but though I perfectly understand the Scotch dialect when I hear it spoken, I could not write it in its charming simplicity, – that honest, truthful brevity, which is so characteristic of this noble people. The smooth tones of the blarney may flatter our vanity, and please us for the moment, but who places any confidence in those by whom it is employed? We know that it is only uttered to cajole and deceive; and when the novelty wears off, the repetition awakens indignation and disgust. But who mistrusts the blunt, straightforward speech of the land of Burns? for good or ill, it strikes home to the heart.

Jeanie Burns was the daughter of a respectable shoe-maker, who gained a comfortable living by his trade in a small town of Ayrshire. Her father, like herself, was an only child, and followed the same vocation, and wrought under the same roof that his father had done before him. The elder Burns had met with many reverses, and now, helpless and blind, was entirely dependent upon the char-ity of his son. Honest Jock had not married until late in life, that he might more comfortably provide for the wants of his aged parents. His mother had been dead for some years. She was a good, pious woman, and Jock quaintly affirmed "that it had pleased the Lord to provide a better inheritance for his dear auld mither than his arm could win, proud an' happy as he wud ha'e been to ha'e sup-ported her, when she was nae langer able to work for him."

Jock's filial love was repaid at last. Chance threw in his way a cannie young lass, baith gude an' bonnie, an' wi' a hantel o' siller. They were united, and Jeanie was the sole fruit of the marriage. But Jeanie proved a host in herself, and grew up the best-natured, the prettiest, and the most industrious girl in the village, and was a general favourite with young and old. She helped her mother in the house, bound shoes for her father, and attended to all the wants of her dear old grandfather, Saunders Burns, who was so much attached to his little handmaid, that he was never happy when she was absent.

Happiness, however, is not a flower of long growth in this world; it requires the dew and sunlight of heaven to nourish it, and it soon withers, removed from its native skies. The cholera visited the remote village; it smote the strong man in the pride of his strength, and the matron in the beauty of her prime, while it spared the helpless and the aged, the infant of a few days, and the patriarch of many years. Both Jeanie's parents fell victims to the fatal disease, and the old blind Saunders and the young Jeanie were left to fight alone a hard battle with poverty and grief.

The truly deserving are never entirely forsaken; God may afflict them with many trials, but he watches over them still, and often provides for their wants in a manner truly miraculous. Sympathizing friends gathered round the orphan girl in her hour of need, and obtained for her sufficient employment to enable her to support her old grandfather and herself, and provide for them the common necessaries of life.

Jeanie was an excellent sempstress, and what between making waistcoats and trousers for the tailors, and binding shoes for the shoemakers, – a business that she thoroughly understood, – she soon had her little hired room neatly furnished, and her grandfather as clean and spruce as ever. When she led him into the kirk of a sabbath morning, all the neighbours greeted the dutiful daughter with an approving smile, and the old man looked so serene and happy that Jeanie was fully repaid for her labours of love.

Her industry and piety often formed the theme of conversation to the young lads of the village. "What a guid wife Jeanie Burns wull mak'!" cried one.

"Aye," said another; "he need na complain of ill fortin who has the luck to get the like o' her."

"An' she's sae bonnie," would Willie Robertson add, with a sigh; "I wud na covet the wealth o' the hale world an' she were mine."

Willie Robertson was a fine active young man, who bore an excellent character, and his comrades thought it very likely that Willie was to be the fortunate man. Robertson was the son of a farmer in the neighbourhood; he had no land of his own, and he was the youngest of a very large family. From a boy he had assisted his father in working the farm for their common maintenance; but after he took to looking at Jeanie Burns at kirk, instead of minding his prayers, he began to wish that he had a homestead of his own, which he could ask Jeanie and her grandfather to share.

He made his wishes known to his father. The old man was prudent. A marriage with Jeanie Burns offered no advantages in a pecuniary view; but the girl was a good, honest girl, of whom any man might be proud. He had himself married for love, and had enjoyed great comfort in his wife.

"Willie, my lad," he said, "I canna gi'e ye a share o' the farm. It is owre sma' for the mony mouths it has to feed. I ha'e laid by a hantel o' siller for a rainy day, an' this I maun gi'e ye to win a farm for yoursel' in the woods of Canada. There is plenty o' room there, an' industry brings its ain reward. If Jeanie Burns lo'es you as weel as your dear mither did me, she will be fain to follow you there."

Willie grasped his father's hand, for he was too much elated to speak, and he ran away to tell his tale of love to the girl of his heart. Jeanie had long loved Robertson in secret, and they were not long in settling the matter. They forgot, in their first moments of joy, that old Saunders had to be consulted, for they had determined to take the old man with them. But here an obstacle occurred, of which they had not dreamed. Old age is selfish, and Saunders obstinately refused to comply with their wishes. The grave that held the remains of his wife and son, was dearer to him than all the comforts promised to him by the impatient lovers in that far foreign land. Jeanie wept, but Saunders, deaf and blind, neither heard nor saw her grief, and like a dutiful child she breathed no complaint to him, but promised to remain with him until his head rested on the same pillow with the dead.

This was a sore and great trial to Willie Robertson, but he consoled himself for the disappointment with the reflection that Saunders, in the course of nature, could not live long; and that he would go and prepare a place for his

Jean, and have everything ready for her reception against the old man died.

"I was a cousin of Willie's," continued James, "by the mither's side, an' her persuaded me to go wi' him to Canada. We set sail the first o' May, an' were here in time to chop a sma' fallow for our fall crop. Willie had more o' the warld's gear than I, for his father had provided him wi' sufficient funds to purchase a good lot o' wild land, which he did in the township of M——, an' I was to wark wi' him on shares. We were amang the first settlers in that place, an' we found the wark before us rough an' hard to our heart's content. Willie, however, had a strong motive for exertion, an' neever did man wark harder than he did that first year on his bush-farm, for the love o' Jeanie Burns. We built a comfortable log-house, in which we were assisted by the few neighbours we had, who likewise lent a han' in clearing ten acres we had chopped for fall crop.

"All this time Willie kept up a correspondence wi' Jeanie; an' he used to talk to me o' her comin' out, an' his future plans, every night when our wark was dune. If I had na lovit and respected the girl mysel', I sud ha'e got unco tired o' the subject.

"We had jest put in our first crop o' wheat, when a letter cam' frae Jeanie bringin' us the news o' her grandfather's death. Weel I ken the word that Willie spak' to me when he closed the letter, – 'Jamie, the auld man's gane at last; an' God forgi'e me, I feel too gladsome to greet. Jeanie is willin' to come whenever I ha'e the means to bring her out; an' hout, man, I'm jest thinkin' that she winna ha'e to wait lang.'

"Guid workmen were gettin' very high wages jest then, an' Willie left the care o' the place to me, an' hired for three months wi' auld squire Jones, in the next township. Willie was an unco guid teamster, an' could put his han' to ony kind o' wark; an' when his term o' service expired, he sent Jeanie forty dollars to pay her passage out, which he hoped she would not delay longer than the spring.

"He got an answer frae Jeanie full o' love an' gratitude; but she thought that her voyage might be delayed until the fall. The guid woman with whom she had lodged sin' her parents died had jest lost her husband, an' was in a bad state o' health, an' she begged Jeanie to bide wi' her until her daughter could leave her service in Edinburg, an' come to tak' charge o' the house. This person had been a kind an' steadfast frin' to Jeanie in a' her troubles, an' had helped her to nurse the auld man in his dyin' illness. I am sure it was jest like Jeanie to act as she did; she had all her life looked more to the comforts of others than to her ain. Robertson was an angry man when he got that letter, an' he said, – 'If that was a' the lo'e that Jeanie Burns had for him, to prefer an auld wife's comfort, wha was naething to her, to her betrothed husband, she might bide awa' as lang as she pleased; he would never fash himsel' to mak' screed o' a pen to her agen.'

"I could na think that the man was in earnest, an' I remonstrated wi' him on his folly an' injustice. This ended in a sharp quarrel atween us, and I left him to gang his ain gate, an' went to live with my uncle, who kept the smithy in the village.

"After a while, we heard that Willie Robertson was married to a Canadian woman, neither young nor good-looking, an' vara much his inferior every way; but she had a guid lot o' land in the rear o' his farm. Of course I thought it was a' broken aff wi' puir Jean, an' I wondered what she wud spier at the marriage.

"It was early in June, an' the Canadian woods were in their first flush o' green, – an' how green an' lightsome they be in their spring dress! – when Jeanie Burns landed in Canada. She travelled her lane up the country, wonderin' why Willie was not at Montreal to meet her, as he had promised in the last letter he sent her. It was late in the afternoon when the steamboat brought her to Cobourg, an' without waitin' to ask ony questions respectin' him, she hired a man an' cart to take her an' her luggage to M——. The road through the bush was vara heavy, an' it was night before they reached Robertson's clearin'. Wi some difficulty the driver fund his way among the charred logs to the cabin door.

"Hearin' the sound o' wheels, the wife – a coarse, ill-dressed slattern – cam' out to spier wha' could bring strangers to sic' an out-o'-the-way place at that late hour. Puir Jeanie! I can weel imagin' the flutterin' o' her heart, when she spiered o' the coarse wife 'if her ain Willie Robertson was at hame?'

" 'Yes,' answered the woman, gruffly; 'but he is not in frae the fallow yet. You maun ken him up yonder, tending the blazing logs.'

"Whiles Jeanie was strivin' to look in the direction which the woman pointed out, an' could na see through the tears that blinded her e'e, the driver jumped down frae the cart, an' asked the puir lass whar he sud leave her trunks, as it was getting late, and he must be aff.

" 'You need na bring thae big kists in here,' quoth Mistress Robertson; 'I ha'e na room in my house for strangers an' their luggage.'

" 'Your house!' gasped Jeanie, catchin' her arm. "Did ye na tell me that *he* lived here? – an' wherever Willie Robertson bides, Jeanie Burns sud be a welcome guest. Tell him,' she continued, tremblin' all owre, – for she telt me afterwards that there was somethin' in the woman's look an' tone that made the cold chills run to her heart, – 'that an auld frind frae Scotland has jest come aff a lang, wearisome journey, to see him.'

" 'You may spier for yoursel',' said the woman, angrily. 'My husband is noo comin' dune the clearin'.'

"The word husband was scarcely out o' her mouth, than puir Jeanie fell as ane dead across the door-stair. The driver lifted up the unfortunat' girl, carried her into the cabin, an' placed her in a chair, regardless o' the opposition of Mistress Robertson, whose jealousy was now fairly aroused, an' she declared that the bold hizzie sud not enter her doors.

"It was a long time afore the driver succeeded in bringin' Jeanie to hersel'; an' she had only jest unclosed her een, when Willie cam' in.

" 'Wife,' he said, 'whose cart is this standin' at the door? an' what do these people want here?'

" 'You ken best,' cried the angry woman. 'That creater is nae acquaintance o' mine; an' if she is suffered to remain here, I will quit the house.'

" 'Forgi'e me, gude woman, for having unwittingly offended you,' said Jeanie, rising; 'but mercifu' Father! how sud I ken that Willie Robertson – my ain Willie – had a wife? Oh, Willie!' she cried, coverin' her face in her hands, to hide a' the agony that was in her heart, 'I ha'e come a lang way, an' a weary, to see ye, an' ye might ha'e spared me the grief, the burnin' shame o' this. Fareweel, Willie Robertson! I will never mair trouble ye nor her wi' my presence; but this cruel deed o' yours has broken my heart!'

"She went her lane weepin', an' he had na the courage to detain her, or speak ae word o' comfort in her sair distress, or attempt to gi'e ony account o' his strange conduct. Yet, if I ken him right, that must ha'e been the most sorrowfu' moment in his life.

"Jeanie was a distant connexion o' my aunt's; an' she found us out that night, on her return to the village, an' tould us a' her grief. My aunt was a kind, guid woman, an' was indignant at the treatment she had received, an' loved and cherished her as if she had been her ain bairn. For two whole weeks she kept her bed, an' was sae ill, that the doctor despaired o' her life; and when she did come amang us agen, the rose had faded aff her cheek, an' the light frae her sweet blue e'e, an' she spak' in a low, subdued voice; but she never accused him o' being the cause o' her grief. One day she called me aside and said –

" 'Jamie, you ken'd how I lo'ed an' trusted him, an' obeyed his ain wish in comin' out to this wearisome country to be his wife. But 'tis a' owre now.' An' she passed her sma' hands tightly owre her breast, to keep doon the swellin' o' her heart. 'Jamie, I ken that this is a' for the best; I lo'ed him too weel, – mair than ony creature sud lo'e a perishin' thing o' earth. But I thought that he wud be sae glad an' sae proud to see his ain Jeanie sae sune. But, oh! – ah, weel; I maun na think o' that. What I wud jest say is this' – and she tuk a sma' packet frae her breast, while the saut tears streamed doon her pale cheeks – 'he sent me forty dollars to bring me owre the sea to him. God bless him for that! I ken he worked hard to earn it, for he lo'ed me then. I was na idle during his absence; I had saved enough to bury my dear auld grandfather, an' to pay my expenses out; an' I thought, like the guid servant in the parable, I wud return Willie his ain wi' interest, an' I hoped to see him smile at my diligence, an' ca' me his dear, bonnie lassie. Jamie, I canna keep his siller; it lies like a weight o' lead on my heart. Tak' it back to him, an' tell him frae me, that I forgi'e him a' his cruel deceit, an' pray God to grant him prosperity, an' restore to him that peace o' mind o' which he has robbed me for ever.'

"I did as she bade me. Willie Robertson looked stupified when I delivered her message. The only remark he made when I gied him back the siller was, 'I maun be gratefu', man, that she did na curse me.' The wife cam' in, an' he hid awa' the packet and slunk aff. The man looked degraded in his ain sight, an' sae wretched, that I pitied him frae my heart.

"When I cam' home, Jeanie met me at the yet. 'Tell me,' she said, in a dowie, anxious voice, – 'tell me, cousin Jamie, what passed atween ye'. Had Willie nae word for me?'

" 'Naething, Jeanie. The man is lost to himsel' – to a' who ance wished him weel. He is na worth a decent body's thought.'

"She sighed sairly; an' I saw that her heart craved after some word or token frae him. She said nae mair; but pale an' sorrowfu', the verra ghaist o' her former sel', went back into the house.

"Frae that hour she never breathed his name to ony o' us; but we all ken'd that it was her lo'e for him that was wearin' out her life. The grief that has nae voice, like the canker-worm, lies ne'est the heart. Puir Jean, she held out durin' the simmer, but when the fa' cam', she jest withered awa', like a flower nipped by the early frost; an' this day we laid her in the earth.

"After the funeral was owre, an' the mourners a' gane, I stood beside her grave, thinking owre the days o' my boyhood, when she an' I were happy weans, an' used to pu' the gowans together, on the heathery hills o' dear auld Scotland. An' I tried in vain to understan' the mysterious providence o' God that had stricken her, who seem sae guid an' pure, an spared the like o' me, who was mair deservin' o' his wrath, when I heard a deep groan, an' I saw Willie Robertson standin' near me, beside the grave.

" 'You may as weel spare your grief noo,' said I, for I felt hard towards him, 'an' rejoice that the weary is at rest.'

" 'It was I killed her,' said he; 'an' the thought will haunt me to my last day. Did she remember me on her death-bed?'

" 'Her thoughts were only ken'd by Him, Willie, wha reads the secrets of a' hearts. Her end was peace; and her Saviour's blessed name was the last sound on her lips. If ever woman died o' a broken heart, there she lies.'

" 'Ah, Jeanie!' he cried, 'my ain darlin' Jeanie! my blessed lammie! I was na worthy o' yer luve. My heart, too, is breakin'. To bring ye back ance mair, I would gladly lay me doon an' dee.'

"An' he flung himsel' upon the fresh piled sods, an' greeted like a child.

"When he grew more calm, we had a long conversation about the past; an' truly I think that the man was na in his right senses, when he married yon wife. At ony rate, he is nae lang for this world; he has fretted the flesh aff his banes, an' afore many months are owre, his heid wul lie as low as puir Jeanie Burns."

MY NATIVE LAND.

"My native land, my native land!
　　How many tender ties,
　Connected with thy distant strand,
　　Call forth my heavy sighs!

"The rugged rock, the mountain stream,
　　The hoary pine-tree's shade,
　Where often in the noon-tide beam,
　　A happy child I played.

"I think of thee, when early light
　　Is trembling on the hill;
　I think of thee at dead of night,
　　When all is dark and still.

"I think of those whom I shall see
　　On this fair earth no more;
　And wish in vain for wings to flee
　　Back to thy much-loved shore."

THIRTEEN

Lost Children

"Oh, how I love the pleasant woods, when silence reigns around,
  And the mighty shadows calmly sleep, like giants on the
    ground,
  And the fire-fly sports her fairy lamp beside the moonlit
    stream,
  And the lofty trees, in solemn state, frown darkly in the beam!"

                                                            S.M.

THERE WAS a poor woman on board the steamer, who
was like myself in search of health, and was going to
the West to see her friends, and to get rid of (if possible) a
hollow, consumptive cough. She looked to me in the last
stage of pulmonary consumption; but she seemed to hope
everything from the change of air.

She had been for many years a resident in the woods,
and had suffered great hardships; but the greatest sorrow
she ever knew, she said, and what had pulled her down the
most, was the loss of a fine boy, who had strayed away
after her through the bush, when she went to nurse a sick
neighbour; and though every search had been made for
the child, he had never been found. "It is a many years
ago," she said, "and he would be a fine young man now, if
he were alive." And she sighed deeply, and still seemed to
cling to the idea that he might possibly be living, with a

sort of forlorn hope, that to me seemed more melancholy than the certainty of his death.

This brought to my recollection many tales that I had been told, while living in the bush, of persons who had perished in this miserable manner. Some of these tales may chance to interest my readers.

I was busy sewing one day for my little girl, when we lived in the township of Hamilton, when Mrs. H——, a woman whose husband farmed our farm on shares, came running in quite out of breath, and cried out –

"Mrs. M——, you have heard the good news? – One of the lost children is found!"

I shook my head, and looked inquiringly.

"What! did not you hear about it? Why, one of Clark's little fellows, who were lost last Wednesday in the woods, has been found."

"I am glad of it. But how were they lost?"

"Oh, 'tis a thing of very common occurrence here. New settlers, who are ignorant of the danger of going astray in the forest, are always having their children lost. I take good care never to let my boys go alone to the bush. But people are so careless in this respect, that I wonder it does not more frequently happen.

"These little chaps are the sons of a poor emigrant who came out this summer, and took up a lot of wild land just at the back of us, towards the plains. Clark is busy logging up his fallow for fall wheat, on which his family must depend for bread during the ensuing year; and he is so anxious to get it ready in time, that he will not allow himself an hour at noon to go home to get his dinner, which his wife generally sends in a basket to the woods by his eldest daughter, a girl of fourteen.

"Last Wednesday, the girl had been sent an errand by her mother, who thought that, in her absence, she might venture to trust the two boys to take the dinner to their father. The boys, who are from five to seven years old, and very smart and knowing for their age, promised to mind all her directions, and went off quite proud of the task, carrying the little basket between them.

"How they came to ramble off into the woods, the younger child, who has been just found, is too much stupified to tell, and perhaps he is too young to remember.

"At night Clark returned from his work, and scolded his wife for not sending his dinner as usual; but the poor woman, (who all day had quieted her fears with the belief that the children had stayed with their father,) instead of paying any regard to his angry words, demanded, in a tone of agony, what had become of her children?

"Tired and hungry as Clark was, he instantly comprehended the danger to which his boys were exposed, and started off in pursuit of them. The shrieks of the distracted woman soon called the neighbours together, who instantly joined in the search. It was not until this afternoon that any trace could be discovered of the lost children, when Brian, the hunter, found the youngest boy, Johnnie, lying fast asleep upon the trunk of a fallen tree, fifteen miles back in the bush."

"And the brother?"

"Will never, I fear, be heard of again. They have searched for him in all directions, and have not discovered him. The story little Johnnie tells is to this effect. During the first two days of their absence, the food they had brought in the basket for their father's dinner sustained life; but to-day, it seems that little Johnnie grew very hungry, and cried continually for bread. William, the eldest boy, promised him bread if he would try and walk farther; but his feet were bleeding and sore, and he could not walk another step. For some time the other little fellow carried him upon his back; but growing tired himself, he bade Johnnie sit down upon a fallen log, (the log on which he was found,) and not stir from the place until he came back. He told the child that he would run on until he found a house, and would return as soon as he could, and bring him something to eat. He then wiped his eyes, and told him not to cry, and not to be scared, for God would take care of him till he came back, and he kissed him several times, and ran away.

"This is all the little fellow knows about his brother; and it is very probable that the generous-hearted boy has been eaten by the wolves that are very plenty in that part of the forest where the child was found. The Indians traced him for more than a mile along the banks of the creek, when they lost his trail altogether. If he had fallen into the water, it is so shallow, that they could scarcely have failed in discovering the body; but they think that he has been dragged into some hole in the bank among the tangled cedars, and devoured.

"Since I have been in the country," continued Mrs. H——, "I have known many cases of children, and even of grown persons, being lost in the woods, who were never heard of again. It is a frightful calamity to happen to any one; for should they escape from the claws of wild animals, these dense forests contain nothing on which life can be supported for any length of time. The very boughs of the trees are placed so far from the ground, that no child could reach or climb to them; and there is so little brush and small bushes among these giant trees, that no sort of fruit can be obtained, on which they might subsist while it remained in season. It is only in clearings, or where the fire has run through the forest, that strawberries or raspberries are to be found; and at this season of the year, and in the winter, a strong man could not exist many days in the wilderness – let alone a child.

"Parents cannot be too careful in guarding their young folks against rambling alone in the bush. Persons, when once they get off the beaten track, get frightened and bewildered, and lose all presence of mind; and instead of remaining where they are when they first discover their misfortune – which is the only chance they have of being found – they plunge desperately on, running hither and thither, in the hope of getting out, while they only involve themselves more deeply among the mazes of the interminable forest.

"Some winters ago, the daughter of a settler in the remote township of Dummer (where my husband took up his grant of wild land, and in which we lived for two years) went with her father to the mill, which was four miles from their log-shanty, and the road lay entirely through the bush. For awhile the girl, who was about twelve years of age, kept up with her father, who walked briskly a-head with his bag of corn on his back; for as their path lay through a tangled swamp, he was anxious to get home before night. After some time, Sarah grew tired with stepping up and down over the fallen logs that strewed their path, and lagged a long way behind. The man felt not the least apprehensive when he lost sight of her, expecting that she would soon come up with him again. Once or twice he stopped and shouted, and she answered, 'Coming, father!' and he did not turn to look after her again. He reached the mill, saw the grist ground, resumed his burden, and took the road home, expecting to meet Sarah by the way. He trode the long path alone; but still he thought that the girl, tired with her walk in the woods, had turned back, and he should find her safe at home.

"You may imagine, Mrs. M——, his consternation, and that of the family, when they found that the girl was lost.

"It was now dark, and all search for her was given up for that night as hopeless. By day-break the next morning the whole settlement, which was then confined to a few lonely log tenements, inhabited solely by Cornish miners, were roused from their sleep to assist in the search.

"The men turned out with guns and horns, and divided into parties, that started in different directions. Those who first discovered Sarah were to fire their guns, which was to be the signal to guide the rest to the spot. It was not long before they found the object of their search, seated under a tree about half a mile from the path she had lost on the preceding day.

"She had been tempted by the beauty of some wild flowers to leave the road; and, when once in the forest, she grew bewildered, and could not find her way back. At first she ran to and fro, in an agony of terror, at finding herself in the woods all alone, and uttered loud and frantic cries; but her father had by this time reached the mill, and was out of hearing.

"With a sagacity beyond her years, and not very common to her class, instead of wandering further into the labyrinth which surrounded her, she sat down under a large tree, covered her face with her apron, said the Lord's prayer – the only one she knew, and hoped that God would send her father back to find her the moment he discovered that she was lost.

"When night came down upon the forest, (and oh! how dark night is in the woods!) the poor girl said that she felt horribly afraid of being eaten by the wolves that abound in those dreary swamps; but she did not cry, for fear they should hear her. Simple girl! she did not know that the scent of a wolf is far keener than his ear; but this was her notion, and she lay down close to the ground and never once uncovered her head, for fear of seeing something dreadful standing beside her; until, overcome by terror and fatigue, she fell fast asleep, and did not awake till roused by the shrill braying of the horns, and the shouts of the party who were seeking her."

"What a dreadful situation! I am sure that I should not have had the courage of this poor girl, but should have died with fear."

"We don't know how much we can bear till we are tried. This girl was more fortunate than a boy of the same age, who was lost in the same township just as the winter set in. The lad was sent by his father, an English settler, in company with two boys of his own age, the sons of neighbours, to be measured for a pair of shoes. George Desne, who followed the double occupation of farmer and shoemaker, lived about three miles from the clearing known as the English line. After the lads left their home, the road lay entirely through the bush. It was a path they had often travelled, both alone and with their parents, and they felt no fear.

"There had been a slight fall of snow, just enough to cover the ground, and the day was clear and frosty. The boys in this country always hail with delight the first fall of snow; and they ran races and slid over all the shallow pools, until they reached George Desne's cabin. He measured young Brown for a strong pair of winter boots, and the boys returned on their homeward path, shouting and laughing in the glee of their hearts.

"About half-way they suddenly missed their companion, and ran back nearly a mile to find him; not succeeding, they thought that he had hidden himself behind some of the trees, and, in order to frighten them, was pretending to be lost; and after shouting his name at the top of their voices, and receiving no answer, they determined to defeat his trick, and ran home without him. They knew he was well acquainted with the road, that it was still broad day, and he could easily find his way home alone. When his father inquired for George, they said he was coming, and went to their respective cabins.

"Night came on and the lad did not return, and his parents began to feel alarmed at his absence. Mr. Brown went over to the neighbouring settlements, and made the lads repeat to him all they knew about his son. The boys described the part of the road where they first missed him; but they had felt no uneasiness about him, for they concluded that he had either run home before them, or had gone back to spend the night with the young Desnes, who had been very importunate for him to stay. This account pacified the anxious father. Early the next morning he went to Desne's himself to bring home the boy, but, to his astonishment and grief, he had not been there.

"His mysterious disappearance gave rise to a thousand strange surmises. The whole settlement turned out in search of the boy. His steps were traced off the road a few yards into the bush, and entirely disappeared at the foot of a large oak tree. The tree was lofty, and the branches so far from the ground, that it was almost impossible for any boy, unassisted, to have raised himself to such a height. There was no track of any animal to be seen on the new fallen snow – no shred of garment, or stain of blood. That boy's fate will always remain a great mystery, for he was never found."

"He must have been carried up the tree by a bear, and dragged down into the hollow trunk," said I.

"If that had been the case, there would have been the track of the bear's feet in the snow. It does not, however, follow that the boy is dead, though it is more than probable. I knew of a case where two boys and a girl were sent into the woods by their mother to fetch home the cows. The children were lost. The parents mourned them for dead, for all search after them proved fruitless. At length, after seven years, the eldest son returned. The children had been overtaken and carried off by a party of Indians, who belonged to a tribe who inhabited the islands in Lake Huron, and who were out on a hunting expedition. They took them many hundred miles away from their forest home, and adopted them as their own. The girl, when she grew up, married one of the tribe; the boys followed the occupation of hunters and fishers, and, from their dress and appearance, might have passed for aborigines of the forest. The eldest boy, however, never forgot his own name, or the manner in which he had been separated from his parents. He distinctly remembered the township and the natural features of the locality, and took the first opportunity of making his escape, and travelling back to the home of his childhood.

"When he made himself known to his mother, who was a widow, but resided on the same spot, he was so dark and Indian-like that she could not believe that it was really her son, until he brought back to her mind a little incident that, forgotten by her, had never left his memory.

" 'Mother, don't you remember saying to me on that afternoon, Ned, you need not look for the cows in the swamp – they went off towards the big hill!'

"The delighted mother immediately caught him to her heart, exclaiming, 'You say truly – you are my own, my long-lost son!'"*

THE CANADIAN HERD-BOY.

"Through the deep woods, at peep of day,
   The careless herd-boy wends his way,
   By piny ridge and forest stream,
   To summon home his roving team –
   Cobos! cobos! from distant dell
   Shy echo wafts the cattle-bell.

"A blithe reply he whistles back,
   And follows out the devious track,
   O'er fallen tree and mossy stone –
   A path to all, save him, unknown.
   Cobos! cobos! far down the dell
   More faintly falls the cattle-bell.

"See the dark swamp before him throws
   A tangled maze of cedar boughs;
   On all around deep silence broods,
   In nature's boundless solitudes.
   Cobos! cobos! the breezes swell,
   As nearer floats the cattle-bell.

"He sees them now – beneath yon trees
   His motley herd recline at ease;
   With lazy pace and sullen stare,
   They slowly leave their shady lair.
   Cobos! cobos! – far up the dell
   Quick jingling comes the cattle-bell!"

*This, and the two preceding chapters, were written for "Roughing it in the Bush," and were sent to England to make a part of that work, but came too late for insertion, which will account to the reader for their appearance here.

FOURTEEN

Toronto

"Fiction, however wild and fanciful,
  Is but the copy memory draws from truth.
  'Tis not in human genius to *create:*
  The mind is but a mirror that reflects
  Realities that are, or the dim shadows
  Left by the past upon its placid surface,
  Recalled again to life."

THE GLOW of early day was brightening in the east, as the steamer approached Toronto. We rounded the point of the interminable, flat, swampy island, that stretches for several miles in front of the city, and which is thinly covered with scrubby-looking trees. The land lies so level with the water, that it has the appearance of being half-submerged, and from a distance you only see the tops of the trees. I have been informed that the name of Toronto has been derived from this circumstance, which in Indian literally means, "*Trees in the water.*"

If the island rather takes from, than adds to, the beauty of the place, it is not without great practical advantages, as to it the city is mainly indebted for its sheltered and very commodious harbour.

After entering the harbour, Toronto presents a long line of frontage, covered with handsome buildings to the eye. A grey mist still hovered over its many domes and spires;

but the new University and the Lunatic Asylum stood out in bold relief, as they caught the broad red gleam of the coming day.

It was my first visit to the metropolitan city of the upper province, and with no small degree of interest I examined its general aspect as we approached the wharf. It does not present such an imposing appearance from the water as Kingston, but it strikes you instantly as a place of far greater magnitude and importance. There is a fresh, growing, healthy vitality about this place, that cannot fail to impress a stranger very forcibly the first time he enters it. He feels instinctively that he sees before him the strong throbbing heart of this gigantic young country, and that every powerful vibration from this ever increasing centre of wealth and civilisation, infuses life and vigour through the whole length and breadth of the province.

Toronto exceeded the most sanguine expectations that I had formed of it at a distance, and enabled me to realize distinctly the rising greatness and rapid improvement of the colony. It is only here that you can form any just estimate of what she now is, and what at no very distant period she must be.

The country, for some miles round the city, appears to the eye as flat as a floor; the rise, though very gradual, is, I am told, considerable; and the land is sufficiently elevated above the lake to escape the disagreeable character of being low and swampy. Anything in the shape of a slope or hill is not distinguishable in the present area on which Toronto is built; but the streets are wide and clean, and contain many handsome public buildings; and the beautiful trees which everywhere abound in the neat, well-kept gardens, that surround the dwellings of the wealthier inhabitants, with the broad, bright, blue inland sea that forms the foreground to the picture, give to it such a lively and agreeable character, that it takes from it all appearance of tameness and monotony.

The wharfs, with which our first practical acquaintance with the city commenced, are very narrow and incommodious. They are built on piles of wood, running out to some distance in the water, and covered with rotten, black-looking boards. As far as comfort and convenience go, they are far inferior to those of Cobourg and Kingston, or even to those of our own dear little "*City of the Bay*," as Belleville has not inaptly been christened by the strange madcap, calling himself the "*Great Orator of the West*."

It is devoutly to be hoped that a few years will sweep all these decayed old wharfs into the Ontario, and that more substantial ones, built of stone, will be erected in their place. Rome, however, was not built in a day; and the magic growth of this city of the West is almost as miraculous as that of Jonah's celebrated gourd.

The steamboat had scarcely been secured to her wharf before we were surrounded by a host of cabmen, who rushed on board, fighting and squabbling with each other, in order to secure the first chance of passengers and their luggage. The hubbub in front of the ladies' cabin grew to a perfect uproar; and, as most of the gentlemen were still in the arms of Morpheus, these noisy Mercuries had it all their own way – swearing and shouting at the top of their voices, in a manner that rivalled civilized Europe. I was perfectly astonished at their volubility, and the pertinacity of their attentions, which were poured forth in the true Milesian fashion – an odd mixture of blarney, self-interest, and audacity. At Kingston these gentry are far more civil and less importunate, and we witnessed none of this disgraceful annoyance at any other port on the lake. One of these Paddies, in his hurry to secure the persons and luggage of several ladies, who had been my fellow-passengers in the cabin, nearly backed his crazy old vehicle over the unguarded wooden wharf into the lake.

We got safely stowed at last into one of these machines, which, internally, are not destitute of either comfort or convenience; and driving through some of the principal avenues of the city, were safely deposited at the door of a dear friend, who had come on board to conduct us to his hospitable home; and here I found the rest and quiet so much needed by an invalid after a long and fatiguing journey.

It was some days before I was sufficiently recovered to visit any of the lions of the place. With a minute description of these I shall not trouble my readers. My book is written more with a view to convey general impressions, than to delineate separate features, – to while away the languid heat of a summer day, or the dreary dulness of a wet one. The intending emigrant, who is anxious for commercial calculations and statistical details, will find all that he can require on this head in "Scobie's Almanack," and Smith's "Past, Present, and Future of Canada," – works written expressly for that purpose.

Women make good use of their eyes and ears, and paint scenes that amuse or strike their fancy with tolerable accuracy; but it requires the strong-thinking heart of man to anticipate events, and trace certain results from particular causes. Women are out of their element when they attempt to speculate upon these abstruse matters – are apt to incline too strongly to their own opinions – and jump at conclusions which are either false or unsatisfactory.

My first visit was to King-street, which may be considered as the Regent-street of Toronto. It is the great central avenue of commerce, and contains many fine buildings, and handsome capacious stores, while a number of new ones are in a state of progress. This fine, broad, airy thoroughfare, would be an ornament to any town or city, and the bustle and traffic through it give to strangers a tolerably just idea of the wealth and industry of the community. All the streets terminate at the water's edge, but Front-street, which runs parallel with it, and may be termed the "west end" of Toronto; for most of the wealthy residents have handsome houses and gardens in this street, which is open through the whole length of it to the lake. The rail-road is upon the edge of the water along this natural terrace. The situation is uncommonly lively, as it

commands a fine view of the harbour, and vessels and
steamboats are passing to and fro continually.

The St. Lawrence market, which is near the bottom of
King-street, is a handsome, commodious building, and
capitally supplied with all the creature-comforts – fish,
flesh, and fowl – besides abundance of excellent fruits and
vegetables, which can be procured at very reasonable
prices. The town-hall is over the market-place, and I am
told – for I did not visit it – that it is a noble room, capable
of accommodating a large number of people with ease
and comfort.

Toronto is very rich in handsome churches, which form
one of its chief attractions. I was greatly struck with the
elegant spire of Knox's church, which is perhaps the most
graceful in the city. The body of the church, however,
seems rather too short, and out of proportion, for the tall
slender tower, which would have appeared to much
greater advantage attached to a building double the
length.

Nothing attracted my attention, or interested me more,
than the handsome, well-supplied book stores. Those of
Armour, Scobie, and Maclean, are equal to many in London in appearance, and far superior to those that were to
be found in Norwich and Ipswich thirty years ago.

This speaks well for the mental improvement of Canada, and is a proof that people have more leisure for
acquiring book lore, and more money for the purchase of
books, than they had some years ago. The piracies of the
Americans have realized the old proverb, "That 'tis an ill
wind that blows nobody any good." Incalculable are the
benefits that Canada derives from her cheap reprints of all
the European standard works, which, on good paper and
in handsome bindings, can be bought at a quarter the
price of the English editions. This circumstance must
always make the Canadas a bad market for English publi-
cations. Most of these, it is true, can be procured by
wealthy individuals at the book stores mentioned above,

but the American reprints of the same works abound a hundred-fold.

Novels form the most attractive species of reading here for the young; and the best of these, in pamphlet form, may be procured from twenty-five to fifty cents. And here I must claim the privilege of speaking a few words in defence of both novel readers and novel writers, in spite of the horror which I fancy I see depicted on many a grave countenance.

There are many good and conscientious persons who regard novels and novel writers with devout horror, – who condemn their works, however moral in their tendency, as unfit for the perusal of responsible and intelligent creatures, – who will not admit into their libraries any books but such as treat of religious, historical, or scientific subjects, imagining, and we think very erroneously, that all works of fiction have a demoralizing effect, and tend to weaken the judgment, and enervate the mind.

We will, however, allow that there is both truth and sound sense in some of these objections; that if a young person's reading is entirely confined to this class of literature, and that of an inferior sort, a great deal of harm may be the result, as many of these works are apt to convey to them false and exaggerated pictures of life. Such a course of reading would produce the same effect upon the mind as a constant diet of sweetmeats would upon the stomach; it would destroy the digestion, and induce a loathing for more wholesome food.

Still, the mind requires recreation as well as the body, and cannot always be engaged upon serious studies without injury to the brain, and the disarrangement of some of the most important organs of the body. Now, we think it could be satisfactorily proved, in spite of the stern crusade perpetually waged against works of fiction by a large portion of well-meaning people, that much good has been done in the world through their instrumentality.

Most novels and romances, particularly those of the modern school, are founded upon real incidents, and, like the best heads in the artist's picture, the characters are drawn from life; and the closer the drawing or story approximates to nature, the more interesting and popular will it become. Though a vast number of these works are daily pouring from the British and American press, it is only those of a very high class that are generally read, and become as familiar as household words. The tastes of individuals differ widely on articles of dress, food, and amusement; but there is a wonderful affinity in the minds of men, as regards works of literature. A book that appeals strongly to the passions, if true to nature, will strike nearly all alike, and obtain a world-wide popularity, while the mere fiction sinks back into obscurity – is once read and forgotten.

The works of Smollett and Fielding were admirable pictures of society as it existed in their day; but we live in a more refined age, and few young people would feel any pleasure in the coarse pictures exhibited in those once celebrated works. The novels of Richardson, recommended by grave divines from the pulpit as perfect models of purity and virtue, would now be cast aside with indifference and disgust. They were considered quite the reverse in the age he wrote, and he was regarded as one of the great reformers of the vices of his time. We may therefore conclude, that, although repugnant to our taste and feelings, they were the means of effecting much good in a gross and licentious age.

In the writings of our great modern novelists, virtue is never debased, nor vice exalted; but there is a constant endeavour to impress upon the mind of the reader the true wisdom of the one, and the folly of the other; and where the author fails to create an interest in the fate of his hero or heroine, it is not because they are bad or immoral characters, like Lovelace in Clarissa Harlowe, and Lord B—— in Pamela, but that, like Sir Charles Grandison, they are too *good* for reality, and their very faultlessness renders them, like the said Sir Charles, affected and unnatural. Where high moral excellence is represented as struggling with the faults and follies common to humanity, sometimes yielding to temptation, and reaping the bitter fruits, and at other times successfully resisting the allurements of vice, all our sympathies are engaged in the contest; it becomes our own, and we follow the hero through all his trials, weep over his fall, or triumph in his success.

Children, who possess an unsophisticated judgment in these matters, seldom feel much interest in the model boy of a moral story; not from any innate depravity of mind, which leads them to prefer vice to virtue, for no such preference can exist in the human breast, – no, not even in the perverted hearts of the worst of men – but because the model boy is like no other boy of their acquaintance. He does not resemble them, for he is a piece of unnatural perfection. He neither fights, nor cries, nor wishes to play when he ought to be busy with his lessons; he lectures like a parson, and talks like a book. His face is never dirty; he never tears his clothes, nor soils his hands with making dirt pies, or puddling in the mud. His hair is always smooth, his face always wears a smile, and he was never known to sulk, or say *I won't!* The boy is a perfect stranger – they can't recognise his likeness, or follow his example – and why? because both are unnatural caricatures.

But be sure, that if the naughty boy of the said tale creates the most interest for his fate in the mind of the youthful reader, it is simply because he is drawn with more truthfulness than the character that was intended for his counterpart. The language of passion is always eloquent, and the bad boy is delineated true to his bad nature, and is made to speak and act naturally, which never fails to awaken a touch of sympathy in beings equally prone to err. I again repeat that few minds (if any) exist than can find beauty in deformity, or aught to admire in the hideousness of vice.

There are many persons in the world who cannot bear to receive instruction when conveyed to them in a serious form, who shrink with loathing from the cant with which too many religious novels are loaded; and who yet might be induced to listen to precepts of religion and morality, when arrayed in a more amusing and attractive garb, and enforced by characters who speak and feel like themselves, and share in all things a common humanity.

Some of our admirable modern works of fiction, or rather truths disguised, in order to make them more palatable to the generality of readers, have done more to ameliorate the sorrows of mankind, by drawing the attention of the public to the wants and woes of the lower classes, than all the charity sermons that have been delivered from the pulpit.

Yes, the despised and reprobated novelist, by daring to unveil the crimes and miseries of neglected and ignorant men, and to point out the abuses which have produced, and are still producing, the same dreadful results, are missionaries in the cause of humanity, the real friends and benefactors of mankind.

The selfish worldling may denounce as infamous and immoral, the heart-rending pictures of human suffering and degradation that the writings of Dickens and Sue have presented to their gaze, and declare that they are unfit to meet the eyes of the virtuous and refined – that no good can arise from the publication of such revolting details – and that to be ignorant of the existence of such horrors is in itself a species of virtue.

Daughter of wealth, daintily nurtured, and nicely educated, *Is blindness nature?* Does your superiority over these fallen creatures spring from any innate principle in your own breast, which renders you more worthy of the admiration and esteem of your fellow-creatures? Are not you indebted to the circumstances in which you are placed, and to that moral education, for every virtue that you possess?

You can feel no pity for the murderer, the thief, the prostitute. Such people may aptly be termed the wild beasts of society, and, like wild beasts, should be hunted down and killed, in order to secure the peace and comfort of the rest. Well, the law has been doing this for many ages, and yet the wild beasts still exist and prey upon their neighbours. And such will still continue to be the case until Christianity, following the example of her blessed Founder, goes forth into the wilderness of life on her errand of mercy, not to condemn, but to seek and to save that which is lost.

The conventional rules of society have formed a hedge about you, which renders any flagrant breach of morality very difficult, – in some cases almost impossible. From infancy the dread commandments have been sounding in your ears, – "Thou shalt not kill! Thou shalt not steal! Thou shalt not commit adultery!" – and the awful mandate has been strengthened by the admonitions of pious parents and good ministers, all anxious for your eternal welfare. You may well be honest; for all your wants have been supplied, and you have yet to learn that where no temptation exists, virtue itself becomes a negative quality. You do not covet the goods which others possess. You have never looked down, with confusion of face and heart-felt bitterness, on the dirty rags that scarcely suffice to conceal the emaciation of your wasted limbs. You have never felt hunger gnawing at your vitals, or shuddered at the cries of famishing children, sobbing around your knees for bread. You have dainties to satiety every day, and know nothing of the agonies of sacrificing your virtue for the sake of a meal. If you are cold, you have a good fire to warm you, a comfortable mansion to protect you from the inclemency of the weather, and garments suitable to every season of the year. How can you be expected to sympathize with the ragged, houseless children of want and infamy!

You cannot bear to have these sad realities presented to your notice. It shocks your nerves. You cannot bring yourself to admit that these outcasts of society are composed of the same clay; and you blame the authors who have dared to run a tilt against your prejudices, and have not only attested the unwelcome fact, but have pointed out the causes which lead to the hopeless degradation and depravity of these miserable fellow-creatures. You cannot read the works of these humane men, because they bid you to step with them into these dirty abodes of guilt and wretchedness, and see what crime really is, and all the horrors that ignorance and poverty, and a want of self-respect, never fail to bring about. You cannot enter into these abodes of your neglected and starving brothers and sisters – these forlorn scions of a common stock – and view their cold hearths and unfurnished tables, their beds of straw and tattered garments, without defilement – or witness their days of unremitting toil, and nights of unrest; and worse, far worse, to behold the evil passions and crimes which spring from a state of ignorance, producing a moral darkness that can be felt.

You are insulted and offended at being seen in such bad company; and cannot for a moment imagine that a change in your relative positions might have rendered you no wiser or better than them. But, let me ask you candidly, has not the terrible scene produced some effect? Can you forget its existence, – its shocking reality? The lesson it teaches may be distasteful, but you cannot shake off a knowledge of its melancholy facts. The voice of conscience speaks audibly to your heart; – that still small voice – that awful record of himself that God has placed in every breast (and woe be to you, or any one, when it ceases to be heard!) – tells you that you cannot, without violating the divine mandate, "*love thy neighbour as thyself*," leave these miserable creatures to languish and die, without making one effort to aid in rescuing them from their melancholy fate.

"But what can I do?" I hear you indignantly exclaim.

Much; oh, how much! You have wealth, a small part of which cannot be better bestowed than in educating these poor creatures; in teaching them to recognise those divine laws which they have broken; in leading them step by step into those paths of piety and peace they have never known. Ignorance has been the most powerful agent in corrupting these perishing criminals. Give them healthful employment, the means of emigrating to countries where labour is amply remunerated, and will secure for them comfort, independence, and self-respect. In Canada, these victims of over-population prove beneficial members of society, while with you they are regarded as a blight and a curse.

Numbers of this class are yearly cast upon these shores, yet the crimes which are commonly committed by their instrumentality in Britain, very rarely occur with us. We could not sleep with unfastened doors and windows near populous towns, if the change in their condition did not bring about a greater moral change in the character of these poor emigrants.

They readily gain employment; their toils are amply remunerated; and they cease to commit crime to procure a precarious existence. In the very worst of these people some good exists. A few seeds remain of divine planting, which, if fostered and judiciously trained, might yet bear fruit for heaven.

The authors, whose works you call disgusting and immoral, point out this, and afford you the most pathetic illustrations of its truth. You need not fear contamination from the vices which they portray. Their depravity is of too black a hue to have the least attraction, even to beings only removed a few degrees from the same guilt. Vice may have her admirers when she glitters in gold and scarlet; but when exposed in filth and nakedness, her most reckless devotees shrink back from her in disgust and horror. Vice, without her mask, is a spectacle too appalling for humanity; it exhibits the hideousness, and breathes of the corruption of hell.

If these reprobated works of fiction can startle the rich into a painful consciousness of the wants and agonies of the poor, and make them, in spite of all the conventional laws of society, acknowledge their kindred humanity, who shall say that their books have been written in vain?

For my own part, I look upon these authors as heaven-inspired teachers, who have been commissioned by the great Father of souls to proclaim to the world the wrongs and sufferings of millions of his creatures, to plead their cause with unflinching integrity, and, with almost superhuman eloquence, demand for them the justice which the world has so long denied. These men are the benefactors of their species, to whom the whole human race owe a vast debt of gratitude.

Since the publication of Oliver Twist, and many other works of the same class, inquiries have been made by thinking and benevolent individuals into the condition of the destitute poor in great cities and manufacturing districts. These works brought to light deeds of darkness, and scenes of oppression and cruelty, scarcely to be credited in modern times and in Christian communities. The attention of the public was directed towards this miserable class of beings, and its best sympathies enlisted in their behalf. It was called upon to assist in the liberation of these *white slaves*, chained to the oar for life in the galleys of wealth, and to recognize them as men and brethren.

Then sprang up the ragged schools, – the institutions for reclaiming the youthful vagrants of London, and teaching the idle and profligate the sublime morality of sobriety and industry.

Persons who were unable to contribute money to these truly noble objects of charity, were ready to assist in the capacity of Sunday-school teachers, and add their mite in the great work of moral reform. In over-peopled countries like England and France, the evils arising out of extreme poverty could not be easily remedied; yet the help thus afforded by the rich, contributed greatly in ameliorating the distress of thousands of the poorer classes. To the same source we may trace the mitigation of many severe laws. The punishment of death is no longer enforced, but in cases of great depravity. Mercy has stepped in, and wiped the blood from the sword of justice.

Hood's "Song of the Shirt" produced an almost electric effect upon the public mind. It was a bold, truthful appeal to the best feelings of humanity, and it found a response in every feeling heart. It laid bare the distress of a most deserving and oppressed portion of the female operatives of London; and the good it did is at this moment in active operation. Witness the hundreds of work-women landed within the last twelve months on these shores, who immediately found liberal employment.

God's blessing upon thee, Thomas Hood! The effect produced by that work of divine charity of thine, will be felt long after thou and thy heart-searching appeal have vanished into the oblivion of the past. But what matters it to thee if the song is forgotten by coming generations? It performed its mission of mercy on earth, and has opened for thee the gates of heaven.

Such a work of fiction as the Caxtons refreshes and invigorates the mind by its perusal; and virtue becomes beautiful for its own sake. You love the gentle humanity of the single-hearted philosopher, the charming simplicity of his loving helpmate, and scarcely know which to admire the most – Catherine in her conjugal or maternal character – the noble but mistaken pride of the fine old veteran Roland, the real hero of the tale – or the excellent young man, his nephew, who reclaims the fallen son, and is not too perfect to be unnatural. As many fine moral lessons can be learned from this novel, as from most works written expressly for the instruction and improvement of mankind; and they lose nothing by the beautiful and attractive garb in which they are presented to the reader.

Our blessed Lord himself did not disdain the use of allegory, which is truth conveyed to the hearer under a symbolical form. His admirable parables, each of which told a little history, were the most popular methods that could be adopted to instruct the lower classes, who, chiefly uneducated, require the illustration of a subject in order to understand it.

Æsop, in his inimitable fables, pourtrayed through his animals the various passions and vices of men, admirably adapting them to the characters he meant to satirize, and the abuses he endeavoured through this medium to reform. These beautiful fictions have done much to throw disgrace upon roguery, selfishness, cruelty, avarice and injustice, and to exalt patience, fidelity, mercy, and generosity, even among Christians who were blessed with a higher moral code than that enjoyed by the wise pagan; and they will continue to be read and admired as long as the art of printing exists to render them immortal.

Every good work of fiction is a step towards the mental improvement of mankind, and to every such writer, we say God speed!

THE EARTHQUAKE.

"Hark! heard ye not a sound?"
         "Aye, 'tis the sullen roar
         Of billows breaking on the shore."
"Hush! – 'tis beneath the ground,
         That hollow rending shock,
         Makes the tall mountains rock, –
The solid earth doth like a drunkard reel;
         Pale nature holds her breath,
         Her tribes are mute as death.
In silent dread the coming doom they feel."

"Ah, God have mercy! – hark! those dismal cries –
         Man knows his danger now,
         And veils in dust his brow.
Beneath, the yawning earth – above, the lurid skies!
         Mortal, behold the toil and boast of years
         In one brief moment to oblivion hurled.
         So shall it be, when this vain guilty world
         Of woe, and sad necessity and tears,
Sinks at the awful mandate of its Lord,
As erst it rose to being at his word."

FIFTEEN

Lunatic Asylum

"Alas! poor maniac;
For thee no hope can dawn – no tender tie
Wake in thy blighted heart a thrill of joy;
The immortal mind is levelled with the dust,
Ere the tenacious chords of life give way!"

S.M.

OUR NEXT visit was to the Lunatic Asylum. The building is of white brick, – a material not very common in Canada, but used largely in Toronto, where stone has to be brought from a considerable distance, there being no quarries in the neighbourhood. Brick has not the substantial, august appearance, that stone gives to a large building, and it is more liable to injury from the severe frosts of winter in this climate. The asylum is a spacious edifice, surrounded by extensive grounds for the cultivation of fruits and vegetables. These are principally worked by the male patients, who are in a state of convalescence, while it affords them ample room for air and exercise.

A large gang of these unfortunates were taking their daily promenade, when our cab stopped at the entrance gate. They gazed upon us with an eager air of childish curiosity, as we alighted from our conveyance, and entered the building.

We were received very politely by one of the gentlemen

belonging to the establishment, who proceeded to show us over the place.

Ascending a broad flight of steps, as clean as it was possible for human hands to make them, we came to a long wide gallery, separated at either end by large folding-doors, the upper part of which were of glass; those to the right opening into the ward set apart for male patients, who were so far harmless that they were allowed the free use of their limbs, and could be spoken to without any danger to the visitors. The female lunatics inhabited the ward to the left, and to these we first directed our attention.

The long hall into which their work-rooms and sleeping apartments opened was lofty, well lighted, well aired, and exquisitely clean; so were the persons of the women, who were walking to and fro, laughing and chatting very sociably together. Others were sewing and quilting in rooms set apart for that purpose. There was no appearance of wretchedness or misery in this ward; nothing that associated with it the terrible idea of madness I had been wont to entertain – for these poor creatures looked healthy and cheerful, nay, almost happy, as if they had given the world and all its cares the go-by. There was one thin, eccentric looking woman in middle life, who came forward to receive us with an air of great dignity; she gave us her hand in a most condescending manner, and smiled most graciously when the gentleman who was with us inquired after her *majesty's* health. She fancies herself Victoria, and in order to humour her conceit, she is allowed to wear a cap of many colours, with tinsel ornaments. This person, who is from the lowest class, certainly enjoys her imaginary dignity in a much greater degree than any crowned monarch, and is perhaps far prouder of her fool's cap than our gracious sovereign is of her imperial diadem.

The madwomen round her appeared to consider her assumption of royalty as a very good joke, for the homage they rendered her was quizzical in the extreme.

There are times when these people seem to have a vague

consciousness of their situation; when gleams of sense break in upon them, and whisper the awful truth to their minds. Such moments must form the drops of bitterness in the poisoned cup of life, which a mysterious Providence has presented to their lips. While I was looking sadly from face to face, as these benighted creatures flitted round me, a tall stout woman exclaimed in a loud voice –

"That's Mrs. M——, of Belleville! God bless her! Many a good quarter dollar I've got from her;" and, running up to me, she flung her arms about my neck, and kissed me most vehemently.

I did not at first recognise her; and, though I submitted with a good grace to the mad hug she gave me, I am afraid that I trembled not a little in her grasp. She was the wife of a cooper, who lived opposite to us during the first two years we resided in Belleville; and I used to buy from her all the milk I needed for the children.

She was always a strange eccentric creature when sane – if, indeed, she ever had enjoyed the right use of her senses; and, in spite of the joy she manifested at the unexpected sight of me, I remember her once threatening to break my head with an old hoop, when I endeavoured to save her little girl from a frightful flagellation from the same instrument.

I had stepped across the street to her husband's workshop, to order a new meat barrel. I found him putting a barrel together, assisted by a fine little girl of ten years of age, who embraced the staves with her thin supple arms, while the father slipped one of the hoops over them in order to secure them in their place. It was a pretty picture; the smiling rosy face of the girl looking down upon her father, as he stooped over the barrel adjusting the hoop, his white curling hair falling over her slender arms. Just then the door was flung open, and Mrs.—— rushed in like a fury. –

"Katrine, where are you?"

"Here, mother," said the child, very quietly.

"How dar'd you to leave the cradle widout my lave?"

"Father called me," and the child turned pale, and began to tremble. "I came for a moment to help him."

"You little wretch!" cried the unjust woman, seizing the child by the arm. "I'll teach you to mind him more nor you mind me. Take that, and *that*."

Here followed an awful oath, and such a blow upon the bare neck of the unhappy child, that she left her hold of the barrel, and fairly shrieked with pain.

"Let the girl alone, Mary; it was my fault," said the husband.

"Yes, it always is your fault! but she shall pay for it;" and, taking up a broken hoop, she began to beat the child furiously.

My woman's heart could stand it no longer. I ran forward, and threw my arms round the child.

"Get out wid you!" she cried; "what business is it of yours? I'll break your head if you are not off out of this."

"I'm not afraid of you, Mrs.——; but I would not see you use a dog in that manner, much less a child, who has done nothing to deserve such treatment."

"Curse you all!" said the human fiend, flinging down her ugly weapon, and scowling upon us with her gloomy eyes. "I wish you were all in –."

A place far too warm for this hot season of the year, I thought, as I walked sorrowfully home. Bad as I then considered her, I have now no doubt that it was the incipient workings of her direful malady, which certainly comes nearest to any idea we can form of demoniacal possession. She is at present an incurable but harmless maniac; and, in spite of the instance of cruelty that I have just related towards her little girl, now, during the dark period of her mind's eclipse, gleams of maternal love struggled like glimpses of sunshine through a stormy cloud, and she inquired of me earnestly, pathetically, nay, even tenderly, for her children. Alas, poor maniac! How could I tell her that the girl she had chastised so undeservedly had died in early womanhood, and her son, a fine young man of twenty, had committed suicide, and flung himself off the bridge into the Moira river only a few months before. Her insanity saved her from the knowledge of events, which might have distracted a firmer brain. She seemed hardly satisfied with my evasive answers, and looked doubtingly and cunningly at me, as if some demon had whispered to her the awful truth.

It was singular that this woman should recognise me after so many years. Altered as my appearance was by time and sickness, my dearest friends would hardly have known me, – yet she knew me at a single glance. What was still more extraordinary, she remembered my daughter, now a wife and mother, whom she had not seen since she was a little girl.

What a wonderful faculty is memory! – the most mysterious and inexplicable in the great riddle of life; that plastic tablet on which the Almighty registers with unerring fidelity the records of being, making it the depository of all our words, thoughts, and deeds – this faithful witness against us for good or evil, at the great assize that hereafter must determine our eternal fate, when conscience, at his dread command, shall open up this book of life! "Keep thy heart, my son, for out of it are the issues of life." Be sure that memory guards well that secret treasure. All that the heart ever felt, the mind ever thought, the restless spirit ever willed, is there.

Another woman – wild, dark, and fierce-looking, with her hands in mufflers – flitted after us from room to room, her black, flashing eyes fixed intently on my daughter. "Yes, it is my own Mary! but she won't speak to me."

The gentleman in attendance begged us to take no notice of this person, as she was apt to be very violent.

Another stout, fair-haired matron, with good features and a very pleasant face, insisted on shaking hands with us all round. Judging from her round, sonsy, rosy face, you never could have imagined her to have been mad. When we spoke in admiration of the extreme neatness and cleanness of the large sleeping apartment, she said very quietly –

"Ah, you would not wonder at that could you see all the water-witches at night cleaning it." Then she turned to me, and whispered very confidentially in my ear, "Are you mad? You see these people; they are all mad – as mad as March hares. Don't come here if you can help it. It's all very well at first, and it looks very clean and comfortable; but when the doors are once shut, you can't get out – no, not if you ask it upon your knees." She then retreated, nodding significantly.

Leaving this ward, we visited the one which contained the male lunatics. They appeared far more gloomy and reserved than the women we had left. One young man, who used to travel the country with jewellery, and who had often been at our house, recognised us in a moment; but he did not come forward like Mrs.—— to greet us, but ran into a corner, and, turning to the wall, covered his face with his hands until we had passed on. Here was at least a consciousness of his unfortunate situation, that was very painful to witness. A gentlemanly man in the prime of life, who had once practised the law in Toronto, and was a person of some consequence, still retained the dress and manners belonging to his class. He had gone to the same school with my son-in-law, and he greeted him in the most hearty and affectionate manner, throwing his arm about his shoulder, and talking of his affairs in the most confidential manner. His mental aberration was only displayed in a few harmless remarks, such as telling us that this large house was his, that it had been built with his money, and that it was very hard he was kept a prisoner in his own dwelling; that he was worth millions, and that people were trying to cheat him of all his money, but that if once he could get out, he would punish them all. He then directed my son-in-law to bring up some law books that he named, on the morrow, and he would give him a dozen suits against the parties from whom he had received so many injuries.

In the balcony, at the far end of the gallery, we found a group of men walking to and fro for the sake of air, or lounging listlessly on benches, gazing, with vacant eyes, upon the fine prospect of wood and water dressed in the gorgeous hues of an autumnal sunset. One very intelligent-looking man, with a magnificent head, was busy writing upon a dirty piece of paper with a pencil, his table furnished by his knee, and his desk the cover of his closed but well worn Bible. He rose as we drew near him, and bowing politely, gave us a couple of poems which he drew from his waistcoat pocket.

"These were written some time ago," he said; "One of them is much better than the other. There are some fine lines in that ode to Niagara – I composed them on the spot."

On my observing the signature of *Delta* affixed to these productions, he smiled, and said, with much complacency, "My name is *David Moir*." This, upon inquiry, we found was really the case, and the mad poet considered that the coincidence gave him a right to enjoy the world-wide fame of his celebrated namesake. The poems which he gave us, and which are still in my possession, contain some lines of great merit; but they are strangely unconnected, and very defective in rhyme and keeping. He watched our countenances intently while reading them, continually stepping in, and pointing out to us his favourite passages. We were going to return them, but he bade us keep them. "He had hundreds of copies of them," he said, "in his head." He then took us on one side, and intreated us in the most pathetic manner to use our influence to get him out of that place. "He was," he said, "a good classic scholar, and had been private tutor in several families of high respectability, and he could shew us testimonials as to character and ability. It is hard to keep me here idling," he continued, "when my poor little boys want me so badly at home; poor fellows! and they have no mother to supply my place." He sighed heavily, and drew his hand across his brow, and looked sadly and dreamily into the blue distance of Ontario. The madman's thoughts were far away with his young sons, or, perhaps, had ranged back to the rugged heathery hills of his own glorious mountain land!

There were two boys among these men who, in spite of their lunacy, had an eye to business, and begged pathetically for coppers, though of what use they could be to them in that place I cannot imagine. I saw no girls under twelve years of age. There were several boys who appeared scarcely in their teens.

Mounting another flight of snowy stairs, we came to the wards above those we had just inspected. These were occupied by patients that were not in a state to allow visitors a nearer inspection than observing them through the glass doors. By standing upon a short flight of broad steps that led down to their ward, we were able to do this with perfect security. The hands of all these women were secured in mufflers; some were dancing, others running to and fro at full speed, clapping their hands, and laughing and shouting with the most boisterous merriment. How dreadful is the laugh of madness! how sorrowful the expressions of their diabolical mirth! tears and lamentations would have been less shocking, for it would have seemed more natural.

Among these raving maniacs I recognised the singular face of Grace Marks – no longer sad and despairing, but lighted up with the fire of insanity, and glowing with a hideous and fiend-like merriment. On perceiving that strangers were observing her, she fled shrieking away like a phantom into one of the side rooms. It appears that even in the wildest bursts of her terrible malady, she is continually haunted by a memory of the past. Unhappy girl! when will the long horror of her punishment and remorse be over? When will she sit at the feet of Jesus, clothed with the unsullied garments of his righteousness, the stain of blood washed from her hand, and her soul redeemed, and pardoned, and in her right mind? It is fearful to look at her, and contemplate her fate in connexion with her crime. What a striking illustration does it afford of that awful text, "Vengeance is mine, I will repay, saith the Lord!"

There was one woman in this ward, with raven hair and eyes, and a sallow, unhealthy complexion, whom the sight of us transported into a paroxysm of ungovernable rage. She rushed to the door, and doubled her fists at us, and began cursing and swearing at a furious rate, and then she laughed – such a laugh as one might fancy Satan uttered when he recounted, in full conclave, his triumph over the credulity of our first mother. Presently she grew outrageous, and had to be thrown to the ground, and secured by two keepers; but to silence her was beyond their art. She lay kicking and foaming, and uttering words too dreadful for human ears to listen to; and Grace Marks came out from her hiding-place, and performed a thousand mad gambols round her: and we turned from the piteous scene, – and I, for one, fervently thanked God for my sanity, and inwardly repeated those exquisite lines of the peasant bard of my native county: –

> "Oh, Thou, who bidd'st the vernal juices rise,
> Thou on whose blast autumnal foliage flies;
> Let peace ne'er leave me, nor my heart grow cold,
> Whilst life and sanity are mine to hold."

We cast but a cursory glance on the men who occupied the opposite ward. We had seen enough of madness, and the shrieks from the outrageous patients above, whom strangers have seldom nerve enough to visit, quickened our steps as we hurried from the place.

We looked into the large ball-room before we descended the stairs, where these poor creatures are allowed at stated times to meet for pleasure and amusement. But such a spectacle would be to me more revolting than the scene I had just witnessed; the delirium of their frightful disease would be less shocking in my eyes than the madness of their mirth. The struggling gleams of sense and memory in these unhappy people reminded me a beautiful passage in "Tupper's Proverbial Philosophy":

> "On all things created remaineth the half-effaced signature
>   of God;
>   Somewhat of fair and good, though blotted by the finger
>   of corruption."

What a sublime truth! How beautifully and forcibly expressed! With what a mournful dignity it invests our fallen nature! Sin has marred the Divine image in which we were made, but the soul in its intense longing after God and good bears, in its sorrowful servitude to evil, the impress of the hand that formed it happy and free. Yes, even in the most abject and fallen, some slight trace of good remains – some spark of the Divine essence that still lingers amid the darkness and corruption of guilt, to rekindle the dying embers, and restore them once more to life and liberty. The madman raving in his chains still remembers his God, to bless or blaspheme his name. We are astonished at his ecstatic dream of happiness, or shocked beyond measure at the blackness of his despair. His superhuman strength fills us with wonder; and, even in the extinction of reason, we acknowledge the eternal presence of God, and perceive flashes of his Spirit breaking through the dark material cloud that shades, but cannot wholly annihilate the light of the soul, the immortality within.

The poor, senseless idiot, who appears to mortal eyes a mere living machine, a body without a soul, sitting among the grass, and playing with the flowers and pebbles in the vacancy of his mind, is still a wonderful illustration of the wisdom and power of God. We behold a human being inferior in instinct and intelligence of the meanest orders of animal life, dependent upon the common charities of his kind for subsistence, yet conscious of the friend who pities his helplessness, and of the hand that administers to his wants. The Spirit of his Maker shall yet breathe upon the dull chaos of his stagnant brain, and open the eyes of this blind of soul into the light of his own eternal day!

What a lesson to the pride of man – to the vain dwellers in houses of clay!

Returning from the asylum, we stopped to examine Trinity College, which is on the opposite side of the road. The architect, K. Tully, Esq. has shown considerable taste and genius in the design of this edifice, which, like the asylum, is built of white brick, the corners, doors, and windows faced with cut stone. It stands back from the road in a fine park-like lawn, surrounded by stately trees of nature's own planting. When the college is completed, it will be one of the finest public buildings in the province, and form one of the noblest ornaments to this part of the city.

THE MANIAC.

"The wind at my casement scream'd shrilly and loud,
And the pale moon look'd in from her mantle of cloud;
Old ocean was tossing in terrible might,
And the black rolling billows were crested with light.
Like a shadowy dream on my senses that hour,
Stole the beautiful vision of grandeur and power;
And the sorrows of life that brought tears to mine eye,
Were forgot in the glories of ocean and sky.

" 'Oh nature!' I cried, 'in thy beautiful face
All the wisdom and love of thy Maker I trace;
Thy aspect divine checks my tears as they start,
And fond hopes long banish'd flow back to my heart!'
Thus musing, I wander'd alone to the shore,
To gaze on the waters, and list to their roar,
When I saw a poor lost one bend over the steep
Of the tall beetling cliff that juts out o'er the deep.

"The wind wav'd her garments, and April's rash showers
Hung like gems in her dark locks, enwreath'd with wild flowers;
Her bosom was bared to the cold midnight storm,
That unsparingly beat on her thin fragile form;

Her black eyes flash'd sternly whence reason had fled,
And she glanc'd on my sight like some ghost of the dead,
As she sang a loud strain to the hoarse dashing surge,
That rang on my ears like the plaint of a dirge.

"And he who had left her to madness and shame,
Who had robb'd her of honour, and blasted her fame –
Did he think in that hour of the heart he had riven,
The vows he had broken, the anguish he'd given? –
And where was the infant whose birth gave the blow
To the peace of his mother, and madden'd her woe?
A thought rush'd across me – I ask'd for her child, –
With a wild laugh of triumph the maniac replied –

" 'Where the dark tide runs strongest, the cliff rises steep,
Where the wild waters eddy, I've rock'd him to sleep:
His sleep is so sound that the rush of the stream,
When the winds are abroad, cannot waken his dream.
And see you that rock, with its surf-beaten side,
There the blood of my false love runs red with the tide;
The sea-mew screams shrilly, the white breakers rave –
In the foam of the billow I'll dance o'er his grave!'

" 'Mid the roar of the tempest, the wind's hollow moan,
There rose on my chill'd ear a faint dying groan;
The billows raged on, the moon smiled on the flood,
But vacant the spot where the maniac had stood.
I turn'd from the scene – on my spirit there fell
A question that sadden'd my heart like a knell;
I look'd up to heav'n, but I breath'd not a word,
For the answer was given – 'Trust thou in the Lord!' "

SIXTEEN

Provincial Agricultural Show

"A happy scene of rural mirth,
    Drawn from the teeming lap of earth,
    In which a nation's promise lies.
    Honour to him who wins a prize! –
    A trophy won by honest toil,
    Far nobler than the victor's spoil."

S.M.

TORONTO was all bustle and excitement, preparing for the Provincial Agricultural Show; no other subject was thought of or talked about. The ladies, too, taking advantage of the great influx of strangers to the city, were to hold a bazaar for the benefit of St. George's Church; the sum which they hoped to realise by the sale of their fancy wares to be appropriated to paying off the remaining debt contracted for the said saint, in erecting this handsome edifice dedicated to his name – let us hope not to his service. Yet the idea of erecting a temple for the worship of God, and calling it the church of a saint of *very doubtful sanctity*, is one of those laughable absurdities that we would gladly see banished in this enlightened age. Truly, there are many things in which our wisdom does not exceed the wisdom of our forefathers. The weather during the two first days of the exhibition was very unpropitious; a succession of drenching thunder showers, succeeded by warm bursts of sunshine, promising better things, and giving rise to hopes in the expectant visitants to the show, which were as often doomed to be disappointed by returns of blackness, storm, and pouring rain.

I was very anxious to hear the opening address, and I must confess that I was among those who felt this annihilation of hope very severely; and, being an invalid, I dared not venture upon the grounds before Wednesday morning, when this most interesting part of the performance was over. Wednesday, however, was as beautiful a September day as the most sanguine of the agricultural exhibitors could desire, and the fine space allotted for the display of the various objects of industry was crowded to overflowing.

It was a glorious scene for those who had the interest of the colony at heart. Every district of the Upper Province had contributed its portion of labour, talent, and ingenuity, to furnish forth the show. The products of the soil, the anvil, and the loom, met the eye at every turn. The genius of the mechanic was displayed in the effective articles of machinery, invented to assist the toils and shorten the labour of human hands, and were many and excellent in their kind. Improvements in old implements, and others entirely new, were shown or put into active operation by the inventors, – those real benefactors to the human race, to whom the exploits of conquerors, however startling and brilliant, are very inferior in every sense.

Mechanical genius, which ought to be regarded as the first and greatest effort of human intellect, is only now beginning to be recognised as such. The statesman, warrior, poet, painter, orator, and man of letters, all have their niche in the temple of fame – all have had their worshippers and admirers; but who among them has celebrated in song and tale the grand creative power which can make inanimate metals move, and act, and almost live, in the wondrous machinery of the present day! It is the mind that conceived, the hand that reduced to practical usefulness these miraculous instruments, with all their complicated works moving in harmony, and performing their appointed office, that comes nearest to the sublime Intelligence that framed the universe, and gave life and motion to that astonishing piece of mechanism, the human form.

In watching the movements of the steam-engine, one can hardly divest one's self of the idea that it possesses life and consciousness. True, the metal is but a dead agent, but the spirit of the originator still lives in it, and sways it to the gigantic will that first gave it motion and power. And, oh, what wonders has it not achieved! what obstacles has it not overcome! how has it brought near things that were far off, and crumbled into dust difficulties which, at first sight, appeared insurmountable. Honour to the clear-sighted, deep-thinking child of springs and wheels, at whose head stands the great Founder of the world, the grandest humanity that ever trode the earth! Rejoice, and shout for joy, ye sons of the rule and line! for was he not one of you? Did he not condescend to bow that God-like form over the carpenter's bench, and handle the plane and saw? Yours should be termed the Divine craft, and those who follow it truly noble. Your great Master was above the little things of earth; he knew the true dignity of man – that virtue conferred the same majesty upon its possessor in the workshop or the palace – that the soul's title to rank as a son of God required neither high birth, nor the adventitious claims of wealth – that the simple name of a good man was a more abiding honour, even in this world, than that of kings or emperors.

Oh! ye sons of labour, seek to attain this true dignity inherent in your nature, and cease to envy the possessors of those ephemeral honours that perish with the perishing things of this world. The time is coming – is now even at the doors – when education shall give you a truer standing in society, and good men throughout the whole world shall recognise each other as brothers.

> "An' o'er the earth gude sense an' worth
> Shall bear the gree an' a' that."

Carried away from my subject by an impetuous current of thought, I must step back to the show from which I derived a great deal of satisfaction and pleasure. The space in which it was exhibited contained, I am told, about sixteen acres. The rear of this, where the animals were shown, was a large grove covered with tall spreading trees, beneath the shade of which, reposing or standing in the most picturesque attitudes, were to be seen the finest breeds of cattle, horses, and sheep, in the province. This inclosure was surrounded by a high boarded fence, against which pens were erected for the accommodation of plethoric-looking pigs, fat sleepy lambs, and wild mischievous goats; while noble horses were led to and fro by their owners or their servants, snorting and curveting in all the conscious pride of strength and beauty. These handsome, proud-looking creatures, might be considered the aristocracy of the animal department; yet, in spite of their prancing hoofs, arched necks, and glances of fire, they had to labour in their vocation as well as the poorest pig that grunted and panted in its close pen. There was a donkey there – a solitary ass – the first of his kind I ever beheld in the province. Unused to such a stir and bustle, he lifted up his voice, and made the grove ring with his discordant notes. The horses bounded and reared, and glanced down upon him in such mad disdain, that they could scarcely be controlled by their keepers. I can imagine the astonishment they must have felt on hearing the first bray of an ass; they could not have appeared more startled at a lion's roar. Whoever exhibited Mr. Braham was a brave man. A gentleman, who settled in the neighbourhood of Peterboro' twenty years ago, brought out a donkey with him to Canada, and until the day of his death he went by no other name than the undignified one of Donkey.

I cannot help thinking, that the donkey would be a very useful creature in the colony. Though rather an untractable democrat, insisting on having things his own way, he is a hardy, patient fellow, and easily kept; and though very obstinate, is by no means insensible of kind treatment, or incapable of attachment; and then, as an *exterminator of Canadian thistles*, he would prove an invaluable reformer by removing these agricultural pests out of the way. Often have I gazed upon the *Canadian thistle* – that prolific, sturdy democrat of the soil, that rudely jostles aside its more delicate and valued neighbours, elbowing them from their places with its wide-spreading and armed foliage – and asked myself for what purpose it grew and flourished so abundantly? Surely, it must have some useful qualities; some good must lie hidden under its hardy structure and coat of mail, independently of its exercising those valuable qualities in man – patience and industry – which must be called into active operation in order to root it out, and hinder it from destroying the fruits of his labour. The time, perhaps, may arrive when its thick milky juices and oily roots may be found to yield nutricious food, or afford a soothing narcotic to alleviate the restless tossings of pain. I firmly believe that nothing has been made in vain; that every animate and inanimate substance has its use, although we may be ignorant of it; that the most perfect and beautiful harmony reigns over the visible world; that although we may foolishly despise those animals, plants, and insects, that we consider noxious, because their real utility has never been tested by experience, they are absolutely necessary as links in the great chain of Providence, and appointed to fulfil a special purpose and end.

"What shall we do for firewood when all the forests are burned?" was a very natural question asked us the other day by a young friend, who, with very scanty means, contemplated with a sort of horror the increased demand for fuel, and its increasing price.

Tupper has an admirable answer for all such queries: –

"Yet man, heedless of a God, counteth up vain reckonings,
Fearing to be jostled and starved out by the too prolific
  increase of his kind,
And asketh, in unbelieving dread, for how few years to come

Will the black cellars of the world yield unto him fuel for his
    winter.
Might not the wide waste sea be bent into narrower bounds?
Might not the arm of diligence make the tangled wilderness a
    garden?
And for aught thou can'st tell, there may be a thousand
    methods
Of comforting thy limbs in warmth, though thou kindle not a
    spark.
Fear not, son of man, for thyself, nor thy seed – with a
    multitude is plenty:
God's blessing giveth increase, and with it larger than enough."

Surely it is folly for any one to despair of the future,
while the providence of God superintends the affairs of
the universe. Is it not sinful to doubt the power of that
Being, who fed a vast multitude from a few loaves and
small fishes? Is His arm shortened, that he can no longer
produce those articles that are indispensable and necessary for the health and comfort of the creatures dependent
upon his bounty? What millions have been fed by the
introduction of the potato plant – that wild, half-poison-
ous native of the Chilian mountains! When first exhibited
as a curiosity by Sir Walter Raleigh, who could have
imagined the astonishing results, – not only in feeding the
multitudes that for several ages in Ireland it has fed, but
that the very blight upon it, by stopping an easy mode of
obtaining food, should be the instrument in the hands of
the great Father to induce these impoverished, starving
children of an unhappy country, to remove to lands where
honest toil would be amply remunerated, and produce
greater blessings for them than the precarious support
afforded by an esculent root? We have faith, unbounded
faith, in the benevolent care of the Universal Father, –
faith in the fertility of the earth, and her capabilities of
supporting to the end of time her numerous offspring.
The over-population of old settled countries may

appear to a casual thinker a dreadful calamity; and yet it is but the natural means employed by Providence to force the poorer classes, by the strong law of necessity, to emigrate and spread themselves over the earth, in order to bring into cultivation and usefulness its waste places. When the world can no longer maintain its inhabitants, it will be struck out of being by the fiat of Him who called it into existence.

Nothing has contributed more to the rapid advance of the province than the institution of the Agricultural Society, and from it we are already reaping the most beneficial results. It has stirred up a spirit of emulation in a large class of people, who were very supine in their method of cultivating their lands; who, instead of improving them, and making them produce not only the largest quantity of grain, but that of the best quality, were quite contented if they reaped enough from their slovenly farming to supply the wants of their family, of a very inferior sort.

Now, we behold a laudable struggle among the tillers of the soil, as to which shall send the best specimens of good husbandry to contend for the prizes at the provincial shows, where very large sums of money are expended in providing handsome premiums for the victors. All the leading men in the province are members of this truly honourable institution; and many of them send horses, and the growth of their gardens, to add to the general bustle and excitement of the scene. The summer before last my husband took the second prize for wheat at the provincial show, and I must frankly own that I felt as proud of it as if it had been the same sum bestowed upon a prize poem.

There was an immense display of farm produce on the present occasion at Toronto, all excellent in their kind. The Agricultural Hall, a large, temporary building of boards, was completely filled with the fruits of the earth and the products of the dairy –

"A glorious sight, if glory dwells below,
Where heaven's munificence makes all the show."

The most delicious butter and tempting cheese, quite equal, perhaps, to the renowned British in every thing but the name, were displayed in the greatest abundance.

A Mr. Hiram Ranney, from the Brock district, contributed a monster cheese, weighing 7 cwt., not made of "double skimmed sky-blue," but of milk of the richest quality, which, from its size and appearance, might have feasted all the rats and mice in the province for the next twelve months. It was large enough to have made the good old deity of heathen times – her godship of the earth – an agricultural throne; while from the floral hall, close at hand, a crown could have been woven, on the shortest notice, of the choicest buds from her own inexhaustible treasury.

A great quantity of fine flax and hemp particularly attracted my attention. Both grow admirably in this country, and at no very distant period will form staple articles for home manufacture and foreign export.

The vast improvement in home-manufactured cloth, blankets, flannels, shawls, carpeting, and counterpanes, was very apparent over the same articles in former years. In a short time Canada need not be beholden to any foreign country for articles of comfort and convenience. In these things her real wealth and strength are shown; and we may well augur from what she has already achieved in this line, how much more she can do – and do well – with credit and profit to herself.

The sheep in Canada are not subject to the diseases which carry off so many yearly in Britain; and though these animals have to be housed during the winter, they are a very profitable stock. The Canadian grass-fed mutton is not so large as it is in England, and in flavour and texture more nearly resembles the Scotch. It has more of a young flavour, and, to my thinking, affords a more whole-

some, profitable article of consumption. Beef is very inferior to the British; but since the attention of the people has
been more intently directed to their agricultural interests,
there is a decided improvement in this respect, and the
condition of all the meat sent to market now-a-days is ten
per cent better than the lean, hard animals, we used to
purchase for winter provisions, when we first came to the
province.

At that time they had a race of pigs, tall and gaunt, with
fierce, bristling manes, that wandered about the roads and
woods, seeking what they could devour, like famished
wolves. You might have pronounced them, without any
great stretch of imagination, descended from the same
stock into which the attendant fiends that possessed the
poor maniacs of Galilee had been cast so many ages ago. I
knew a gentleman who was attacked in the bush by a sow
of this ferocious breed, who fairly tried him in the woods
of Douro, and kept him on his uncomfortable perch during several hours, until his swinish enemy's patience was
exhausted, and she had to give up her supper of human
flesh for the more natural products of the forest, acorns
and beech-mast.

Talking of pigs and sheep recals to my mind an amusing
anecdote, told to me by a resident of one of our back
townships, which illustrates, even in a cruel act of retaliation, the dry humour which so strongly characterizes the
lower class of emigrants from the emerald isle. I will give it
in my young friend's own words: –

"In one of our back townships there lived an old
Dutchman, who was of such a vindictive temper that none
of his neighbours could remain at peace with him. He
made the owners of the next farm so miserable that they
were obliged to sell out, and leave the place. The farm
passed through many hands, and at last became vacant,
for no one could stay on it more than a few months; they
were so worried and annoyed by this spiteful old man,
who, upon the slightest occasion, threw down their fences
and injured their cattle. In short, the poor people began to

suspect that he was the devil himself, sent among them as a punishment for their sins.

"At last an Irish emigrant lately out was offered the place very cheap, and, to the astonishment of all, bought it, in spite of the bad *karacter*, for the future residence of himself and family.

"He had not been long on the new place when one of his sheep, which had got through a hole in the Dutchman's fence, came hobbling home with one of its legs stuck through the other. Now, you must know that this man, who was so active in punishing the trespasses of his neighbours' cattle and stock, was not at all particular in keeping his own at home. There happened to be an old sow of his, who was very fond of Pat's *potaties*, and a constant *throuble* to him, just then in the field when the sheep came home. Pat took the old sow (not very tenderly, I'm afraid) by the ear, and drawing out his jack-knife, very deliberately slit her mouth on either side as far as he could. By and by, the old Dutchman came puffing and blowing along; and seeing Pat sitting upon his door-step, enjoying the evening air, and comfortably smoking his pipe, he asked him if he had seen anything of his sow?

" 'Well, neighbour,' said Pat, putting on one of his gravest faces, 'one of the strangest things happened a short while ago that I ever saw. A sheep of mine came home with its leg slit and the other put through it, and your old sow was so amused with the odd sight that she split her jaws with laughing.' "

This turned the tables upon the spiteful old man, and completely cured him of all his ill-natured tricks. He is now one of the best neighbours in the township.

This was but a poor reparation to the poor sheep and the old sow. Their sufferings appear to have been regarded by both parties as a very minor consideration.

The hall set apart for the display of fancy work and the fine arts appeared to be the great centre of attraction, for it was almost impossible to force your way through the dense crowd, or catch a glimpse of the pictures exhibited by native artists. The show of these was highly creditable indeed. Eight pictures, illustrative of Indian scenery, character, and customs, by Mr. Paul Kane, would have done honour to any exhibition. For correctness of design, beauty of colouring, and a faithful representation of the peculiar scenery of this continent, they could scarcely be surpassed.

I stood for a long time intently examining these interesting pictures, when a tall fellow, in the grey homespun of the country, who, I suppose, thought that I had my share of enjoyment in that department, very coolly took me by the shoulders, pulled me back into the crowd, and possessed himself of my vacant place. This man should have formed a class with the two large tame bears exhibited on the ground appropriated to the poultry; but I rather think that Bruin and his brother would have been ashamed of having him added to their fraternity; seeing that their conduct was quite unexceptionable, and they could have a set a good example to numbers of the human bipeds, who pushed and elbowed from side to side anything that obstructed their path, while a little common courtesy would have secured to themselves and others a far better opportunity of examining everything carefully. The greatest nuisance in this respect was a multitude of small children, who were completely hidden in the press, and whose feet, hands, and head, dealt blows, against which it was impossible to protect yourself, as you felt severely without being able to ward off their home-thrusts. It is plain that they could not *see* at all, but were determined that every one should sensibly *feel* their disappointment. It was impossible to stop for a moment to examine this most interesting portion of the Exhibition; and one was really glad to force a passage out of the press into the free air.

Large placards were pasted about in the most conspicuous places, warning visitors to the grounds to look out for pickpockets! Every one was on the alert to discover these gentry – expecting them, I suppose, to be classed like the animal and vegetable productions of the soil; and the vicinity of a knowing-looking, long-bearded pedlar, who was selling Yankee notions at the top of his voice, and always surrounded by a great mob, was considered the most likely locality for these invisible personages, who, I firmly believe, existed alone in the fancy of the authors of the aforesaid placards.

There was a very fine display of the improved and foreign breeds of poultry; and a set of idle Irish loungers, of the lower class, were amusing themselves by inserting the bowls of their pipes into the pens that contained these noble fowls, and giving them the benefit of a good smoking. The intoxicating effects of the fumes of the tobacco upon the poor creatures appeared to afford their tormentors the greatest entertainment. The stately Cochin-China cocks shook their plumed heads, and turned up their beaks with unmistakeable signs of annoyance and disgust; and two fine fowls that were lying dead outside the pens, were probably killed by this novel sport.

I was greatly struck by the appearance of Okah Tubee, the celebrated Indian doctor, who was certainly the most conspicuous-looking person in the show, and on a less public occasion would have drawn a large number of spectators on his own hook.

Okah Tubee is a broad, stout, powerfully built man, with a large fat face, set off to the least possible advantage by round rings of braided hair, tied with blue ribbons, and with large gold ear-rings in his ears. Now, it certainly is true that a man has a perfect right to dress his hair in this fashion, or in any fashion he pleases; but a more absurd appearance than the blue ribbons gave to his broad, brown, beardless face, it is impossible to imagine. The solemn dignity, too, with which he carried off this tomfoolery was not the least laughable part of it. I wonder which of his wives – for I was told he had several – braided all these small rings of hair, and confined them with the blue love knots; but it is more than probable that the grave Indian performed his own toilet. His blue surtout

beaver hat accorded ill with his Indian leggings and moc-
cassins. I must think that the big man's dress was in
shocking bad taste, and decided failure. I missed the sight
of him carrying a flag in the procession, and mounted on
horseback; if his riding-dress matched his walking costume, it must have been rich.

Leaving the show-ground, we next directed our steps to
the Ladies' Bazaar, that was held in the government buildings, and here we found a number of well-dressed, elegant
women, sitting like Mathew at the receipt of custom; it is
to be hoped that their labours of love received an ample
recompense, and that the sale of their pretty toys completely discharged the debt that had been incurred for
their favourite saint. Nor was the glory of old England
likely to be forgotten amid such a display of national flags
as adorned the spacious apartment.

THE BANNER OF ENGLAND.

> "The banner of old England flows
>   Triumphant in the breeze –
> A sign of terror to our foes,
>   The meteor of the seas.
> A thousand heroes bore it
>   In battle fields of old;
> All nations quail'd before it,
>   Defended by the bold.

> "Brave Edward and his gallant sons
>   Beneath its shadow bled;
> And lion-hearted Britons
>   That flag to glory led.
> The sword of kings defended,
>   When hostile foes drew near;
> The sheet whose colours bended –
>   Memorials proud and dear!

> "The hist'ry of a nation
>   Is blazon'd on its page,

A brief and bright relation
  Sent down from age to age.
O'er Gallia's hosts victorious,
  It turn'd their pride of yore;
Its fame on earth is glorious,
  Renown'd from shore to shore.

"The soldier's heart has bounded
  When o'er the tide of war;
Where death's brief cry resounded,
  It flash'd a blazing star.
Or floating over leaguer'd wall,
  It met his lifted eye;
Like war-horse to the trumpet's call,
  He rush'd to victory!

"No son of Britain e'er will see
  A foreign band advance,
To seize the standard of the free,
  That dared the might of France.
Bright banner of our native land,
  Bold hearts are knit to thee;
A hardy, brave, determined band,
  Thy champions yet shall be!"

SEVENTEEN

Niagara

"Come and worship at a shrine,
  Rear'd by hands eternal,
Where the flashing waters shine,
  And the turf is ever vernal,
And nature's everlasting voice
For ever cries – rejoice, rejoice!"

S.M.

T HE NIGHT had been one of pouring rain, and the day
  dawned through a thick veil of misty clouds, on the
morning of which we were to start from Toronto to visit
the Falls of Niagara.

"It is always so," I thought, as I tried to peer through
the dense mist that floated round the spire of St. George's
church, in order to read what promise there might lurk
behind its gray folds of a fine day. "What we most wish
for is, for some wise purpose inscrutable to our narrow
vision, generally withheld. But it may clear up after all. At
all events, we must 'bide the chance and make the
experiment."

By seven o'clock we were on board the "Chief Justice,"
one of the steamers that daily ply between Toronto and
Queenstone. A letter that I got, in passing the post-office,
from the dear children at home, diverted my thoughts for
a long while from the dull sky and the drizzling rain; and

when it had been read and re-read, and pondered over for some time, and God inwardly thanked for the affection that breathed in every line, and the good news it contained, the unpromising mist had all cleared away, and the sun was casting bright silvery gleams across the broad bosom of the beautiful Ontario.

We did not meet with a solitary adventure on our very pleasant voyage; the deep blue autumnal sky, and the gently-undulating waters, forming the chief attraction, and giving rise to pleasant trains of thought, till the spirit blended and harmonized with the grand and simple elements that composed the scene.

There were no passengers in the ladies' cabin, and we never left the deck of the steamer until she came to her wharf at Queenstone.

The lake for some miles before you reach the entrance of the Niagara river assumes a yellowish-green tint, quite different from the ordinary deep blue of its waters. This is probably owing to the vast quantity of soil washed down by the rapids from the high lands above.

The captain told us that after a storm, such as we had experienced on the preceding night, this appearance, though it always existed, was more apparent. You catch a distant glance of the Falls from this part of the lake; but it is only in the shape of a light silvery cloud hovering on the edge of the horizon. We listened in vain for any sound to give us an indication of their near vicinity. The voice of nature was mute. The roar of the great cataract was not distinguishable at that distance.

The entrance to the Niagara river is very interesting. You pass between the two strong stone forts, raised for the protection of their respective countries; and a hostile vessel would stand but a small chance of keeping clear from danger in passing either Cerberus. It is devoutly to be hoped that all such difficulties will be avoided, by the opposite shores remaining firm friends and allies.

The town of Niagara is a quaint, old-fashioned looking place, and belongs more to the past than the present of

Canada; for it has not made much progress since it ceased to be the capital of the Upper Province, in spite of its very advantageous and beautiful locality.

As you approach Queenstone, the river is much contracted in its dimensions, and its banks assume a bold and lofty appearance, till they frown down upon the waters in stern and solemn grandeur, and impart a wild, romantic character to the scene, not often found in the Upper Province.

I never beheld any water that resembled the deep green of the Niagara. This may be owing, perhaps, to the immense depth of the river, the colour of the rocks over which it flows, or it may be reflected from the beautiful trees and shrubs that clothe its precipitous banks; but it must strike every person who first gazes upon it as very remarkable. You cannot look down into it, for it is not pellucid but opaque in its appearance, and runs with a smooth surface more resembling oil than water.

The waters of the St. Lawrence are a pale sea-green, and so transparently clear that you see through them to a great depth. At sunrise and sunset they take all the hues of the opal. The Ottawa is a deep blue. The Otonabee looks black, from the dark limestone bed over which it foams and rushes. Our own Moira is of a silvery or leaden hue, but the waters of the Niagara are a bright deep green; and did any painter venture to transfer their singular colour to his canvas, it would be considered extravagant and impossible.

The new Suspension Bridge at Queenstone is a beautiful object from the water. The river here is six hundred feet in width; the space between the two stone towers that support the bridge on either shore is eight hundred and fifty feet; the height above the water, two hundred feet. The towers are not built on the top of the bank, but a platform for each has been quarried out of the steep sides of the precipice, about thirty feet below the edge of the cliffs. The road that leads up from the Queenstone ferry has been formed by the same process. It is a perilous ascent, and hangs almost over the river, nor is there any sufficient barrier to prevent a skittish horse from plunging from the giddy height into the deep, swift stream below. I should not like to travel this romantic road of a dark October night, even on foot. The Queenstone cab-drivers rattle up and down this fearful path without paying the least regard to the nerves of their passengers. At the entrance to the bridge, a space is quarried out of the bank to allow heavy teams to turn on to the bridge, which is done with the greatest ease and safety.

Several heavy loaded teams were crossing from the other side, and it was curious to watch the horses, when they felt the vibratory motion, draw back close to the vehicles, and take high, short steps, as if they apprehended some unknown danger. It is surprising how well they behave on this trying occasion, for a horse, though a very brave animal, is one of the most nervous ones in creation.

These beautiful, airy-looking structures, are a great triumph of mechanical art over a barrier which had long been considered as insurmountable, except by water. The ready mode of communication which by their means has been established between the opposite shores, must prove of incalculable advantage to this part of the colony.

It is to be hoped that similar bridges will soon span the many rapid rivers in Canada. A sudden spring thaw gives such volume and power to most of the streams, that few bridges constructed on the old plan are long able to resist the impetuosity of the current, but are constantly liable to be carried away, occasioning great damage in their vicinity.

The Suspension Bridge, by being raised above the possible action of the water, is liable to none of the casualties that operate against the old bridge, whose piers and arches, though formed of solid masonry, are not proof against the powerful battering-rams formed by huge blocks of ice and heavy logs of wood, aided by the violent opposing force of the current.

The light and graceful proportions of the Suspension

Bridge add a great charm to the beauty of this charming landscape. It is well worth paying a visit to Niagara, if it possessed no object of greater interest in its neighbourhood than these wonderful structures.

The village of Queenstone is built at the foot of the hill, and is a very pretty romantic-looking place. Numerous springs wind like silvery threads along the face of the steep bank above; and wherever the waters find a flat ledge in their downward course, water-cresses of the finest quality grow in abundance, the sparkling water gurgling among their juicy leaves, and washing them to emerald brightness. Large portions of the cliff are literally covered with them. It was no small matter of surprise to me when told that the inhabitants made no use of this delicious plant, but laugh at the eagerness with which strangers seek it out.

The Queenstone Heights, to the east of the village, are a lofty ridge of land rising three hundred feet above the level of the country below. They are quite as precipitous as the banks of the river. The railroad winds along the face of this magnificent bank. Gigantic trees tower far above your head, and a beautiful fertile country lies extended at your feet. There, between its rugged banks, winds the glorious river; and, beyond forest and plain, glitters the Ontario against the horizon, like a mimic ocean, blending its blue waters with the azure ocean of heaven. Truly it is a magnificent scene, and associated with the most interesting historical events connected with the province.

Brock's monument, which you pass on the road, is a melancholy looking ruin, but by no means a picturesque one, resembling some tall chimney that has been left standing after the house to which it belonged had been burnt down.

Some time ago subscriptions were set on foot to collect money to rebuild this monument; but the rock on which it stands is, after all, a more enduring monument to the memory of the hero, than any perishable structure raised to commemorate the desperate struggle that terminated on this spot. As long as the heights of Queenstone remain, and the river pours its swift current to mingle with the Ontario, the name of General Brock will be associated with the scene. The noblest tablet on which the deeds of a great man can be engraved, is on the heart of his grateful country.

Were a new monument erected on this spot tomorrow, it is more than probable that it would share the fate of its predecessor, and some patriotic American would consider it an act of duty to the great Republic to dash it out of *creation*.

From Queenstone we took a carriage on to Niagara, a distance of about eight miles, over good roads, and through a pleasant, smiling tract of country. This part of the province might justly be termed the garden of Canada, and partakes more of the soft and rich character of English scenery.

The ground rises and falls in gentle slopes; the fine meadows, entirely free from the odious black stumps, are adorned with groups of noble chestnut and black walnut trees; and the peach and apple orchards in full bearing, clustering around the neat homesteads, give to them an appearance of wealth and comfort, which cannot exist for many years to come in more remote districts.

The air on these high table lands is very pure and elastic; and I could not help wishing for some good fairy to remove my little cottage into one of the fair enclosures we passed continually by the roadside, and place it beneath the shade of some of the beautiful trees that adorned every field.

Here, for the first time in Canada, I observed hedges of the Canadian thorn – a great improvement on the old snake fence of rough split timber which prevails all through the colony. What a difference it would make in the aspect of the country if these green hedgerows were in general use! It would take from the savage barrenness given to it by these crooked wooden lines, that cross and recross the country in all directions: no object can be less picturesque or more unpleasing to the eye. A new clearing reminds one of a large turnip field, divided by hurdles into different compartments for the feeding of sheep and cattle. Often, for miles on a stretch, there is scarcely a tree or bush to relieve the blank monotony of these ugly, uncouth partitions of land, beyond charred stumps and rank weeds, and the uniform belt of forest at the back of the new fields.

The Canadian cuts down, but rarely plants trees, which circumstance accounts for the blank look of desolation that pervades all new settlements. A few young maples and rock elms, planted along the roadsides, would, at a very small expense of labour, in a very few years remedy this ugly feature in the Canadian landscape, and afford a grateful shade to the weary traveller from the scorching heat of the summer sun.

In old countries, where landed property often remains for ages in the same family, the present occupant plants and improves for future generations, hoping that his son's sons may enjoy the fruit of his labours. But in a new country like this, where property is constantly changing owners, no one seems to think it worth their while to take any trouble to add to the beauty of a place for the benefit of strangers.

Most of our second growth of trees have been planted by the beautiful hand of nature, who, in laying out her cunning work, generally does it in the most advantageous manner; and chance or accident has suffered the trees to remain on the spot from whence they sprung.

Trees that grow in open spaces after the forest has been cleared away, are as graceful and umbrageous as those planted in parks at home. The forest trees seldom possess any great beauty of outline; they run all to top, and throw out few lateral branches. There is not a tree in the woods that could afford the least shelter during a smart shower of rain. They are so closely packed together in these dense forests, that a very small amount of foliage, for the size and length of the trunk, is to be found on any individual tree. One wood is the exact picture of another; the uniformity dreary in the extreme. There are no green vistas to be seen; no grassy glades beneath the bosky oaks, on which the deer browse, and the gigantic shadows sleep in the sunbeams. A stern array of rugged trunks, a tangled maze of scrubby underbrush, carpetted winter and summer with a thick layer of withered buff leaves, form the general features of a Canadian forest.

A few flowers force their heads through this thick covering of leaves, and make glad with their beauty the desolate wilderness; but those who look for an Arcadia of fruits and flowers in the Backwoods of Canada cannot fail of disappointment. Some localities, it is true, are more favoured than others, especially those sandy tracts of table land that are called plains in this country; the trees are more scattered, and the ground receives the benefit of light and sunshine.

Flowers – those precious gifts of God – do not delight in darkness and shade, and this is one great reason why they are so scarce in the woods. I saw more beautiful blossoms waving above the Niagara river, from every crevice in its rocky banks, than I ever beheld during my long residence in the bush. These lovely children of light seem peculiarly to rejoice in their near vicinity to water, the open space allowed to the wide rivers affording them the air and sunshine denied to them in the close atmosphere of the dense woods.

The first sight we caught of the Falls of Niagara was from the top of the hill that leads directly into the village. I had been intently examining the rare shrubs and beautiful flowers that grew in an exquisite garden surrounding a very fine mansion on my right hand, perfectly astonished at their luxuriance, and the emerald greenness of the turf at that season, which had been one of unprecedented drought, when, on raising my head, the great cataract burst on my sight without any intervening screen, producing an overwhelming sensation in my mind which amounted to pain in its intensity.

Yes, the great object of my journey – one of the fondest anticipations of my life – was at length accomplished; and for a moment the blood recoiled back to my heart, and a tremulous thrill ran through my whole frame. I was so bewildered – so taken by surprise – that every feeling was absorbed in the one consciousness, that the sublime vision was before me; that I had at last seen Niagara; that it was now mine forever, stereotyped upon my heart by the unerring hand of nature; producing an impression which nothing but madness or idiotcy could efface! It was some seconds before I could collect my thoughts, or concentrate my attention sufficiently to identify one of its gigantic features. The eye crowds all into the one glance, and the eager mind is too much dazzled and intoxicated for minor details. Astonishment and admiration are succeeded by curious examination and enjoyment; but it is impossible to realize this at first. The tumultuous rush of feeling, the excitement occasioned by the grand spectacle, must subside before you can draw a free breath, and have time for thought.

The American Fall was directly opposite, resembling a vast rolling cylinder of light flashing through clouds of silvery mist, and casting from it long rays of indescribable brightness. I never could realize in this perfect image of a living and perpetual motion, a *fall* of waters; it always had to my eyes this majestic, solemn, rotatory movement, when seen from the bank above. The Horse-shoe Fall is further on to the right, and you only get a side view of it from this point.

The Falls are seen to the least possible advantage from the brow of the steep bank. In looking down upon them, you can form no adequate idea of their volume, height, and grandeur; yet that first glance can never be effaced. You feel a thrilling, triumphant joy, whilst contemplating this master-piece of nature – this sublime idea of the Eternal – this wonderful symbol of the power and strength of the divine Architect of the universe.

It is as if the great heart of nature were laid bare before

you, and you saw and heard all its gigantic throbbings, and watched the current of its stupendous life flowing perpetually forward.

I cannot imagine how any one could be disappointed in this august scene; and the singular indifference manifested by others; – it is either a miserable affectation of singularity, or a lamentable want of sensibility to the grand and beautiful. The human being who could stand unmoved before the great cataract, and feel no quickening of the pulse, no silent adoration of the heart towards the Creator of this wondrous scene, would remain as indifferent and as uninspired before the throne of God!

Throwing out of the question the romantic locality, – the rugged wooded banks, the vast blocks of stone scattered at the edge of the torrent, the magic colour of the waters, the overhanging crags, the wild flowers waving from the steep, the glorious hues of the ever-changing rainbow that spans the river, and that soft cloud of silvery brightness for ever flowing upward into the clear air, like the prayer of faith ascending from earth to heaven, – the enormous magnitude of the waters alone, their curbless power, and eternal motion, are sufficient to give rise to feelings of astonishment and admiration such as never were experienced before.

Not the least of these sensations is created by the deep roar of the falling torrent, that shakes the solid rocks beneath your feet, and is repeated by the thousand hidden echoes among those stern craggy heights.

It is impossible for language to convey any adequate idea of the grandeur of the Falls, when seen from below, either from the deck of the "Maid of the Mist," – the small steamer that approaches within a few yards of the descending sheet of the Horse-shoe Falls – or from the ferry boat that plies continually between the opposite shores. From the frail little boat, dancing like a feather upon the green swelling surges, you perhaps form the best notion of the vastness and magnitude of the descending waters, and of your own helplessness and insignificance.

They flow down upon your vision like moving mountains of light; and the shadowy outline of black mysterious-looking rocks, dimly seen through clouds of driving mist, adds a wild sublimity to the scene. While the boat struggles over the curling billows, at times lifted up by the ground-swells from below, the feeling of danger and insecurity is lost in the whirl of waters that surround you. The mind expands with the scene, and you rejoice in the terrific power that threatens to annihilate you and your fairy bark. A visible presence of the majesty of God is before you, and, sheltered by His protecting hand, you behold the glorious spectacle and live.

The dark forests of pine that form the background to the Falls, when seen from above, are entirely lost from the surface of the river, and the descending floods seem to pour down upon you from the skies.

The day had turned out as beautiful as heart could wish; and though I felt very much fatigued with the journey, I determined to set all aches and pains at defiance whilst I remained on this enchanted ground.

We had just time enough to spare before dinner to walk to the table rock, following the road along the brow of the steep bank. On the way we called in at the Curiosity Shop, kept by an old grey-haired man, who had made for himself a snug little California by turning all he touched into gold; his stock-in-trade consisting of geological specimens from the vicinity of the Falls – pebbles, plants, stuffed birds, beasts, and sticks cut from the timber that grows along the rocky banks, and twisted into every imaginable shape. The heads of these canes were dexterously carved to imitate snakes, snapping turtles, eagles' heads, and Indian faces. Here, the fantastic ends of the roots of shrubs from which they were made were cut into a grotesque triumvirate of legs and feet; here a black snake, spotted and coloured to represent the horrid reptile, made you fancy its ugly coils already twisting in abhorrent folds about your hands and arms. There was no end to the old man's imaginative freaks in this department, his wares bearing a proportionate price to the dignity of the location from which they were derived.

A vast amount of Indian toys, and articles of dress, made the museum quite gay with their tawdry ornaments of beads and feathers. It is a pleasant lounging place, and the old man forms one of its chief attractions.

Proceeding on to the table rock, we passed many beautiful gardens, all bearing the same rich tint of verdure, and glowing with fruit and flowers. The showers of spray, rising from the vast natural fountain in their neighbourhood, fill the air with cool and refreshing moisture, which waters these lovely gardens, as the mists did of yore that went up from the face of the earth to water the garden of Eden.

The Horse-shoe Fall is much lower than its twin cataract on the American side; but what it loses in height, it makes up in power and volume, and the amount of water that is constantly discharged over it. As we approached the table rock, a rainbow of splendid dyes spanned the river; rising from out the driving mist from the American Fall, until it melted into the leaping snowy foam of the great Canadian cataract. There is a strange blending, in this scene, of beauty and softness with the magnificent and the sublime: a deep sonorous music in the thundering of the mighty floods, as if the spirits of earth and air united in one solemn choral chant of praise to the Creator; the rocks vibrate to the living harmony, and the shores around seem hurrying forward, as if impelled by the force of the descending torrent of sound. Yet, within a few yards of all this whirlpool of conflicting elements, the river glides onward as peacefully and gently as if it had not received into its mysterious depths this ever-falling avalanche of foaming waters.

Here you enjoy a splendid view of the Rapids. Raising your eyes from the green, glassy edge of the Falls, you see the mad hubbub of boiling waves rushing with headlong fury down the watery steep, to take their final plunge into the mist-covered abyss below. On, on they come – that white-crested phalanx of waves – pouring and crowding upon each other in frantic chase!

> "Things of life, and light, and motion,
> Spirits of the unfathom'd ocean,
> Hurrying on with curbless force,
> Like some rash unbridled horse;
> High in air their white crests flinging,
> And madly to destruction springing."

These boiling breakers seem to shout and revel in a wild ecstasy of freedom and power; and you feel inclined to echo their shout, and rejoice with them. Yet it is curious to mark how they slacken their mad speed when they reach the ledge of the fall, and melt into the icy smoothness of its polished brow, as if conscious of the superior force that is destined to annihilate their identity, and dash them into mist and spray. In like manner the waves of life are hurried into the abyss of death, and absorbed in the vast ocean of eternity.

Niagara would be shorn of half its wonders divested of these glorious Rapids, which form one of the grandest features in the magnificent scene.

We returned to our inn, the Clifton House, just in time to save our dinner: having taken breakfast in Toronto at half-past six, we were quite ready to obey the noisy summons of the bell, and follow our sable guide into the eating room.

The Clifton House is a large, handsome building, directly fronting the Falls. It is fitted up in a very superior style, and contains ample accommodations for a great number of visitors. It had been very full during the summer months, but a great many persons had left during the preceding week, which I considered a very fortunate circumstance for those who, like myself, came to see instead of to be seen.

The charges for a Canadian hotel are high; but of course you are expected to pay something extra at a place of such general resort, and for the grand view of the Falls, which can be enjoyed at any moment by stepping into the handsome balcony into which the saloon opens, and which runs the whole length of the side and front of the house. The former commands a full view of the American, the latter of the Horse-shoe Fall; and the high French windows of this elegantly furnished apartment give you the opportunity of enjoying both.

You pay four dollars a-day for your board and bed; this does not include wine, and every little extra is an additional charge. Children and servants are rated at half-price, and a baby is charged a dollar a-day. This item in the family programme is something new in the bill of charges at an hotel in this country; for these small gentry, though they give a great deal of trouble to their lawful owners, are always entertained gratis at inns and on board steamboats.

The room in which dinner was served could have accommodated with ease treble the number of guests. A large party, chiefly Americans, sat down to table. The dishes are not served on the table; a bill of fare is laid by every plate, and you call for what you please.

This arrangement, which saves a deal of trouble, seemed very distasteful to a gentleman near us, to whom the sight of good cheer must have been almost as pleasant as eating it, for he muttered half aloud – "that he hated these new-fangled ways; that he liked to see what he was going to eat; that he did not choose to be put off with kickshaws; that he did not understand the French names for dishes. He was not French, and he thought that they might be written in plain English."

I was very much of the same opinion, and found myself nearly in the same predicament with the grumbler at my left hand; but I did not betray my ignorance by venturing a remark. This brought forcibly to my mind a story that had recently been told me by a dear primitive old lady, a daughter of one of the first Dutch settlers in the Upper Province, over which I had laughed very heartily at the time; and now it served as an illustration of my own case.

"You know, my dear," said old Mrs. C——, "that I went lately to New York to visit a nephew of mine, whom I had not seen from a boy. Well, he has grown a very great man since those days, and is now one of the wealthiest merchants in the city. I never had been inside such a grandly furnished house before. We know nothing of the great world in Canada, or how the rich people live in such a place as New York. Ours are all bread and butter doings when compared with their grand fixings. I saw and heard a great many things, such as I never dreamed of before, and which for the life of me I could not understand; but I never let on.

"One morning, at luncheon, my nephew says to me, 'Aunty C——, you have never tasted our New York cider; I will order up some on purpose to see how you like it.'

"The servant brought up several long-necked bottles on a real silver tray, and placed them on the table. 'Good Lord!' thinks I, 'these are queer looking cider bottles. P'raps it's champagne, and he wants to get up a laugh against me before all these strange people.' I had never seen or tasted champagne in all my life, though there's lots of it sold in Canada, and our head folks give champagne breakfasts, and champagne dinners; but I had heard how it acted, and how, when you drew the corks from the bottles, they went pop – pop. So I just listened a bit, and held my tongue; and the first bounce it gave, I cried out, 'Mr. R——, you may call that cider in New York, but we call it champagne in Canada!'

"'Do you get champagne in Canada, Aunty?' says he, stopping and looking me straight in the face.

"'Oh, don't we?' says I; 'and it's a great deal better than your *New York cider*.'

"He looked mortified, I tell you, and the company all laughed; and I drank off my glass of champagne as bold as you please, as if I had been used to it all my life. When you are away from home, and find yourself ignorant of a thing or two, never let others into the secret. Watch and wait, and you'll find it out by and by."

Not having been used to French dishes during my long sojourn in Canada, I was glad to take the old lady's advice, and make use of my eyes and ears before I ordered my own supplies.

It would have done Mrs. Stowe's heart good to have seen the fine corps of well-dressed negro waiters who served the tables, most of whom were runaway slaves from the States. The perfect ease and dexterity with which they supplied the guests, without making a single mistake out of such a variety of dishes, was well worthy of notice.

It gave me pleasure to watch the quickness of all their motions, the politeness with which they received so many complicated orders, and the noiseless celerity with which they were performed. This cost them no effort, but seemed natural to them. There were a dozen of these blacks in attendance, all of them young, and some, in spite of their dark colouring, handsome, intelligent looking men.

The master of the hotel was eloquent in their praise, and said that they far surpassed the whites in the neat and elegant manner in which they laid out a table, – that he scarcely knew what he would do without them.

I found myself guilty of violating Lord Chesterfield's rules of politeness, while watching a group of eaters who sat opposite to me at table. The celerity with which they despatched their dinner, and yet contrived to taste of everything contained in the bill of fare, was really wonderful. To them it was a serious matter of business; they never lifted their eyes from their plates, or spoke a word beyond ordering fresh supplies, during feeding time.

One long-ringletted lady in particular attracted my notice, for she did more justice to the creature comforts than all the rest. The last course, including the dessert, was served at table, and she helped herself to such quantities of pudding, pie, preserves, custard, ice, and fruit, that such a medley of rich things I never before saw heaped upon one plate. Some of these articles she never tasted; but she seemed determined to secure to herself a portion of all, and to get as much as she could for her money.

I wish nature had not given me such a quick perception of the ridiculous – such a perverse inclination to laugh in the wrong place; for though one cannot help deriving from it a wicked enjoyment, it is a very troublesome gift, and very difficult to conceal. So I turned my face resolutely from contemplating the doings of the long-ringletted lady, and entered into conversation with an old gentleman from the States – a *genuine* Yankee, whom I found a very agreeable and intelligent companion, willing to exchange, with manly, independent courtesy, the treasures of his own mind with another; and I listened to his account of American schools and public institutions with great interest. His party consisted of a young and very delicate looking lady, and a smart active little boy of five years of age. These I concluded were his daughter and grandson, from the striking likeness that existed between the child and the old man. The lady, he said, was in bad health – the boy was hearty and wide-awake.

After dinner the company separated; some to visit objects of interest in the neighbourhood, others to the saloon and the balcony. I preferred a seat in the latter; and ensconcing myself in the depths of a large comfortable rocking chair, which was placed fronting the Falls, I gave up my whole heart and soul to the contemplation of their glorious beauty.

I was roused from a state almost bordering on idolatry by a lady remarking to another, who was standing beside her, "that she considered the Falls a great humbug; that there was more fuss made about them than they deserved; that she was satisfied with having seen them once; and that she never wished to see them again."

I was not the least surprised, on turning my head, to behold in the speaker the long-ringletted lady.

A gentleman to whom I told these remarks laughed heartily. – "That reminds me of a miller's wife who came from Black Rock, near Buffalo, last summer, to see the Falls. After standing here, and looking at them for some minutes, she drawled through her nose – "Well, I declare, is that all? And have I come eighteen miles to look at you? I might ha' spared myself the expense and trouble; my husband's mill-dam is as good a sight, – only it's not just as *high*."

This lady would certainly have echoed the sublime sentiment expressed by our friend the poet, –

> "Oh, what a glorious place for washing sheep
> Niagara would be!"

In the evening my husband hired a cab, and we drove to see the Upper Suspension Bridge. The road our driver took was very narrow, and close to the edge of the frightful precipice that forms at this place the bank of the river, which runs more than two hundred feet below.

The cabman, we soon discovered, was not a member of the temperance society. He was very much intoxicated; and, like Jehu the son of Nimshi, he drove furiously. I felt very timid and nervous. Sickness makes us sad cowards, and what the mind enjoys in health, becomes an object of fear when it is enfeebled and unstrung by bodily weakness.

My dear husband guessed my feelings, and placed himself in such a manner as to hide from my sight the danger to which we were exposed by our careless driver. In spite of the many picturesque beauties in our road, I felt greatly relieved when we drove up to the bridge, and our short journey was accomplished.

The Suspension Bridge on which we now stood – surveying from its dizzy height, two hundred and thirty feet above the water, the stream below – seems to demand from us a greater amount of interest than the one at Queenstone, from the fact of its having been the first experiment of the kind ever made in this country, – a grand and successful effort of mechanical genius over obstacles that appeared insurmountable.

The river is two hundred feet wider here than at Queenstone, and the bridge is of much larger dimensions. The height of the stone tower that supports it on the American side is sixty-eight feet, and of the wooden tower on the Canadian shore fifty feet. The number of cables for the bridge is sixteen; of strands in each cable, six hundred; of strands in the ferry-cable, thirty-seven, the diameter of which is seven-eighths of an inch. The ultimate tension is six thousand five hundred tons, and the capacity of the bridge five hundred. A passage across is thrillingly exciting.

The depth of the river below the bridge is two hundred and fifty feet, and the water partakes more largely of that singular deep green at this spot than I had remarked elsewhere. The American stage crossed the bridge as we were leaving it, and the horses seemed to feel the same mysterious dread which I have before described. A great number of strong wooden posts that support the towers take greatly from the elegance of this bridge; but I am told that these will shortly be removed, and their place supplied by a stone tower and buttresses. We returned by another and less dangerous route to the Clifton House, just in time to witness a glorious autumnal sunset.

The west was a flood of molten gold, fretted with crimson clouds; the great Horse-shoe Fall caught every tint of the glowing heavens, and looked like a vast sheet of flame, the mist rising from it like a wreath of red and violet-coloured smoke. This gorgeous sight, contrasted by the dark pine woods and frowning cliffs which were thrown into deep shade, presented a spectacle of such surpassing beauty and grandeur, that it could only be appreciated by those who witnessed it. Any attempt to describe it must prove a failure. I stood chained to the spot, mute with admiration, till the sun set behind the trees, and the last rays of light faded from the horizon; and still the thought uppermost in my mind was – who could feel disappointed at a scene like this? Can the wide world supply such another?

The removal of all the ugly mills along its shores would improve it, perhaps, and add the one charm it wants, by being hemmed in by tasteless buildings, – the sublimity of solitude.

Oh, for one hour alone with Nature, and her great master-piece Niagara! What solemn converse would the soul hold with its Creator at such a shrine, – and the busy hum of practical life would not mar with its jarring discord, this grand "thunder of the waters!" Realities are unmanageable things in some hands, and the Americans are gravely contemplating making their sublime Fall into a motive power for turning machinery.

Ye gods! what next will the love of gain suggest to these gold-worshippers? The whole earth should enter into a protest against such an act of sacrilege – such a shameless desecration of one of the noblest works of God.

Niagara belongs to no particular nation or people. It is an inheritance bequeathed by the great Author to all mankind, – an altar raised by his own almighty hand, – at which all true worshippers must bow the knee in solemn adoration. I trust that these free glad waters will assert their own rights, and dash into mist and spray any attempt made to infringe their glorious liberty.

But the bell is ringing for tea, and I must smother my indignation with the reflection, that "sufficient for the day is the evil thereof."

A FREAK OF FANCY.

"I had a dream of ocean,
    In stern and stormy pride;
With terrible commotion,
    Dark, thundering, came the tide.
High on the groaning shore
    Upsprang the wreathed spray;
Tremendous was the roar
    Of the angry, echoing bay.

"Old Neptune's snowy coursers
    Unbridled trode the main,
And o'er the foaming waters
    Plunged on in mad disdain:
The furious surges boiling,
    Roll mountains in their path;
Beneath their white hoofs coiling,
    They spurn them in their wrath.

"The moon at full was streaming
    Through rack and thunder-cloud,
Like the last pale taper gleaming
    On coffin, pall, and shroud.
The winds were fiercely wreaking
    Their vengeance on the wave,
A hoarse dirge wildly shrieking
    O'er each uncoffin'd grave.

"I started from my pillow –
    The moon was riding high,
The wind scarce heav'd a billow
    Beneath that cloudless sky.
I look'd from earth to heaven,
    And bless'd the tranquil beam;
My trembling heart had striven
    With the tempest of a dream."

EIGHTEEN

Goat Island

"Adown Niagara's giant steep,
　The foaming breakers crowding leap,
　　With wild tumultuous roar;
　The mighty din ascends on high,
　In deafening thunder to the sky,
　　And shakes the rocky shore."

S.M.

T HE LADY with the ringlets was absent with her party
from the tea-table; I was not sorry to learn that she
was gone. I had conceived a prejudice against her from the
remark I heard her make about the Falls. Her gustative-
ness predominated so largely over her ideality, that she
reminded me of a young lady who, after describing to me
a supper of which by her own account she had largely
partaken, said, with a candour almost shocking in its simplicity –

"To tell you the plain truth, my dear Mrs. M——, my
art (she was English, and cockney, and dreadfully
mangled the letter *h* whenever it stumbled into a speech) is
in my *stomach*."

The cup of excellent tea was most refreshing after the
fatigues of the day; and, while enjoying it, I got into an
agreeable chat with several pleasant people, but we were
all strangers even in name to each other.

The night was misty and intensely dark, without moon or stars. How I longed for one glimpse of the former, to shed if only a wandering gleam upon the Falls! The awful music of their continuous roar filled the heavens, and jarred the windows of the building with the tremulous motion we feel on board a steam-boat. And then I amused myself with picturing them, during one of our desolating thunderstorms, leaping into existence out of the dense darkness, when revealed by the broad red flashes of lightning; and I wished that my limited means would allow me to remain long enough in their vicinity, to see them under every change of season and weather. But it was not to be; and after peering long and anxiously into the dark night, I retreated to an unoccupied sofa in a distant part of the saloon, to watch and listen to all that was passing around me.

Two young American ladies, not of a highly educated class, were engaged in a lively conversation with two dashing English officers, who, for their own amusement, were practising upon their credulity, and flattering their national prejudices with the most depreciating remarks on England and the English people.

"I am English," cried number one; "but I am no great admirer of her people and institutions. The Americans beat them hollow."

"All the world think so but themselves," said the younger lady; "they are such a vain, arrogant set!"

"Decidedly so. The men are bad enough, but the women, – I dare say you have heard them called handsome?"

"Ah, yes," in a very lively tone; "but I never believed it. I never in my life saw a pretty English woman among all that I have seen in New York. To my thinking, they are a sad set of frights. Stiff, formal, and repulsive, they dress in shocking bad taste, and consider themselves and their uncouth fashions as the standards of perfection."

"My dear madam, you are right. They are odious creatures. The beauty for which they were once renowned has vanished with the last generation. Our modern English girls are decided barbarians. It is impossible to meet with a pretty English woman now-a-days. I have made a vow to cut them altogether; and if ever I commit such a foolish thing as matrimony, to take to myself an *American* wife."

"Are you in earnest?" with a very fascinating smile, and flashing upon him her fine dark eyes.

"Quite so. But, now, you must not take me for a rich English Cœlebs in search of a wife. I am an unfortunate scapegrace, have run out all my means, and am not worth a York shilling to jingle on a tombstone. I was obliged to borrow money of my landlord – he's a capital fellow – to pay my washerwoman's bill this morning. So don't fall in love with me. I assure you, on my honour, it would be a bad spec."

"Don't be alarmed," returned the dark-eyed girl, evidently much pleased with her odd companion. "Are you very young?"

"I was never young. My mother told me that I had cut my wisdom-teeth when I was born. I was wide awake, too, like your clever people, and have kept my eyes open ever since."

"You have seen a great deal of the world?"

"Yes, too much of it; but 'tis a tolerable world to live in after all."

"Were you ever in the United States?"

"Only crossed from the other side a few days ago. Did you not notice the arrival of Mr. P—— among the list of distinguished foreigners that honoured your great city with their presence?"

"And what struck you most when you got there?"

"Oh, the beauty and elegance of the women, of course."

"You flatter us."

"Fact, upon honour," with a quizzical application of his hand to his heart.

"What did you admire in them?"

"Their straight up and down figures. They have no vulgar redundancies – no red cheeks and pug noses; and

then their voices are so sweet and harmonious, their pro-
nunciation so correct, so every way superior to the boisterous, hearty frankness of our British girls!"

"English women have very bad noses – I have remarked
that; and they are so horribly fat, and they laugh so loud,
and talk in such a high key! My! I often wondered where
they learned their manners."

"Oh! 'tis all natural to them – it comes to them without
teaching."

"I have been told that London is a shocking place."

"Dreadful; and the climate is disgusting. It rains there
every day, and fogs are so prevalent that during the winter
months, they burn candles all day to see to eat. As to the
sun, he never comes out but once or twice during the
summer, just to let us know that he has not been struck
out of creation. And the streets, my dear young lady, are
so filthy that the women have to wear pattens in their
carriages."

"You don't say?"

"Just to keep their petticoats out of the mud, which is
so deep that it penetrates through the bottom of the
carriages."

"I never will go to England, I declare."

"You will be better appreciated in your free and glorious country. Slavery thrives there, and you make slaves of
us poor men."

"Now, do stop there, and have done with your blarney."

"Blarney! I'm not Irish. Englishmen always speak the
truth when talking to the ladies."

Here he paused, quite out of breath, and his companion
in mischief commenced with the other lady.

"Who is that tall, stout, handsome man, with the fat
lady on his arm, who has just entered the room?"

"That's an American from the south; he's worth his
weight in gold, and that fleshy woman's his wife. My! is he
not handsome! and he's so clever – one of our greatest
senators."

"If size makes a man great, and he has the distinguished

honour of being one of *your* senators, he must be a great – a very great man."

"He's a splendid orator; you should hear him speak."

"He has kept his mouth shut all day; and when he does open it, it is only to speak in French to his wife. My curiosity is excited; it would be quite a treat to hear him talk on any subject."

"When *he* speaks, it's always to the purpose. But there's no one here who is able to appreciate talents like his."

"He's an American aristocrat."

"We have no aristocrats with us. He's a great slave-owner, and immensely rich."

"Very substantial claims to distinction, I must confess. You are wiser in these matters than we are. What do you think of Canada?"

"I don't know; it's very well for a young place. I only came here with sister last night; we are on our way to Quebec."

"To visit friends?"

"We have no friends in Canada. We want to see Lord Elgin."

"Lord Elgin!"

"Yes. We have seen a great many curious things, but we never saw an English lord."

"And you are going to Quebec for no other purpose than to look at Lord Elgin? His lordship should feel himself highly flattered. What sort of an animal do you suppose him to be?"

"A man, of course; but I assure you that the Boston ladies thought a great deal of him. Sister and I have plenty of time and money at our disposal, and we wanted to see if their opinion was correct."

"Well, I hope you may be gratified, and agree with the Boston ladies that he is a very clever man."

"Is he handsome?"

"He has an English nose."

"Oh, shocking!"

"A decided Anglo-Saxon face."

"I'm sure I shan't admire him."

"But I'll not anticipate. A man may be a fine looking fellow in spite of his nose. But what do you think of the Falls?"

"Well, I have not *quite* made up my mind about them. I should like to ride down to the edge of the river to look at them from below."

"I will order a carriage to-morrow morning, and drive you down."

"Thank you; I can do that for myself, if I have a mind to. I should like to ride down on horseback."

"The path is too steep; no one ventures down that terrible road on horseback."

"But I'm a capital rider."

"No matter; they use cows for that purpose here."

"Cows!"

"They are very safe, sure-footed animals. All the ladies ride down to the Falls on cows."

"Are they fools?"

"Wise women. Did not you see that fine drove of cows pass the hotel at sunset?"

"I did. I thought they were driven into the yard to be milked."

"Why, yes; but those cows are making Mr. ——'s fortune. They serve a double purpose, providing delicious butter and cream for his customers, and acting as horses for the ladies. I will pick out the most docile among them for your excursion to-morrow morning, and see it bridled and saddled myself."

This was too much for the gravity of any one. My son-in-law ran out of the room, and I laughed aloud. The poor girls began to find out that they were sold, and retreated into the balcony. An hour afterwards, as I was pacing through the long gallery that led to our sleeping apartment, one of the many doors on either side softly opened, and the youngest of these bright-eyed damsels stole out.

"I want to ask you a question," she said, laying her very

white hand confidingly on my arm; "were those English-men quizzing my sister and me?"

"Need you ask that question?" said I, not a little amused at her simplicity.

"I never suspected it till I saw your son laughing to himself, and then I guessed something was wrong. It was a great shame of those rude fellows to amuse themselves at our expense; but your son is quite a different person – so handsome and gentlemanly. We admire him so much. Is he married?"

"His wife is my daughter."

I can't tell why my answer struck the fair inquirer dumb; she drew back suddenly into her chamber, and closed the door without bidding me good night, and that was the last time I saw or heard of her and her companion.

"A summer spent at the Clifton House would elicit more extraordinary traits of character than could be gathered from the chit-chat of a dozen novels," thought I, as I paced on to No. 50, the last room on the long tier.

I was up by daybreak the next morning to see the Falls by sunrise, and was amply repaid for leaving my warm bed, and encountering the bright bracing morning air, by two hours' enjoyment of solemn converse alone with God and Niagara. The sun had not yet lifted his majestic head above the pine forest, or chased with his beams the dark shadows of night that rested within the curved sides of the great Horse-shoe. The waters looked black as they rolled in vast smooth masses downward, till, meeting the pro-jecting rocks, they were tossed high into the air in clouds of dazzling foam – so pure, so stainlessly white, when contrasted with the darkness, that they looked as if belonging to heaven rather than to earth. Anon, that dancing feathery tumult of foam catches a rosy gleam from the coming day. A long stream of sunlight touches the centre of the mighty arch, and transforms the black waters into a mass of smooth transparent emerald green, and the spray flashes with myriads of rubies and dia-monds; while the American Fall still rolls and thunders on in cold pure whiteness, Goat Island and its crests of dark pines shrouding it in a robe of gloom. The voice of the waters rising amidst the silence that reigns at that lovely calm hour, sounds sonorous and grand. Be still, O my soul! earth is pouring to her Creator her morning anthem of solemn praise!

Earth! how beautiful thou art! When will men be worthy of the paradise in which they are placed? Did our first father, amidst the fresh young beauty of his Eden, ever gaze upon a spectacle more worthy of his admiration than this? We will except those moments when he held converse with God amid the cool shades of that delicious garden.

"That's a sublime sight!" said a voice near me.

I turned, and found the old American gentleman at my side.

"I can see a change in the appearance of these Falls," he continued, "since I visited them some forty years ago. Time changes everything; I feel that I am changed since then. I was young and active, and clambered about these rugged banks with the careless hardihood of a boy who pants for excitement and adventure, and how I enjoyed my visit to this place! A change has taken place – I can scarcely describe in what respect; but it looks to me very different to what it did then."

"Perhaps," I suggested, "the fall of that large portion of the table-rock has made the alteration you describe."

"You have just hit it," he said; "I forgot the circumstance. The Horse-shoe is not so perfect as it was."

"Could these Falls ever have receded from Queenstone?" said I.

He turned to me with a quick smile – "If they have, my dear Madam, the world is much older by thousands of ages than we give it credit for; but –" continued he, gazing at the mighty object in dispute, "it is possible that these Falls are of more recent date than the creation of the world. An earthquake may have rent the deep chasm that forms the bed of that river, and in a few seconds of time the same cause might break down that mighty barrier, and drain the upper lakes, by converting a large part of your fine province into another inland sea. But this is all theory. Fancy, you know, is free, and I often amuse myself by speculating on these things."

"Your daughter, I hope, is not ill," I said; "I did not see her at tea last night with her little son."

Instead of his usual shrewd smile, the old man laughed heartily. "So you take that young lady for my daughter!"

"Is she not? The child, however, must be your grandson, for he is the picture of you."

"I flatter myself that he is. That young lady is my wife – that little boy my son. Isn't he a fine clever little chap?" and his keen grey eye brightened at the growing promise of his boy. "I have another younger than him."

"Heavens!" thought I, "what a mistake I have made! How M—— will laugh at me, and how delighted this old man seems with my confusion!" I am always making these odd blunders. Not long ago I mistook a very old-looking young man for his father, and congratulated him on his daughter's marriage; and asked a young bride who was returning her calls, and who greatly resembled a married cousin who lived in the same town, *how her baby was?* And now I had taken a man's wife for his daughter – his son for a grandson. But I comforted myself with the idea that the vast disparity between their ages was some excuse, and so slipped past one of the horns of that dilemma.

As soon as we had taken breakfast, we set off in company with the American and his little boy to pay a visit to Goat Island, and look at the Falls from the American side. The child fully realized his father's description. He was a charming, frank, graceful boy, full of life and intelligence, and enjoyed the excitement of crossing the river, and the beauties it revealed to us, with a keen appreciation of the scene, which would have been incomprehensible to some of the wonder-seekers we had met the day before. All nature contributed to heighten our enjoyment. The heavens were so blue and cloudless, the air so clear and transparent, the changing tints on the autumnal foliage so rich, the sun so bright and warm, that we seemed surrounded by an enchanted atmosphere, and the very consciousness of existence was delightful; but, with those descending floods of light towering above us, and filling the echoing shores with their sublime melody, we were doubly blessed!

When our little boat touched the American shore, the question arose as to which method would be the best to adopt in ascending the giddy height. A covered way leads to the top of the bank, which is more than two hundred feet in perpendicular height. Up this steep our ingenious neighbours have constructed on an inclined plane of boards a railway, on which two cars run in such a manner that the weight of the descending car draws up the other to the top of the bank. Both are secured by a strong cable. By the side of this railway, and under the same roof, 200 steps lead to the road above. I was too weak to attempt the formidable flight of steps; and though I felt rather cowardly while looking at the giddy ascent of the cars, there was no alternative between choosing one or the other, or remaining behind. The American and his little boy were already in the car, and I took my seat behind them. When we were half-way, the question rose in my mind – "What if the cable should give way, where should we land?" "You'll know that when the tail breaks," as the Highlander said when holding on to the wild boar; and I shut my eyes, determined not to disturb my mind or waken my fears by another glance below.

"Why do you shut your eyes?" said the American. "I thought the English were all brave."

"I never was a coward till after I came to North America," said I, laughing; and I felt that I ought to be as brave as a lion, and not injure the reputation of my glorious country by such childish fears.

When the car stopped, we parted company with the

American and his brave little son. He had friends to visit in Manchester, and I saw them no more.

Our path lay through a pretty shady grove to the village. Groups of Indian women and children were reposing beneath the shade of the trees, working at their pretty wares, which they offered for sale as we passed by. Following the winding of the road, we crossed a rural bridge, from which we enjoyed a fine view of the glorious Rapids, and entered Goat Island.

This beautiful spot is still in forest, but the underbrush has been cleared away, and a path cut entirely round it. The trunks of these trees are entirely covered with the names and initials of persons who at different times have visited the spot, and they present the most curious appearance.

After a few minutes' walk through the wood, we reached the bank of the river, which here is not very high, and is covered with evergreen shrubs and wild flowers; and here the wide world of tumbling waters are flashing and foaming in the sunlight – leaping and racing round the rocky, pine-covered islands, that vainly oppose their frantic course. Oh, how I longed to stem their unstemmed tides; to land upon those magic islands which the foot of man or beast never trode, whose beauty and verdure are guarded by the stern hand of death! The Falls are more wonderful, but not more beautiful, than this sublime confusion and din of waters –

> "Of glad rejoicing waters,
> Of living leaping waters."

Their eternal voice and motion might truly be termed the "joy of waves."

On the American side, the view of the great cataracts is not so awful and overwhelming, but they are more beautiful in detail, and present so many exquisite pictures to the eye. They are more involved in mystery, as it were; and so much is left for the imagination to combine into every varied form of beauty. You look down into the profound abyss; you are wetted with that shower of silvery spray that rises higher than the tree tops, and which gives you in that soft rain an actual consciousness of its living presence.

I did not cross the bridge, which extends within a few yards of the great plunge, or climb to the top of the tower; for my strength had so entirely failed me, that it was with difficulty I could retrace my steps. I sat for about an hour beneath the shadow of the trees, feasting my soul with beauty; and with reluctance, that drew tears from my eyes, bade adieu to the enchanting spot – not for ever, I hope, for should God prolong my life, I shall try and visit the Falls again. Like every perfect work, the more frequently and closely they are examined, the more wonderful they must appear; the mind and eye can never weary of such an astonishing combination of sublimity and power.

We stopped at a pretty cottage at the edge of the wood to get a glass of water, and to buy some peaches. For these we had to pay treble the price at which they could be procured at Toronto; but they proved a delicious refreshment, the day was very warm, and I was parched with thirst. Had time permitted, I should have enjoyed greatly a ramble through the town; as it was, my brief acquaintance with the American shores left a very pleasing impression on my mind.

The little that I have seen of intelligent, well-educated Americans, has given me a very high opinion of the people. Britain may be proud of these noble scions from the parent tree, whose fame, like her own, is destined to fill the world. "The great daughter of a great mother," America claims renown for her lawful inheritance; and it is to be deeply regretted that any petty jealousy or party feeling should ever create a rivalry between countries so closely united by the ties of blood; whose origin, language, religion and genius are the same; whose industry, energy, and perseverance, derived from their British sires, have procured for them the lofty position they hold, and made them independent of the despots of earth.

THE LAND OF OUR BIRTH.

"There is not a spot in this wide-peopled earth,
  So dear to the heart as the land of our birth;
  'Tis the home of our childhood! the beautiful spot
  By mem'ry retain'd when all else is forgot.
      May the blessing of God
      Ever hallow the sod,
  And its valleys and hills by our children be trode!

"Can the language of strangers, in accents unknown,
  Send a thrill to the bosom like that of our own!
  The face may be fair, and the smile may be bland,
  But it breathes not the tones of our dear native land.
      There's no spot on earth
      Like the home of our birth,
  Where heroes keep guard o'er the altar and hearth.

"How sweet is the language that taught us to blend
  The dear names of father, of husband, and friend;
  That taught us to lisp on our mother's fond breast,
  The ballads she sang as she rock'd us to rest!
      May the blessing of God
      Ever hallow the sod,
  And its valleys and hills by our children be trode!

"May old England long lift her white crest o'er the wave,
  The birth-place of science, the home of the brave!
  In her cities may peace and prosperity dwell!
  May her daughters in beauty and virtue excel!
      May their beauty and worth
      Bless the land of their birth,
  While heroes keep guard o'er the altar and hearth!"

NINETEEN

Conclusion

"Why dost thou fear to speak the honest truth?
Speak boldly, fearlessly, what thou think'st right,
And time shall justify thy words and thee!"

S.M.

WE LEFT Niagara at noon. A very pleasant drive brought us to Queenstone, and we stepped on board the "Chief Justice" steamboat, that had just touched the wharf, and was on her return trip to Toronto.

Tired and ill, I was glad to lie down in one of the berths in the ladies' cabin to rest, and, if possible, to obtain a little sleep. This I soon found was out of the question. Two or three noisy, spoiled children kept up a constant din; and their grandmother, a very nice-looking old lady, who seemed nurse-general to them all, endeavoured in vain to keep them quiet. Their mother was reading a novel, and took it very easy; reclining on a comfortable sofa, she left her old mother all the fatigue of taking care of the children, and waiting upon herself.

This is by no means an uncommon trait of Canadian character. In families belonging more especially to the middle class, who have raised themselves from a lower to a higher grade, the mother, if left in poor circumstances, almost invariably holds a subordinate position in her wealthier son or daughter's family. She superintends the servants, and nurses the younger children; and her time is occupied by a number of minute domestic labours, that allow her very little rest in her old age.

I have seen the grandmother in a wealthy family ironing the fine linen, or broiling over the cook-stove, while her daughter held her place in the drawing-room. How differently in my own country are these things ordered! where the most tender attention is paid to the aged, all their wants studied, and their comfort regarded as a sacred thing.

Age in Canada is seldom honoured. You would imagine it almost a crime for any one to grow old – with such slighting, cold indifference are the aged treated by the young and strong. It is not unusual to hear a lad speak of his father, perhaps, in the prime of life, as the "old fellow," the "old boy," and to address a grey-haired man in this disrespectful and familiar manner. This may not be apparent to the natives themselves, but it never fails to strike every stranger that visits the colony.

To be a servant is a lot sufficiently hard – to have all your actions dictated to you by the will of another – to enjoy no rest or recreation, but such as is granted as a very great favour; but to be a humble dependent in old age on children, to whom all the best years of your life were devoted with all the energy of maternal love, must be sad indeed. But they submit with great apparent cheerfulness, and seem to think it necessary to work for the shelter of a child's roof, and the bread they eat.

The improved circumstances of families, whose parents, in the first settlement of the country, had to work very hard for their general maintenance, may be the cause of this inversion of moral duties, and the parents not being considered properly on an equality with their better dressed and better educated offspring; but from whatever cause it springs, the effect it produces on the mind of a stranger is very painful. It is difficult to feel much respect for any one who looks down upon father or mother as an inferior being, and, as such, considers them better qualified to perform the coarse drudgeries of life. Time, we hope, will remedy this evil, with many others of the same class.

There was a bride, too, on board – a very delicate looking young woman, who was returning from a tour in the States to her native village. She seemed very much to dread the ordeal she had yet to pass through – in sitting dressed up for a whole week to receive visitors. Nor did I in the least wonder at her repugnance to go through this trying piece of ceremonial, which is absolutely indispensable in Canada.

The Monday after the bride and bridegroom make their first appearance at church, every person in the same class prepares to pay them a visit of congratulation; and if the town is large, and the parties well known, the making of visits to the bride lasts to the end of the week.

The bride, who is often a young girl from sixteen to twenty years of age, is doomed for this period to sit upon a sofa or reclined in an easy chair, dressed in the most expensive manner, to receive her guests.

Well she knows that herself, her dress, the furniture of her room, even her cake and wine, will undergo the most minute scrutiny, and be the theme of conversation among all the gossips of the place for the next nine days. No wonder that she feels nervous, and that her manners are constrained, and that nothing looks easy or natural about her, from her neck-ribbon to her shoe-tie.

"Have you seen the bride yet? What do you think of her? How was she dressed? Is she tall, or short? Pretty, or plain? Stupid, or clever? Lively, or quiet?" are all questions certain to be asked, and answered according to the taste and judgment of the parties to whom they are put; besides those thousand little interludes which spring from envy, ill-nature, and all uncharitableness. The week following they, in courtesy, must return all these visits; and, oh, what a relief it must be when all this stiff complimentary nonsense is over, and they are once more at home to themselves and their own particular friends!

There is another custom, peculiar to Canada and the United States, which I cordially approve, and should be very much grieved for its discontinuance.

On New-Year's day all the gentlemen in the place call upon their friends, to wish them a happy new year, and to exchange friendly greetings with the ladies of the family, who are always in readiness to receive them, and make them a return for these marks of neighbourly regard, in the substantial form of rich cakes, fruit, wine, coffee, and tea. It is generally a happy, cheerful day; all faces wear a smile, old quarrels are forgotten, and every one seems anxious to let ill-will and heart-burnings die with the old year.

A gentleman who wishes to drop an inconvenient acquaintance, has only to omit calling upon his friend's wife and daughters on New-Year's day, without making a suitable apology for the omission of this usual act of courtesy, and the hint is acknowledged by a direct cut the next time the parties meet in public.

It is an especial frolic for all the lads who have just returned from school or college to enjoy their Christmas holidays. Cakes and sweetmeats are showered upon them in abundance, and they feel themselves of vast importance, while paying their compliments to the ladies, and running from house to house, with their brief congratulatory address – "I wish you all a happy New Year!"

It would be a thousand pities if this affectionate, time-honoured, hospitable custom, should be swept away by the march of modern improvement. Some ladies complain that it gives a number of vulgar, under-bred men, the opportunity of introducing themselves to the notice and company of their daughters. There may be some reasonable truth in this remark; but after all it is but for one day, and the kindly greetings exchanged are more productive of good than evil.

The evening of New-Year's day is generally devoted to dancing parties, when the young especially meet to enjoy themselves.

The Wesleyan Methodists always "pray the old year out and the new year in," as it is termed here, and they could not celebrate its advent in a more rational and improving manner. Their midnight anthem of praise is a sacred and beautiful offering to Him, whose vast existence is not meted out like ours, and measured by days and years.

Large parties given to very young children, which are so common in this country, are very pernicious in the way in which they generally operate upon youthful minds. They foster the passions of vanity and envy, and produce a love of dress and display which is very repulsive in the character of a child. Little girls who are in the constant habit of attending these parties, soon exchange the natural manners and frank simplicity so delightful at their age, for the confidence and flippancy of women long hacked in the ways of the world.

For some time after I settled in the town, I was not myself aware that any evil could exist in a harmless party of children playing together at the house of a mutual friend. But observation has convinced me that I was in error; that these parties operate like a forcing bed upon young plants, with this difference, that they bring to maturity the seeds of *evil*, instead of those of goodness and virtue, and that a child accustomed to the heated atmosphere of pleasure, is not likely in maturer years to enjoy the pure air and domestic avocations of home.

These juvenile parties appear to do less mischief to boys than to girls. They help to humanize the one, and to make heartless coquets of the other. The boys meet for a downright romping play with each other; the girls to be caressed and admired, to show off their fine dresses, and to gossip about the dress and appearance of their neighbours.

I know that I shall be called hard-hearted for this assertion; but it is true. I have frequently witnessed what I relate, both at my own house and the houses of others; and those who will take the pains to listen to the conversation of these miniature women, will soon yield a willing assent to my observations, and keep their little ones apart from such scenes, in the pure atmosphere of home. The garden or the green field is the best place for children, who can always derive entertainment and instruction from nature and her beautiful works. Left to their own choice, the gay party would be a *bore*, far less entertaining than a game of blind-man's buff in the school-room, when lessons were over. It is the vanity of parents that fosters the same spirit in their children.

The careless, disrespectful manner often used in this country by children to their parents, is an evil which in all probability originates in this early introduction of young people into the mysteries of society. They imagine themselves persons of consequence, and that their opinion is quite equal in weight to the experience and superior knowledge of their elders. We cannot imagine a more revolting sight than a young lad presuming to treat his father with disrespect and contempt, and daring presumptuously to contradict him before ignorant idlers like himself.

"You are wrong, Sir; it is not so" – "Mamma, that is not true; I know better," are expressions which I have heard with painful surprise from young people in this country; and the parents have sunk into silence, evidently abashed at the reproof of an insolent child.

These remarks are made with no ill-will, but with a sincere hope that they may prove beneficial to the community at large, and be the means of removing some of the evils which are to be found in our otherwise pleasant and rapidly-improving society.

I know that it would be easier for me to gain the approbation of the Canadian public, by exaggerating the advantages to be derived from a settlement in the colony, by praising all the good qualities of her people, and by throwing a flattering veil over their defects; but this is not my object, and such servile adulation would do them no good, and degrade me in my own eyes. I have written what I consider to be the truth, and as such I hope it may do good, by preparing the minds of emigrants for what they will *really find*, rather than by holding out fallacious hopes that can never be realized.

In "Roughing it in the Bush," I gave an honest personal statement of *facts*. I related nothing but what had really happened; and if illustrations were wanting of persons who had suffered *as much*, and been reduced to the same straits, I could furnish a dozen volumes without having to travel many hundred miles for subjects.

We worked hard and struggled manfully with overwhelming difficulties, yet I have been abused most unjustly by the Canadian papers for revealing some of the mysteries of the Backwoods. Not one word was said *against the country* in my book, as was falsely asserted. It was written as a warning to well-educated persons not to settle in localities for which they were unfitted by their *previous habits and education*. In this I hoped to confer a service both on them and Canada; for the *prosperous* settlement of such persons on cleared farms must prove more beneficial to the colony than their *ruin in the bush*.

It was likewise very cruelly and falsely asserted, that I had spoken ill of the *Irish people*, because I described the revolting scene we witnessed at Grosse Isle, the actors in which were principally Irish emigrants of the *very lowest class*. Had I been able to give the whole details of what we saw on that island, the terms applied to the people who furnished such disgusting pictures would have been echoed by their own countrymen. This was one of those cases in which it was *impossible* to reveal the *whole truth*.

The few Irish characters that occur in my narrative have been drawn with an *affectionate*, not a malignant hand. We had very few Irish settlers round us in the bush, and to them I never owed the least obligation. The contrary of this has been asserted, and I am accused of *ingratitude* by one editor for benefits I never received, and which I was too proud to ask, always preferring to work with my own hands, rather than to *borrow* or *beg* from others. All the kind acts of courtesy I received from the *poor Indians* this gentleman thought fit to turn over to the Irish, in order to hold me up as a monster of ingratitude to his countrymen.

In the case of Jenny Buchannon and John Monaghan, *the only two Irish people* with whom I had anything to do, the benefits were surely mutual. Monaghan came to us a runaway apprentice, – not, by-the-bye, the best recommendation for a servant. We received him starving and ragged, paid him good wages, and treated him with great kindness. The boy turned out a grateful and attached creature, which cannot possible confer the opposite character upon us.

Jenny's love and affection will sufficiently prove *our ingratitude* to *her*. To the good qualities of these people I have done ample justice. In what, then, does my ingratitude to the *Irish people* consist? I should feel much obliged to the writer in the *London Observer* to enlighten me on this head, or those editors of Canadian papers, who, without reading for themselves, servilely copied a *falsehood*.

It is easy to pervert people's words, and the facts they may represent, to their injury; and what I have said on the subject of education may give a handle to persons who delight in misrepresenting the opinions of others, to accuse me of republican principles; I will, therefore, say a few words on this subject, which I trust will exonerate me from this imputation.

That all men, morally speaking, are equal in the eyes of their Maker, appears to me a self-evident fact, though some may be called by His providence to rule, and others to serve. That the welfare of the most humble should be as dear to the country to which he belongs as the best educated and the most wealthy, seems but reasonable to a reflective mind, who looks upon man as a responsible and immortal creature; but, that *perfect equality* can exist in a world where the labour of man is required to procure the common necessaries of life – where the industry of one will create wealth, and the sloth of another induce poverty – we cannot believe.

Some master spirit will rule, and the masses will bow down to superior intellect, and the wealth and importance which such minds never fail to acquire. The laws must be enforced, and those to whom the charge of them is committed will naturally exercise authority, and demand respect.

Perfect equality never did exist upon earth. The old republics were more despotic and exclusive in their separation of the different grades than modern monarchies; and in the most enlightened, that of Greece, the plague-spot of slavery was found. The giant republic, whose rising greatness throws into shade the once august names of Greece and Rome, suffers this heart-corroding leprosy to cleave to her vitals, and sully her fair fame, making her boasted vaunt of *equality* a base lie – the scorn of all Christian men.

They thrust the enfranchised African from their public tables – born beneath their own skies, a native of their own soil, a free citizen by their own Declaration of Independence; yet exclaim, in the face of this *black* injustice – "Our people enjoy equal rights." Alas! for Columbia's *sable sons!* Where is their equality? On what footing do they stand with their white brethren? What value do they place upon the negro beyond his price in dollars and cents? Yet is he equal in the sight of Him who gave him a rational soul, and afforded him the means of attaining eternal life.

We are advocates for *equality of mind* – for a commonwealth of intellect; we earnestly hope for it, ardently pray for it, and we feel a confident belief in the possibility of our theory. We look forward to the day when honest labour will be made honourable; when he who serves, and he who commands, will rejoice in this freedom of soul together; when both master and servant will enjoy a reciprocal communion of mind, without lessening the respect due from the one to the other.

But equality of station is a dream – an error which is hourly contradicted by reality. As the world is at present constituted, such a state of things is impossible. The rich and the educated will never look upon the poor and ignorant as their equals; and the voice of the public, that is ever influenced by wealth and power, will bear them out in their decision.

The country is not yet in existence that can present us a better government and wiser institutions than the British. Long may Canada recognise her rule, and rejoice in her sway! Should she ever be so unwise as to relinquish the privileges she enjoys under the sovereignty of the mother country, she may seek protection *nearer* and "*fare worse!*" The sorrows and trials that I experienced during my first eight years' residence in Canada, have been more than counterbalanced by the remaining twelve of comfort and peace. I have long felt the deepest interest in her prosperity and improvement. I no longer regard myself as an alien on her shores, but her daughter by adoption, – the happy mother of Canadian children, – rejoicing in the warmth and hospitality of a Canadian Home!

May the blessing of God rest upon the land! and her people ever prosper under a religious, liberal, and free government!

FOR LONDON.
A National Song.

"For London! for London! how oft has that cry
From the blue waves of ocean been wafted on high,
When the tar through the grey mist that mantled the tide,
The white cliffs of England with rapture descried,
And the sight of his country awoke in his heart
Emotions no object save home can impart!
For London! for London! the home of the free,
There's no part in the world, royal London, like thee!

"Old London! what ages have glided away,
Since cradled in rushes thy infancy lay!
In thy rude huts of timber the proud wings lay furl'd
Of a spirit whose power now o'ershadows the world,

And the brave chiefs who built and defended those towers,
Were the sires of this glorious old city of ours.
For London! for London! the home of the free,
There's no city on earth, royal London, like thee!

"The Roman, the Saxon, the Norman, the Dane,
Have in turn sway'd thy sceptre, thou queen of the main!
Their spirits though diverse, uniting made one,
Of nations the noblest beneath yon bright sun;
With the genius of each, and the courage of all,
No foeman dare plant hostile flag on thy wall.
For London! for London! the home of the free,
There's no city on earth, royal London, like thee!

"Old Thames rolls his waters in pride at thy feet,
And wafts to earth's confines thy riches and fleet;
Thy temples and towers, like a crown on the wave,
Are hail'd with a thrill of delight by the brave,
When, returning triumphant from conquests afar,
They wreathe round thy altars the trophies of war.
For London! for London! the home of the free,
There's no part in the world, royal London, like thee!

"Oh, London! when we, who exulting behold
Thy splendour and wealth, in the dust shall be cold,
May sages, and heroes, and patriots unborn,
Thy altars defend, and thy annals adorn!
May thy power be supreme on the land of the brave,
The feeble to succour, the fallen to save,
And the sons and the daughters now cradled by thee,
Find no city on earth like the home of the free!"

THE END

Afterword

BY CAROL SHIELDS

As readers, we like to think that books are prompted into print through a sense of authorial urgency, and that a writer picks up a pen out of the heat of intense conviction. We imagine that the resulting manuscript goes on to forge a mystical bond with an editor – wise, principled – who instantly grasps the historical significance of the work and foresees how its pertinent observations and narrative leaps will fuse with the consciousness of a contemporary audience, speaking with its authentic voice and awakening its best instincts.

This romantic notion holds little truth today, as we all know, nor did it in the summer of 1852 when the English publisher, Richard Bentley, wrote to Susanna Moodie of Belleville asking if she would consider writing a second book on the subject of life in Canada. His terms of reference were genial but specific:

> If you could render your picture of the state of society in the large towns and cities of Canada, interesting to the idle reader, at the same time you make it informing to those who are looking for facts it would be acceptable. Present them to the reader's eye as they were years ago and as they are now, and are still every year I imagine rapidly prospering it might form a good work as a pendant to "Roughing It in the Bush."

In November she replied. She was eager to begin, so eager

that she enclosed a partial manuscript. She was, she explained to Bentley, recovering from a life-threatening illness, and at the urging of her doctors had recently undertaken a restorative boat trip to Niagara Falls.

"My idea was," she wrote, "to describe as much of the country, as I could in my trip to Niagara, beginning with Belleville, and going through our lovely Bay, sketching the little villages along its shores, and introducing as many incidents and anecdotes illustrative of the *present state of Canada*, as I could collect or remember, to form a sort of apendix [sic] to *Roughing It in the Bush*."

Considering the differences of geography and privilege, gender and sensibility that lay between Bentley and Moodie, it is impossible to say whether his "pendant" bore any resemblance to her "appendix." Bentley's intentions can be imagined; he was a gentleman, but also a businessman with an eye to capitalizing on the romance of immigration and on the widespread need for practical information.

Moodie's expectations were more complex. She was understandably anxious to profit from the success of her previous book and ever in need of money for "bread, butter and tea," and she also hoped to correct what she perceived to be the public's grave misunderstanding of *Roughing It in the Bush*. She had never, she maintained, discouraged immigration to Canada; she had only warned that life on an uncleared farm offered hardship, isolation, and ruin for those of the middle or higher classes who were unfit for hard labour. Far more suitable for such settlers were farms already under cultivation or positions in Canada's progressive and prosperous towns.

It seems likely that Bentley anticipated a new manuscript, freshly conceived and composed, but Moodie, ever practical and always resourceful, saw the book as a chance to reissue old work, both published and unpublished. Thrifty housewife that she was, she emptied her drawers, added a few new chapters and a thin tissue of connecting material, and quickly arrived at a complete manuscript.

It is little wonder that the book she wrote was not the

book that she promised. Once settled in Canada, Moodie scarcely ever travelled more than a few miles from Belleville, and so she was far from being a knowledgeable and objective witness to the state of contemporary society. Her sensibility, too, was firmly rooted in pre-Victorian England, and her syntax was shaped – decorously, protectively – for a readership she had long since lost touch with. The "facts" specified by Bentley in his letter of contract for *Life in the Clearings versus the Bush* either sink beneath the weight of Moodie's didactic commentary or are annihilated by her indefatigable enthusiasm. Also fragmented along the way is her proposed structural device, the journey to Niagara Falls in search of health.

The idea of such a pilgrimage is an ancient one, and so, particularly, is the idea that water possesses restorative properties: the pure spring, the enchanted fountain, the sacred river, the calm lake, the bracing seaside. A change of air, a change of scene – these held out the promise of a renewal of the body and spirit, and what more abundant source of refreshment could there be than the waters of Niagara. Here the power and purity of nature merged, and here too was a tourist attraction that Moodie shrewdly judged would interest her English readers.

But she seems unable to decide whether this is a literary or historical journey. Again and again in the early chapters she pleads for postponement – "My dear reader, before we proceed further on our journey . . ." – and imposes her own agenda. From time to time she catches herself, briefly relocating the reader on the map and painting in a few landmarks. Only the final chapters accommodate themselves to the journey scheme, but these suggest an anecdotal travelogue rather than an Odyssian voyage. The vision soon deteriorates, and the vigour with which she devours information, consumes scenery, and thirsts after vignettes refutes her claims to physical frailty.

Life in the Clearings, then, succeeds by default. Moodie was ill-equipped to write the kind of book Bentley commissioned, and she quickly loses control of her organizing framework. Her voice is discursive, euphemistic, over-blown, and sometimes oppressive – in the way that all storytellers are oppressive – but it is unmistakably authentic.

When we speak of the voice of a period, we most often mean a voice of authority and munificence, the far-ranging voice of the lavishly gifted or the arbitrarily powerful. In the past that voice frequently was both aristocratic and male, securely located, rich with certitude and learning, a voice either self-anointed or baptized by the circumstantial unfolding of a literary tradition.

An *authentic* voice is something else. We know it when we hear it. The texture of the quotidian is in it, and every cultural moment secured suggests a thousand others. Even its self-consciousness, even its silences, can make a statement. It whines and falters, but manages to catch enough thieving narrative to reveal the configuration of a society and how it invests itself with meaning.

Susanna Moodie's life spanned the greater part of the nineteenth century. Her lifetime coincided with enormous shifts in political dominion and, more important, with dramatic new concepts of personal power. To these phenomena, she is a perplexed but never disinterested witness. She immigrated to Canada when she was close to thirty years old, and so her consciousness was stretched across two cultures, two continents, and two political philosophies. Her adopted culture exposed her to the new radical democracy, but failed to erase her conflicting instincts of privilege. "That all men, morally speaking, are equal in the eyes of their Maker, appears to me to be a self-evident fact," Moodie says in one chapter, but goes on in the next breath to say that "equality of station is a dream." Her fixed view of society was shaken, finally, by her growing suspicion that many of the grievances of the lower classes were justified, and that immigration and education offered at least a measure of class mobility.

Happily, Moodie's comments are never deformed by that critical strait-jacket; unity of vision, and her struggle to maintain her idealistic vision in a harsh landscape provides *Life in the Clearings* with much of its tension. Romanticism and realism, those competing forces, not only reflect the turbulence of the period, but also that element in her nature that urged her toward decency and fairness. She examines, she vacillates, she contradicts herself.

Her contradictions are her chief delight. She is one minute praising the natural beauties of the land and the next minute smarting under the bad manners of her fellow tourists. She enjoys local folk customs while longing for those at home. Always a woman to relish irony in human behaviour, she was perhaps unaware of the way in which her own bewilderment and indecisiveness gave weight to her account. Writing for Moodie was both a financial opportunity and a personal outlet; she is forever trying to reconcile the two, and never realizing that she has succeeded. To her work she brings a kind of fortuitous innocence, mingling the historical and the sentimental with results that are sometimes earnestly clumsy, at other times vividly dramatic.

The experience of her life is so long and varied, so splintered and buffeted by social upheavals, that she is obliged to create a new form. *Roughing It in the Bush* and *Life in the Clearings* are both books that generously and disconcertingly embrace elements of travel writing, the literary sketch, narrative fiction, meditation, factual material, and poetry. The tone varies widely, from injured and defensive to astringent and bright, and the theme of dislocation and adaptation is anchored to the seemingly random ceremonies and stories with which she shapes her sense of the world. *Life in the Clearings* is the kind of patchwork, unofficial document that allows us to "read" a slice of our national history, and a rather large slice at that.

Trying to place such a text in a governing tradition is to miss the book itself. The form is Susanna Moodie's invention; it fits like a comfortable hand-knitted sweater. She is

at home with her divagations, liberated by them, in fact.
"Allow me a woman's privilege," she begs us, "of talking
of all sorts of things by the way." Her digressions are only
superficially intrusive, however, since they carry us into
unmapped territory and provide us with an interlinear
gloss, giving her voice not just authenticity, but
particularity.

For today's reader, the ringing subtext reveals even
more. Beneath Moodie's "enthusiasm" (a favourite word
of hers and also the title of her 1831 volume of poems) is a
sense of woman making the best of things, of bitter longing transcended by fervour and commitment. Moodie is a
Crusoe baffled by her own heated imagination, the dislo-
cated immigrant who never fully accepts or rejects her
adopted country. When her methodology wobbles, her
reflexes can be counted on. Her acts of re-imagination rise
from an unconscious strategy of survival; she states her
belief in male dominance, for instance, but reserves for
women characters like Jeanie Burns qualities of courage
and endurance. She struggles with the image of a beautiful
lake disfigured by a new saw mill – natural harmony con-
fronted by necessary progress – and is unable to resolve
her feelings.

It is precisely this human ambivalence of Moodie's, as
well as her shifting focus and telling silences, that defines
her for the modern reader and places *Life in the Clearings
versus the Bush* near the heart of our developing
literature.

BY SUSANNA MOODIE

AUTOBIOGRAPHY
Roughing It in the Bush; or, Life in Canada (1852)
Life in the Clearings versus the Bush (1853)

FICTION
Mark Hurdlestone; or, The Gold Worshipper (1853)
Flora Lyndsay; or, Passages in an Eventful Life (1854)
Matrimonial Speculations (1854)
Geoffrey Moncton; or, The Faithless Guardian (1855)
The World before Them (1868)

FICTION FOR YOUNG ADULTS
Spartacus: A Roman Story (1822)
The Little Quaker; or, The Triumph of Virtue (n.d.)
The Sailor Brother; or, The History of Thomas Saville (n.d.)
The Little Prisoner; or, Passion and Patience (n.d.)
Hugh Latimer; or, The School-Boy's Friendship (1828)
Rowland Massingham; or, I Will Be My Own Master (n.d.)
Profession and Principle; or, The Vicar's Tales (n.d.)
George Leatrim; or, The Mother's Test (1875)

LETTERS
Letters of a Lifetime [eds. Carl Ballstadt, Elizabeth Hopkins,
and Michael Peterman] (1985)

POETRY
Patriotic Songs [with Agnes Strickland] (1830)
Enthusiasm; and Other Poems (1831)